St. Nicholas

A Closer Look at Christmas

Joe Wheeler & Jim Rosenthal

NELSON REFERENCE & ELECTRONIC
A Division of Thomas Nelson Publishers
Since 1798

www.thomasnelson.com

COPYRIGHT & ACKNOWLEDGMENTS

The authors would like to thank Greg Johnson, Connie Wheeler, Veronica Elks, and the staff of Thomas Nelson, especially Wayne Kinde, Michael Stephens, Barbara West, Vicki Hargis, and Robin Crosslin for their efforts to make this book a reality.

Copyright © 2005 by Joe Wheeler and Jim Rosenthal

ISBN 1-4185-0407-6

Published in Nashville, Tennessee, by Thomas Nelson, Inc.

Published in association with the literary agency of WordServe Literary Group, 10152 Knoll Circle, Highlands Ranch, Colorado 80130.

Scripture marked KJV is taken from The Holy Bible, King James Version.

Coca-Cola related images printed by permission of the Archives, The Coca-Cola Company.

"Christmas: Santa Reading Mail" (SEP 12/21/35) by Norman Rockwell. Printed by permission of the Norman Rockwell Family Agency. Copyright © 1935 by the Norman Rockwell Family Entities.

"The Discovery" (SEP 12/29/56) by Norman Rockwell. Printed by permission of the Norman Rockwell Family Agency. Copyright © 1956 by the Norman Rockwell Family Entities.

"To lose one's faith surpass" in *The Poems of Emily Dickinson*, edited by Thomas H. Johnson. Reprinted by permission of the publishers and the Trustees of Amherst College from THE POEMS OF EMILY DICKINSON, Thomas H. Johnson, ed. Cambridge, Mass.: The Belknap Press of Harvard University Press, Copyright © 1951, 1955, 1979, 1983 by the President and Fellows of Harvard College.

Unless otherwise noted, the images used in this book are from the collection of and owned by Canon James Rosenthal and are part of a world-class collection of St Nicholas items. This collection has been housed in the Archbishop's Old Palace Canterbury, England from 1997–2005. It includes numerous icons, paintings, statues, crafts, cards, moulds, stamps, books, music and ornaments.

Acknowledgements of certain images and illustrations appear in the body of the book.

Book design and typesetting by Crosslin Creative, Thompson Station, Tennessee

Printed in the United States of America

1 2 3 4 5 6 7 8 – 09 08 07 06 05

DEDICATION

This book is dedicated to the rainbow children of God's world today and to all who honor St. Nicholas.

ST. NICHOLAS CENTER AND ST. NICHOLAS SOCIETY
The contribution of the above organizations to this work is most appreciated.
   www.stnicholascenter.org and www.stnicholassociety.com

Author's note: The various spellings of our saint, Nicholas, are used throughout the book. They include Nicholas/most common, Nicolas/French, Nicolaas/Dutch, Nikolaus/German, Nikolai/Russian, Nicola/Italian, Nikolo/Austrian, Niklaas/Flemish, and Nick/American. All are correct. —Jim Rosenthal

CONTENTS

by Joe Wheeler

Last Christmas season, our five-year-old grandson, Taylor, without seeking counsel from anyone, wrote a letter to Santa Claus and sealed it in an envelope. He took it to his mother and asked her how to address it. Then he slowly and laboriously wrote,

SANTA

NORTH POLE

His mother gave him a stamp, and Taylor took the precious letter out to the road, placed it in the mailbox, raised the flag, and sat down on the steps to wait for the mailman. Only when the truck drove away did he reenter the house.

The very next day, there was a letter in the box addressed to Taylor. It was from Santa!

Some weeks later, the family drove north to spend Christmas with Taylor's other grandparents, in Oshawa, Ontario. Several days after their arrival in Canada, everyone went to a mall to do some last-minute Christmas shopping. One of the Santas there called out to Taylor, "Hey! What do you want for Christmas?" Taylor just stood there for a moment, in shocked disbelief. Then he shot back angrily, "I already *told* you! *Don't you remember?*" and walked away.

Sabrina, a friend of Taylor's, puzzled about what she saw almost everywhere she went, asked, "How can Santa be in all the shopping malls at once?"

A year passed, and Taylor, now six, came to Colorado with his family to spend Christmas with us. Again he wrote a letter to Santa. Our daughter, Michelle, cornered me in our utility room. "Dad, what do we *do*? Do I tell him Santa isn't real? That he's just make-believe? Or do I encourage that belief—it's so cute, so sweet—and hope it all works out okay?"

This card shows that St. Nicholas was obviously not foreign to the English-speaking world in the early 1900s.

What could I say? Taylor was already six years into Santa-belief. That evening, during family story hour, I tried to clarify just who and what Santa was. The next day, in an old inn near Evergreen, Colorado, Taylor climbed up on a Santa's lap and placed his order; his three-year-old brother, Seth, followed him.

Here's hoping Old Saint Nick will smile at you on CHRISTMAS

C-203

Afterward, another child got down from Santa's lap, and as she and her mother walked away, her mother had said to her, "You know, dear, that Santa Claus isn't real—he's just make-believe."

The Santa turned to me as I was signing books at an adjacent table and groused, "I hate it when parents disillusion their children like that!"

The very next day, Taylor mailed his letter to Santa, just to make *sure* his message got through. This one was never answered.

After returning to Annapolis, Taylor was instructed by his mother to write thank-you notes for all the Christmas presents he'd received. After writing all those on his list, he looked up at his mother with joy on his face and said, "Oh! I need to write a letter to Santa to thank him, too!"

His mother smiled down tenderly and said, "A great idea! Why don't you *do* it!"

Later, Taylor's father, Duane, having overheard, told Michelle, in a low voice, "So much for telling him the truth about Santa!"

She retorted, "But it was so *cute!*"

A Confusing Cast of Characters

Every post office in America greeted the first Christmas of the new Millennium with a large poster. The poster depicted four stamps, each picturing a bearded fatherly Christmas figure carrying toys and a small Christmas tree. The banner headline read: "GREETINGS FROM ST. NICK." Untold millions of those stamps have since then been mailed all over the world.

Not Santa Claus, but St. Nick.

Why?

Detail from a U.S. Postal Service poster advertising the 2001 holiday stamps. Used by permission.

A Happy Christmas

In the Western world, almost one quarter of our lives is devoted to the Christmas season. Back-to-school sales begin in late July and last until mid-September. Then, with breathtaking speed, the transformation takes place—in almost every store you enter, it's Christmas. And it stays that way until the second week of January.

The mixture of Christmas can be confusing to children. On one hand, the Christian church emphasizes Joseph, Mary, and Jesus, along with the Magi and the shepherds. On the other hand, secular folklore has Father Christmas, *Pelznickel*, *Krampus*, Santa Claus, and Rudolph the Red-nosed Reindeer. Which figures will children believe in? Since believing gives meaning and structure to childhood, and since children gradually structure their lives on these beliefs, it *is* important to make wise choices.

Ask any small child the question: "Is there a Santa Claus?" and you'll be greeted with shocked eyes. Ask any teenager the same question, and eyes will roll heavenward. Clearly, somewhere between childhood and adolescence, a dramatic shift in perception takes place. Is that good? Is it bad?

Awaiting St. Nicholas, postcard from 1909

Ask these same people the question: "Is there a St. Nicholas?" and your answers will vary a lot more. Rarely will anyone fail to recognize the name itself, but since his Christmas role varies so much from country to country, synthesis is difficult to achieve.

Even more confusing to most people are these questions: "Who is the true St. Nicholas?" "Is he the same person as Santa Claus?" "Are all his European counterparts the same person?" "Is there a *real* St. Nicholas? Or are they all mythical?"

All this is confusing enough in America, where we only have two competitors: Santa Claus and St. Nicholas. Europeans have a much more difficult time sorting out the competition. For starters, there is a very old gentleman known as "Father Christmas" (in English-speaking countries), "*Pere Noel*" (French), "*Weihnachtsmann*" (German), and "Grandfather Frost" to the Russian people. One of Father Christmas's ancestors is the god Saturn, who in Roman days "ruled over" a December festival called the "Saturnalia." The Romans brought him to England. But in truth, Father Christmas is little more than a Protestant Reformation repackaging of St. Nicholas.

In Italy, there is a fascinating Christianized pagan called *Befana*. In Germanic countries it really gets confusing—perhaps because Germany as we know it is so recently an addition to the family of nations (it has traditionally been a collection of many small dukedoms, principalities, and kingdoms). Among others, they may choose from *Krampus, Pelznickel, Hans Trapp, Hans Muff, Knecht Ruprecht, Bartel, Berchta, Aschen Klaus,* and *Gumphinkel.* In Denmark, they have *Juletomte* (or his female counterpart, *Julenisse*); in Sweden, *Tompte Gubbe*; in old Czechoslovakia, *Svaty Mikulas*; and in Romania, *Mos Craicun*. Directly or indirectly, most of these owe allegiance to St. Nicholas. And we haven't even mentioned St. Nicholas's assistants (most dark in color and pre-Christian in origin), such as Holland's *Zwarte Piet* (Black Pete) and Luxembourg's *Hoêsecker*.

A traditional Dutch cartoon image of Sint Nicolaas delivering toys at a fireplace. Notice that he brought his donkey indoors.

Painting by Haddon Sundblom of Santa at the fireplace. Courtesy of the Archives, The Coca-Cola Company. Used by Permission.

To muddy the waters further, keep in mind the fact that all across Christendom another figure seeks to hold its own: The Christchild; in Germany he is called *Christkindel*; in Spain, *Niño Jesús*; in France, *Petit Noel*; in Italy, *Gesu Bambino*; and in the Middle East, *Baba Noel*.

Then there is the great forefather of these Christmas gift-givers, St. Nicholas himself, still going strong after 1,700 years. There is also his nineteenth-century secularized double, Santa Claus, who, having already consolidated much of America behind him, now seeks to conquer the rest of the world.

Is it any wonder that so many of us are confused about who is real and who is not? How do we separate the genuine from the fake? Is there an original who deserves to be first among all these peers?

That is what we seek to find out in this book.

Does Any of this Really Matter?

This is a *big* question! We will be discussing this question in this book. We will also take up volatile questions like these:

Does it really matter what our children believe as long as they believe in *something*?

Should we encourage our children to believe in their illusions? How long, to what age, should our children retain those illusions?

When those illusions are finally lost, will our child's faith in everything else we've advocated be lost as well? Will our child ever believe us again? When those illusions are lost, what should we attempt to replace them with?

Does Christmas as we know it really matter anymore? Is it merely a convenient vehicle for persuading people to buy more products than they can afford? Why not greet people with "Happy Holidays!" "Season's Greetings!" or "Happy Winter Solstice!" instead?

How about the Christmas season itself? Just what does it accomplish in today's society? Should it be only a day long? a month? two months?

If most of the Christmas gift-bearers are essentially benign, does it really matter which one we emphasize most?

St. Nicholas crossed the Atlantic to America as *Sinterklaas*. In New York, the words were anglicized to Santa Claus. Now Santa is returning to Europe seeking ascendancy over St. Nicholas and all the others. Does the outcome matter at all?

Now that we have Santa Claus, do we even need St. Nicholas? Don't they really mean about the same?

A card from Flanders for St. Nicholas day

Is it not important that each of us parents realize at the very inception of our parenting just how serious a matter it is to be worthy of the complete trust of our children? What if we should lose that trust by failing to be completely honest with our children?

Stately saint in stained glass in Castle Hedingham Church, England

So it does matter what we say to a child about Santa Claus, about St. Nicholas. It matters far more than generations of parents have realized.

Dennis E. Engleman, in his insightful little book, *The Saint Nicholas Secret*, remembers how in his childhood he was a true believer and wrote to St. Nicholas religiously every year. He fully believed that Santa and his elves could build enough toys in their North Pole workshop to give every good child on earth one or two. "Nor was it any trouble to believe that he could fit millions of gifts into his bag and deliver them all over the world via an airborne sled in a single night, Christmas Eve. Santa's omniscience in knowing what each person deserved was as credible as the proposition that this rotund old man could slide down the narrowest of chimneys unscathed—including those that led to gas furnaces!" (Engleman, 19).

But as he grew older, doubt began to creep in. Especially when he encountered Santas in mall after mall, of so many sizes and shapes. Finally, one memorable day, he decided to find out once and for all if the stories were true or not.

Down the chimney with good St. Nick

Classic elegance and kindliness of gentle Bishop Nicholas

"Mother, is there really a St. Nicholas?" I asked one night, trembling.

"She glanced up from a sink full of dishes with a strange look on her face. Maybe she felt regret—or maybe relief—but she only shrugged her shoulders and said simply, 'No, there isn't.'

"Mother did not explain how there could be no St. Nicholas when I had been told so many times that he was real. She did not say why I had been taught to believe in something that could be snatched away with a word. . . .

"Finally, after I had stared sightlessly at the yellow and green patterns on the linoleum floor for a long time, Mother said, 'Now you are older. Now you can understand more. You don't need to believe in miracles.'

"After that, I went to my room and quietly closed the door. I had an empty feeling inside, for a door in my heart was also quietly closing—a door to the chamber of childhood dreams, where hope and faith are nurtured in the light of trust. And after that I could not keep hoping and believing, for a world without miracles was a world without anything to hope for or to believe in" (Engleman, 23–4).

True indeed! After that, things could never be the same again: the magic had gone out of his life. In time he grew up, married, and had three children of his own. Eventually, the moment of reckoning came: how should he deal with the subject in his own home? He tried in every way possible to avoid the issue, but somehow his children assimilated the St. Nicholas/Santa Claus story without him. This he discovered by chance, overhearing his children talking among themselves. All that work for naught! "So in spite of parental blockades, St. Nicholas had already climbed down the chimney and taken up residence in our home! Does it always happen this way, I wondered? Does he always kindle childhood faith sort of miraculously?" What should he do? "In the eager faces of John, Lily, and Victoria, a familiar hope and faith glowed that had nothing to do with wanting gifts. The doors to their chambers of childhood dreams stood wide open, allowing the gentle light of trust to shine forth" (Engleman, 30–1).

Time passed, and this father knew full well that the dreaded moment was not far off: the question would be asked any day now. He pondered the issue in his mind, recognizing that "Innocent hearts can believe and be saved or be broken and lost. Children naturally entertain various immature notions about reality; in the normal course of time many such ideas fall away without consequence. But if the subject touches on life's essential nature, meaning, or purpose, disillusionment can be devastating" (Engleman, 34–5).

The answer came as a result of considerable research into the subject. Research that carried him to Chartres, to Rome, to Florence, to Bari. It was in Bari, in the ancient basilica of St. Nicholas, that the father discovered the truth: St. Nicholas was *real*. He

This postcard from Holland shows St. Nicholas using a ladder to put toys in a chimney.

Card featuring St. Nicholas and his donkey delivering gifts

It must be St. Nick. The bishop's miter is the real clue

wept, and the heartbreak of the years began to ebb away. "A pool of betrayed faith and devastated hope drained away, leaving only quiet emptiness" (Engleman, 63). At *last*, he was ready to face his children.

For us, too, the answer to our dilemma can be found in the past. Back to Bari, and even further back, to a quiet Turkish town on the shores of the Mediterranean, that sea St. Paul knew so well.

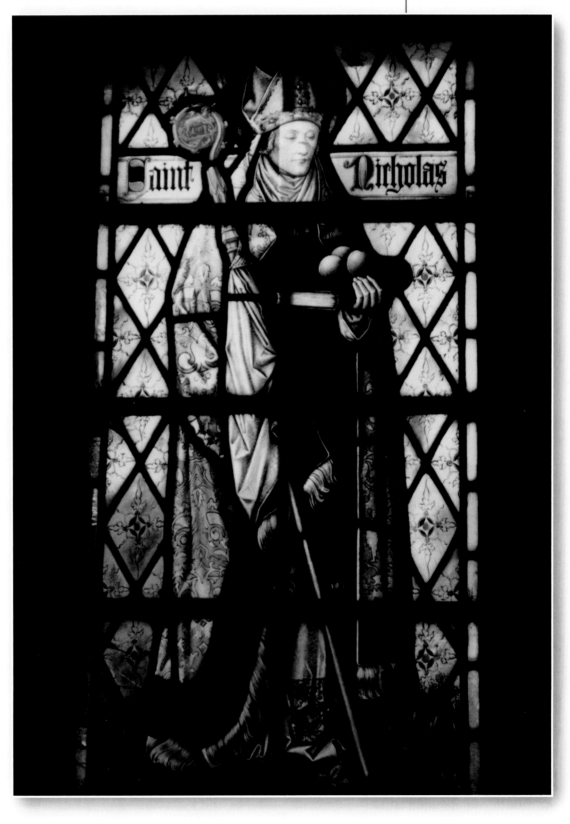

Cloister window at Chichester Cathedral in England

CHAPTER 1

Born into a Dark World

It is evening. The simple meal has been eaten, and the dishes cleared away. As darkness descends, several lamps are lit and the family gathers around them. So do all the animals that have free run of the house. Demetrius, the youngest child, is first to break the silence: "Father . . . tell us a story!"

For thousands of years it has been this way, and for well over another thousand years, almost all knowledge (family, social, historical, and spiritual) will be communicated by storytellers. True enough, somewhere here and there a literate monk spends his lifetime laboriously copying ancient manuscripts by hand, but few can read the words he writes.

Hence story continues to be, century after century, millennium after millennium, the central part of life. Over time, listeners memorize what they hear, then become storytellers to *their* children. Little is different in the palaces and castles of the nobility except that travelers and troubadours who know the wider world tell or sing their stories.

Truth? What is that? Who can validate a story, separating fact from fiction? Few indeed are these consolidators of known knowledge, and those few are revered, almost worshiped. But with the fastest speed known to travelers being the galloping horse or the wind-propelled ship, just getting to a scholar who might know the truth about something would likely take weeks—even months. Perhaps years.

The world? It is too vast to even conceptualize! No map-maker has ever mapped it. In the Mediterranean, the world ends for most folks with the Pillars of Hercules (the region of Gibraltar) to the west, the frozen world of Nordic barbarians to the north, the vast desert we know as the Sahara to the south, and Asia that is so far away it fades into the mists of myth to the east.

Life itself is an enigma. You are born, then struggle for survival in large families. Since almost any disease is likely to prove fatal, few children survive to adulthood. Doctors are usually poorly trained and kill as many patients as they help. The average man

Opposite:
Lycian rock
tombs in Myra

1

(up until the twentieth century) will marry at least three times, because so many women die of childbirth complications. Neither midwives nor doctors know anything about germs, so they do not wash their hands between patients. Disease and the plagues that periodically kill millions are called "Acts of God." No one knows what causes them or how to stop them.

So it should come as no surprise that the average person, lacking the education twenty-first-century people will take for granted, is deeply superstitious. Since neither life nor death make much sense, even the wildest and most improbable stories are accepted as truth. And since God—however God is conceptualized—represents the only bedrock society knows, miracles are accepted as a matter of course.

Such is the world Nicholas was born into.

The rock formation, caves, and tombs of Patara in modern Turkey

But all this has to do with that by-gone world, generally speaking. Now let's get specific and step backward in time to the decade of the 270s, only 240-50 years after the death, resurrection, and ascension of Christ (a time interval comparable to our looking backward today to the time of George Washington).

The Mediterranean world had turned dark. Rome the republic, where all were equal before the law, where men ruled as patriarchs and women taught their children to believe in goodness and integrity, where gods were to be believed in and worshiped, and family was sacred—that Rome was no more. In its place was now Impe-

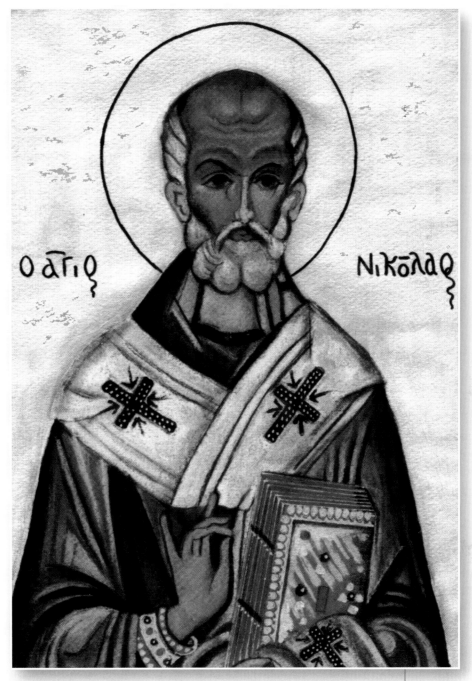

An icon of St. Nicholas by Winitha Fernando of Canterbury, England, in classic Byzantine style

rial Rome, where there were no longer absolutes. Everything was now relative, and laws were for the breaking. The gods and religion were a laugh, and neither marriage nor the family unit meant anything. Unwanted children were thrown out on the streets to fend for themselves (these children were known to the Romans as "alumni"). In this ever more hedonistic society, power, excess, pleasure, debauchery, and violence ruled. All-powerful emperors now ruled as tyrannical gods and lived in splendor almost beyond belief. In this later Rome, emperors openly pandered to the rabble, everything and everyone was for sale, and no one was safe.

But a counter-force had arisen. Christ's disciples were turning the world upside down with a belief system that could not

possibly have been more different from that of dissolute Rome. This new religion of goodness, purity, integrity, constancy, kindness, and love made life worth living and made death a door into the hereafter. Thus these early Christians not only had no fear of death, they welcomed it—for an eternity with God awaited them. To the millions who felt that life was a dead-end street under the Romans, Christianity was Good News indeed! And it spread like wildfire.

The Caesars, who insisted that they be worshiped as divine, unleashed their fury on Christians who maintained that only God was worthy of such worship. Untold thousands were slain by the sword or axe, or were killed by fierce animals in the public arenas. Still others were burned alive on posts as human torches.

The setting for the life of Nicholas would be the twin cities of Patara and Myra in what was then called Lycia. Patara was first built about 1,500 years earlier and had become one of the most important harbor cities in that region, first in the Lycian kingdom, and later in the Medo-Persian, Greek, and Roman empires. Myra was only seven centuries old but had grown into a city rivaling Patara. Most of the ships traveling between Egypt and Rome stopped in Myra. St. Paul landed here on his third missionary voyage, while traveling from Ephesus to Tyre (Acts 21:1–2). He stayed long enough to raise up a company of believers. On his final journey, he landed once again at Myra, but this time he was in chains, on his long voyage to Rome, where he would die for his faith (Acts 27:5). Nicholas was born into a family descended from converts St. Paul had left behind two hundred years earlier.

Which brings us to a crucial point in our story: Was Nicholas a real person? Or was he only a convenient fabrication. Let's settle that issue at the very start.

First of all, we must deal with one reality: no other part of our world has suffered more bloodshed and upheaval than the Mediterranean. Even under the *Pax Romana*, life was never safe.

By the 270s, the emperors were always facing attacks, both from within and without. It only got worse. As Rome began to crumble, it was like the feeding frenzy of ravenous sharks. Towns and cities were burned and ransacked, the men and children were killed or sold as slaves, the women were violated and enslaved. The city of Rome became a ghost town, the population plummeting from 1,500,000 to a paltry 40,000. Goat herds grazed on its

A banner found in St. Nicholas Anglican Church in Southern Africa. Photo: St Nicholas Center/Myers.

seven hills. It would remain that way for a thousand years. What law and order remained would be in the Byzantine East.

Many succumbed to disease. One plague outbreak (542–594) killed off half the population of Europe! Also untold thousands of records were destroyed during the periodic destruction of iconography. A side-effect of all this is that much of the church-related records in the East were destroyed. Consequently, it's amazing that any record survived! Especially when you realize that they didn't have any paper to write on. They had only papyrus, parchment, or velum. These were incredibly fragile and subject to disintegration, so they had to be periodically recopied by hand. The Chinese had paper by the second century, but it didn't arrive in Spain until the tenth century, Constantinople until the eleventh, the Italian Peninsula until the twelfth, the Germanic states until the thirteenth, and England until the fourteenth. Mechanized printing was not available in Europe until 1453.

Ancient bas relief map on the wall in the Antalya Museum in Turkey. The inset shows the location of Myra.

But now let's look at what survived in spite of all that.

After 450, more and more clergy chose or were assigned the name Nicholas. This never happens by chance, for there has to be a prototype, a reason for such a thing to occur. Also, there were four early popes named Nicholas. Certainly, the one minor figure by this name in the New Testament would not have caused it.

The first surviving Nicholas reference to which we may attribute a measure of validity dates back to the period of A.D. 510–515. The writer was Theodor, Lector of Byzantium. His *Tripartite History* depends entirely on three historians of the fifth century (Socrates, Sozomen, and Theodoret). Nicholas's name appears on the tenth line of this A.D. 510 manuscript in his list of participants in the famed Council of Nicaea. The 151st attendee was listed as "Nicholas of Myra of Lycia."

The Encyclopedia Britannica declares that "He was bishop of Myra in the time of the Emperor Diocletian, was persecuted, tortured, and kept in prison until the more tolerant reign of Constantine, though Athanasius, who knew all the notable bishops of the period, never mentions Nicholas. The oldest monument of the cult of St. Nicholas seems to be the church of S. S. Priscus and Nicholas built at Constantinople by the Emperor Justinian" (*Encyclopedia Britannica*, vol. 16, 416).

The Eastern Roman Emperor, Theodosius II (401–450), ordered that a great church be constructed in Myra. It became known as the Church of St. Nicholas. The last great Roman Emperor of the East, Justinian (527–565), codifier of Roman laws and builder of the *Hagia Sophia* (still one of the wonders of our world), restored another St. Nicholas church. It was rebuilt just outside the summer palace of Blachernes (the primary imperial palace on the Golden Horn). This church was burned by the Slavs and Avars in 626 but was restored and was still standing in 1350. It is inconceivable that a monarch of the stature of Justinian would have constructed

The statue of St. Nicholas in the sanctuary of the Bari Basilica

such a church next to his palace had he had any doubts about the tradition of St. Nicholas. This would have been no more than 200 years after the bishop's death. *The Life of Nicholas of Sion* (written two centuries after the bishop's death) specifically refers to the church dedicated to Nicholas in Myra, also to another dedicated to him at Kastellon, and to an annual feast in his honor of such significance that the bishops of the region used it as an occasion for annual conclaves.

Simeon Metaphrastes's biography was the most widely read and generally accepted canonical text on St. Nicholas. Completed the last year of Justinian's reign (565), it clearly reveals that the people of Lycia deeply venerated the memory of St. Nicholas. It also corroborates the story of "The Three Generals." In this text we find one of the earliest known references to the church in Myra dedicated to St. Nicholas. It testifies to the annual celebration that took place on his feast day.

About 570 an anonymous author wrote a biography of St. Nicholas. Another followed twelve years later.

Michael the Arachimaindrite (814–842) wrote that "Others have written about St. Nicholas before me." His is the earliest manuscript to survive intact.

Also writing about Nicholas were Peter Damian (d. 1072), cardinal bishop of Ostia; Honorius of Autun (d. 1130); Adam of St-Victor (d. 1192), precentor of the Cathedral of Notre Dame and author of the renowned *Sequences*; Vincent of Beauvais (c. 1194–1264); St. Bonaventure; St. Thomas Aquinas; Dante Alighieri; Jean Gerson; Robert Wace; John the Deacon; Jean Bodel; and James of Voragine, author of the *Golden Legend*.

Will Durant also affirms the historicity of St. Nicholas: "St. Nicholas, in the fourth century, modestly filled the episcopal see of Myra in Lycia, never dreaming that he was to be the patron saint of Russia, of thieves and boys and girls, and at last, in his Dutch name as Santa Claus, to enter into the Christmas mythology of half the Christian world" (Durant, *The Age of Faith*, 62).

Bari image from the collection of Professor Nino Lavaromocca, the foremost scholar on San Nicola di Bari

In the center of a community that is 99 percent Muslim, stands the original church in Myra/Demre. Amidst the minarets of the mosque, the church is hopeful once again of being an active congregation.

Clearly, with this evidence before us, we can abandon any remaining reservations as to whether or not Nicholas was a real person.

But this is about all that we know for sure. Truth and myth have become so intertwined during the last seventeen centuries that a biography in the modern sense is impossible. We are left with stories. Hagiographers (scholars specializing in the literature of venerated figures) tell us that, while many saint-related stories are somewhat suspect and almost impossible to prove one way or another, a good share of them are based on historically true accounts. Over time, those true accounts have evolved into wildly improbable stories that have little relation to the originals.

There is something Velcro-ish about stories. Once imbedded in the mind or heart, they are incredibly difficult to dislodge. And truth has little to do with whether or not a given story survives or dies. Take, for instance, Parson Weems's story of little George Washington's chopping down his father's cherry tree. Though Americans have known for well over a century that the story is pure fabrication, the myth refuses to die: it is more real than real, thus proving once again Machiavelli's contention that perception is more significant than reality. Ironically, chances are that if you

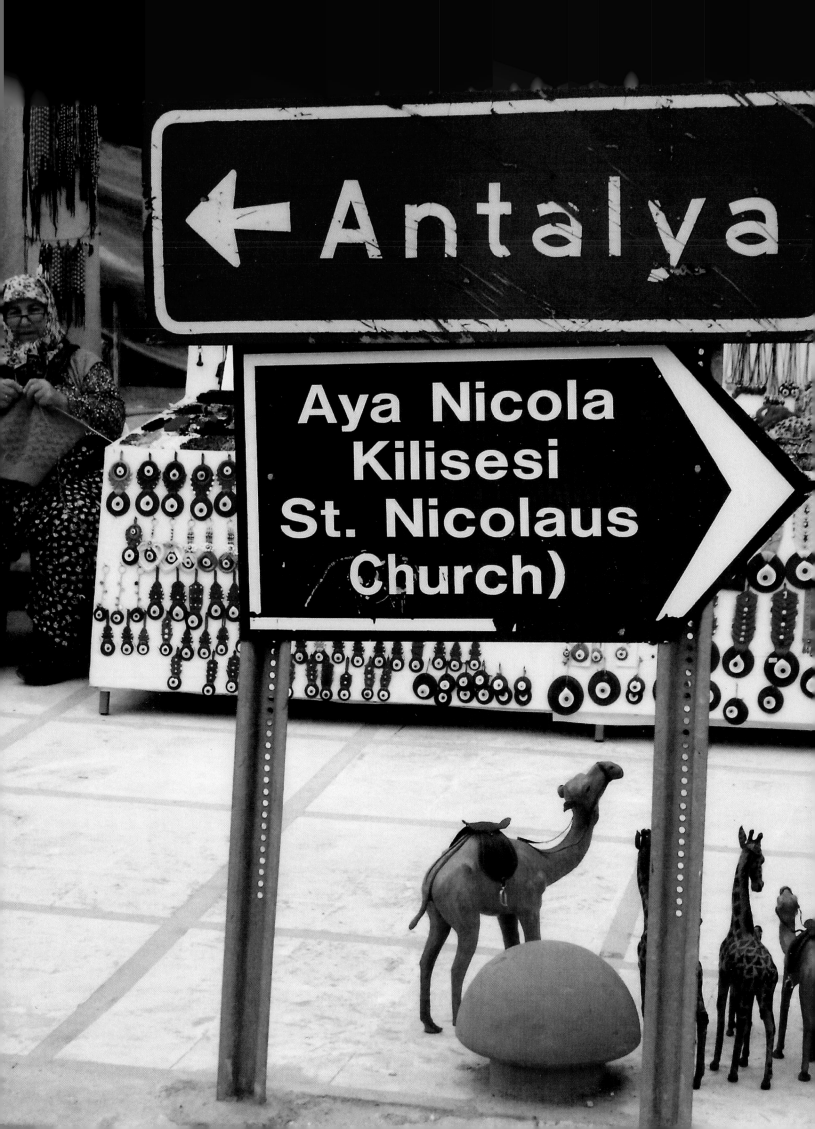

St. Nicolas as found in the chapel in Braga Cathedral, Portugal

were asked to come up with just one story about Washington's life, it would be the cherry tree story. Grant Wood's painting of little George and his axe has made the fiction even more real.

The same is true of the St. Nicholas stories. Whether some are less true than others is really a moot question, for they have already achieved immortality by still being vibrantly alive almost seventeen centuries after Nicholas's death. This is no more an issue than whether the characters of Homer's *Iliad* and *Odyssey* are literally true some twenty-eight centuries after he wrote them. Who questions the reality of Tolstoy's reflective Prince Andre and bewitching Natasha? Or Sienkiewicz's patrician Vinitius and devout Lygia? Or Moliere's bombastic Tartuffe or Cervantes's Don Quixote?

The St. Nicholas stories may be divided into three types: (1) those that are true or appear to be true to the spirit of the original act (most of these were probably first told during his lifetime or shortly thereafter); (2) those that appear to be based on actual incidents but were subsequently embellished; (3) those that are so heavily dependent on the supernatural that modern scholars might be tempted to doubt the story's authenticity. But the early Christians didn't see it that way at all. Ancelet-Hustache maintains that "Our ancestors in the faith cared little for critical accuracy. They loved marvels, and lived by them. The greater scale on which a miracle flouted the laws of nature, the better they liked it, for the more it showed the ever-fresh omnipotence of God's love. They were like children who want their stories repeated again and again" (Ancelet-Hustache, 19). Ancelet-Hustache also points out that since most of us believe in a Higher Power, and believe that God is capable of performing miracles, how then can we metaphorically remove that possibility from the lives of the early Christians?

These miracle stories—such as those having to do with St. Nicholas—were not only retold in Latin and Greek but also in all the regional dialects. And the very nature of oral transmission means that rarely would a retelling be an exact one. Furthermore, storytellers tended to cut and paste their story parts, applying them indiscriminately from one saint to another.

Now that we realize that we need to approach the stories about St. Nicholas with the same willing suspension of disbelief

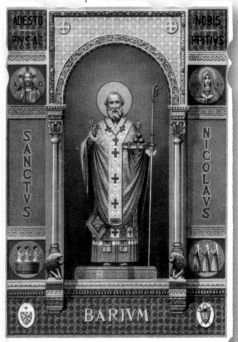

Holy card of St. Nicholas of Bari

we use when dealing with imaginative literature, we are ready to hear some of the most memorable ones.

A Selfless Life

According to the story that has come down to us, Nicholas's parents had long wished for a child but had been unable to conceive. As was true with Samuel's mother Hannah in Scripture, the mother (some call her Ona, some Johane) and the father (some call him Theopannes, some Epiphanes), finding themselves unable to conceive, prayed for God to grant them a child. If the child were to be a boy, they promised to dedicate his life to God's service. Late in life, their prayers were finally answered, and Nicholas (meaning "People's Victor") was born. True to their vow, his wealthy parents dedicated him to God. Since no other children came their way, he was given *all* of their attention.

Reportedly, when the baby Nicholas was placed in a bath right after birth, he immediately stood up by himself. Also, he apparently was granted religious knowledge not usually given to babies: he would refuse his mother's breast on Wednesdays and Fridays (the traditional days of fasting). Such precociousness was equated with God's special favor by early Christians.

The boy's childhood was generally a joyful one. "Generally," because the plague came to Patara early in his youth. The disease quickly spread from house to house, and soon people began to die. In the end, the plague took both the boy's parents. An uncle was a bishop, and he accepted the responsibility of the boy's upbringing, education, and mentoring. Nicholas, being by nature deeply religious, fit in well with the priests and sisters.

Life in the church compound was simple and austere. Even at this early age, it was clear that Nicholas was generous and deeply concerned for the problems and needs of others. Not only did the priests and sisters love him, but so did all the others who came in contact with him. As he daily observed the ebb and flow of suffering humanity

Card depicting the story of the infant Nicholas standing by himself when he was given a bath immmediately after his birth

GENTILE DA FABRIANO   *The Birth of St Nicholas*

Eastern Europe knows well St. Nicholas and the traditions surrounding him.

14

Pozdrav od Mikuláše

Issued in 1987 by the Vatican Post to mark the ninth centenary of the translation of the relics from Turkey to Bari. This stamp shows a different representation of the very popular legend of the gold coins for the girls with no dowries.

seeking help from the bishop and his associates, he pondered long about his legacy and wondered how he could make a difference with it. One thing he was sure of was that his wealth would be distributed in Christ's name, not his.

As the boy grew into adulthood, he found many ways in which to make a difference, to step in surreptitiously and help where the need was greatest. Little by little, he began to give his wealth away, but in secret. The most beloved Nicholas story coming out of his early years is that of the Three Dowerless Daughters.

In those days, men did not marry women who were destitute. Unless the father offered the suitor a dowry, the poor daughter was doomed. The alternatives were equally grim: being sold as a slave or becoming a woman of the streets. A neighbor Nicholas knew had three beautiful daughters who were of age. Each had suitors. Unfortunately, however, the once affluent nobleman had recently lost his fortune. It wasn't hard, in those days of piracy, to lose all one owned in one attack on a trading ship. Now the father faced the darkest days of his life—what should he do? He made it a matter of continual prayer: that God would save his daughters from a fate worse than death. But finally the time came when the decision could be delayed no longer. For the benefit of the other two, the eldest would have to be sacrificed; with this money, the other two could survive a while longer, and perhaps a modest dowry for one of them could somehow be eked out. The daughters had no say in the matter, for in those days a father's word was law, and women had very few rights. Word spread throughout the community of the family's terrible plight; and the story finally reached young Nicholas.

It didn't take Nicholas long to come up with a plan of action. Knowing that the father would never have accepted charity, and furthermore being determined to remain anonymous, he decided to act that very night. All his life Nicholas was known for moving into action when the need was greatest. Late that night, approaching the home of the father and his three daughters, Nicholas reached in through an open window and dropped a bag of gold coins on the floor (some maintain that Nicholas climbed up on the roof and dropped the sack of gold down the chimney). Next morning, to the family's joy and astonishment, there was the bag of gold! Weeping in joy and relief, all knelt down to thank God for this unexpected miracle. With this gold, the oldest daughter was able to be dowered and married, as well as leaving her father and sisters enough to live on for some time.

An altar frontal covering from St. Nicholas Anglican Church, Chiswick, London, featuring the legend of the poor girls and the bags of gold coins

Supporting Romanian orphans is this card from the organization FARA. It shows Nicholas with the Nativity scene on his priestly vestments. The design is a statue of St. Nicholas made by Steven Nemethy (1950-2004) for the FARA home in Suceava.

Christmas Greetings

But alas! Before too long, that money was all but gone, and the unthinkable once again had to be faced. Nicholas, who had been secretly monitoring the situation, found out just in time. That night, once again, through the open window went another bag of gold. Next morning, once again there was joy, thanksgiving, tears, and prayers of gratitude to God. With this gold, the second daughter was dowered and married, and there was quite a bit left to live on.

Considerable time passed, and the money held out a long time. But at last it too was gone, and the father informed his youngest that three miracles in a row was just too much to expect. Bowing to her tears, he kept delaying that irreversible act, hoping and praying that somehow God would also save his third daughter. But he strongly suspected that a human being had been God's instrument in saving his two older daughters, and he determined to stay awake all night so that he might catch the anonymous donor in the act and express his gratitude. Night after night he struggled against sleep as he kept his vigil, but to no avail. Finally, when delay was no longer possible, in the dead of night in came another sack of gold, this one landing in a stocking hung up to dry by the fireplace. This woke the father, and he chased his fleeing benefactor, shouting all the while, "Stop! Don't run away! I want to talk to you!" With an almost superhuman effort, the father finally caught up with Nicholas. Gasping for breath, he fell to his knees and tried to kiss his benefactor's feet. But Nicholas would have none of it. Reaching down, he raised the man to his feet. Then he told the father that God alone should be thanked for the three bags of gold. Furthermore, he made the father swear a solemn vow that the secret of where the gold came from would never be revealed while Nicholas lived. Reluctantly, the father made that promise. And kept it. Not until after Nicholas's death was the story told (most likely by the daughters). But, thanks to that third bag of gold, the youngest daughter was able to be dowered and married.

Although this act was the most famous, many other acts of similar selfless generosity took place. Whenever his identity was discovered, Nicholas exacted a similar promise. A number of these had to do with money; many others involved assistance of a dif-

Opposite right: A very Santa-looking St. Nicolas in Wales, in a parish church and village called St. Nicolas, near Cardiff

Far right: In St. Nicholas Anglican Church, Halewood, near Liverpool, England, is this stained-glass image of Nicholas and child. It is the creation of famed artist Sir Edward Burne-Jones.

ferent kind. Whatever help it might be, Nicholas always insisted that no credit or thanks be given to him, but to God only. In this, Nicholas was responding to Christ's repeated injunction that each of us should give in secret, for only in so doing could the giver be blessed. Not surprisingly, in a relatively small community such as Myra, it was not easy to keep this many secrets. Gradually, the people of that region became aware that among them was a selfless human being who went about doing good and directing all praise and gratitude to God.

It also became increasingly clear that Nicholas would never wall himself off from human suffering, for he was a man of the people. Like his Lord, he could not even conceive of a life being spent other than in daily service. The great brawling, hurting world would evermore be his pasture.

This altar frontal adorns the holy table in St. Nicholas Chapel in the great Anglican cathedral, York Minster, England.

It has been assumed that Nicholas was ordained by his uncle, first as a deacon, and later as a priest. As for his creature comforts, they were mighty few. Nicholas early on disciplined himself to fast every day, eating only in the evening, and then only one dish of food. Furthermore, he conditioned himself to either sleep on the floor or on rush matting.

Upon growing into adulthood, he became convicted that he should follow in the steps of his uncle and visit the Holy Land. In this quest, his uncle undoubtedly encouraged him. Finally, Nicholas boarded an Egyptian ship bound for Palestine. This was by choice, for he wanted to be alone on this journey, free to think, to pray, and to dream, without having to interact with friends and acquaintances. Nevertheless, other pilgrims bound for the same destination boarded, too.

The first night, as the ship was cutting its way through the choppy waters of what the ancients called "The Great Sea," Nicholas fell into a deep sleep. During the night, he dreamed the devil was in the process of cutting the ropes that supported the ship's main mast. In the morning, he accosted the sailors and told them of his dream. Interpreting it for them, he told them he was convinced that God had thereby warned him of a coming storm. Even though it would be a fierce one, he told them to fear not: "Trust in God because He will protect you from death." (To this day Greek vessels generally have an icon of St. Nicholas on board.)

Hardly had he finished speaking when the storm struck, dark clouds first, then the wind whipped the waves into a maelstrom. The crew lost all control of the ship, so they pulled down the sails and just let their bark wallow in the deep troughs and teeter on the crests of the monstrous waves. The terrified sailors begged Nicholas to pray for their lives. High above, the ropes securing the mast threatened to come loose. A sailor was given the perilous task of climbing the swaying mast in order to tighten the rope supports. After having tightened them, during a lurch of the ship the poor sailor lost his footing and plunged to his death on the deck far below.

Saint Nicolas, évêque.

Dep. 3928

A French holy card showing St. Nicholas, patron saint of sailors and mariners, praying for safety on the turbulent seas

To the people of his time, if anyone deserved to be called a saint, it was Nicholas.

Gradually the storm subsided, as Nicholas had predicted it would. But the sailor's death had cast a pall over everyone. Nicholas felt impressed to ask God, if it be His will, to bring the sailor back to life. Quickly, and miraculously, God answered his prayer and restored the sailor to life. Furthermore, it was as though he had merely been asleep: he awoke without any pain whatsoever.

When the ship reached port, word of the miracle raced ahead. Many people afflicted by all kinds of diseases streamed down to the dock; they all asked Nicholas if he would pray for their recovery. Nicholas did so, and many were healed by those intercessory prayers. After a day spent ministering to their needs, Nicholas proceeded to Jerusalem, where he visited the Holy Sepulchre, Golgotha, and other holy sites. He also journeyed to Bethlehem and settled in what is known as *Beit Jala* only a short distance

Postcard from Sweden, 1906

from what is today the Church of the Nativity. Apparently, he spent a number of his days in a cave similar to the cave that housed the Baby Jesus. (Visitors today can still find this cave in an Orthodox church dedicated to St. Nicholas in *Beit Jala.*) According to Simeon Metaphrastes, Nicholas had originally planned to stay in the Holy Land for some time, but "an angel of the Lord" ordered him to return home.

Back at the port, Nicholas finally was able to arrange passage on a ship. But the captain proved devious: once at sea, he changed directions. According to Symeon, God "raised a violent storm that caused the ship's rudder to be damaged beyond repair." As a result, the ship drifted rudderless across the sea, but "quite purposefully in a specific direction." Much later, the captain and his crew were awestruck to see the Patara harbor directly ahead.

Not long after his return, as he was meditating one afternoon in a chapel, Nicholas fell asleep. In his dream he had a vision in which Jesus informed him that a high calling (a significant leadership role) awaited him. In that dream Jesus told him that his calling was to serve his people. Nicholas awoke deeply puzzled. Just what did it all mean?

It wasn't many months before he found out. The aged bishop of Myra (his mentor and father-figure) died suddenly. Thousands came to the funeral service in the cathedral, and Nicholas joined them in mourning the bishop's passing. The announcement was made that a great Synod would be called during the next few days

In the midst of the Israeli-Palestinian conflict stands one of the greatest St. Nicholas shrines, in the Greek Orthodox Church in Beit Jala, just minutes from Bethlehem. It is believed that Nicholas used this crypt cave as his home when he was in the Holy Land. There are bullet holes in the doors and windows of the church.

to elect a successor. It was a heavy responsibility, for the Diocese of Myra was an extremely important one in that part of the empire.

Prayers and deliberations went on for days without any consensus. Who among them had the moral and spiritual stature to fill such shoes? One night a voice spoke to the most revered bishop in the Synod, commanding him to rise early and station himself at the doors of the cathedral before daybreak and to consecrate as bishop the first man entering the sanctuary who answered to the name "Nicholas." Several hours later, he shared the injunction with his hastily assembled fellow bishops and urged them to pray that God would bring the right person in at the right time.

Shortly after dawn, the doors were opened for Mattins, the early morning prayer service. As the bishop stood in the center aisle, the blinding Mediterranean sun blazed down through the great doorway. Who would come first?

Colorful windows from the Victorian era at St. Nic's Church, Nottingham, England.

Nicholas had awakened earlier than usual that morning and was strongly impressed to hurry over to the cathedral. As he walked into the foyer, he cast a shadow on the nave floor. An elderly bishop he didn't recognize abruptly stopped him and asked his name. Respectfully, he answered, "My name is Nicholas, your servant for Jesus Christ's sake." The bishop could contain his joy no longer but exclaimed in a loud voice that echoed through the empty cathedral, "Thanks be to God, Alleluia!" At this point the members of the Synod (a great number) entered through the cloister door.

Nicholas just stood there stunned: *What could all of this mean?*

The old bishop announced triumphantly, "Here, my brothers, is Nicholas. My dream is true! Let us greet our new bishop." The Synod members began to chant and sing. It was all too much for the young man: he turned to flee, but the verger stopped him.

Nicholas, come forward!" ordered the old bishop.

Still bewildered by it all, Nicholas finally obeyed and was slowly led to the bishop's throne. In the weeks that followed, the news of the new bishop's appointment spread quickly throughout the diocese and beyond. The great day finally arrived, and people came from many miles away to take part in the celebration. They cheered as their friend Nicholas entered the cathedral dressed in a simple cassock. Several hours later, the crowds outside who had been unable to get in saw the massive doors open and Nicholas, bishop of Myra, come forth to bless them and the city. Only now, as he stood there listening to their singing and clapping, as he wore the Golden Mitre, the colorful robes of a bishop with the pallium, and held the Gospel book, did his dreams begin to make sense.

As time passed and the people of Myra came to know their bishop better, it became increasingly clear that he remained the same Nicholas he had always been: humble, honest, energetic, caring, dedicated, and devoted to his Lord and his flock. His well-

Matthew Bell of St. Nicholas Anglican Cathedral, Newcastle upon Tyne, England, created this prize-winning drawing of the patron saint of the cathedral.

known compassion and generosity altered not at all in his new position. When he taught the gospel, people said listening to him was like receiving precious gems. Always he was concerned about the poor, those who were in trouble, those who were mistreated, and the children. His parishioners were quick to note that his giving tended to be done in secret, and many began to emulate him.

The Crucible

The altar at San Nicolas di Bari Church in Burgos, Spain, is breathtaking to behold.

Before long, however, a testing time came to the young bishop and his flock. Emperor Galerius, seeing in Christianity the last obstacle to absolute rule, urged his chief, Diocletian, to restore the Roman gods. Diocletian held back, believing there would be a high price to pay for such a step. Galerius waited, certain that Christians would make a mistake he could capitalize on. It happened one day at an imperial sacrifice: a Christian made the sign of the Cross to ward off evil demons. Evidently, it worked: the imperial priests were unable to find the marks on sacrificed animals they hoped to interpret. In order to find out who had intervened, Diocletian commanded that all who had been in attendance that day had to offer sacrifice to the gods or be flogged; and that all the soldiers in the army should also conform, or lose their positions. When many Christians refused to offer those sacrifices, the stage was set. At Galerius's instigation, in February of 303, the four caesars decreed the destruction of all Christian churches, the burning of all Christian books, the dissolution of all Christian congregations, the confiscation of all property belonging to Christians, the exclusion of all Christians from public office, and if Christians dared to meet together, they would be put to death. The signal to start this empire-wide attack on the Christian faith was the burning to the ground of the great cathedral at Nicomedia by imperial soldiers.

Christians were now, however, numerous enough to retaliate. Twice they set fire to Diocletian's palace. Hundreds of Christians were arrested, accused of arson, and tortured. Nicholas, knowing that if he were to go into hiding, his parishioners would suffer all the more because of it, calmly waited for the tread of the imperial soldiery outside the building where he ate and slept. He didn't have long to wait. One night, a thunderous knock ordered those inside to open the door immediately—that it was Caesar's will. Nicholas calmly opened it, even though he knew he might never see his people again.

Death would have been easier to take than the fiendish tortures the Romans used to break down the resistance of their victims. But somehow, thanks to his faith in the Christ who had endured the anguish of the Cross, Nicholas found the strength to hold out. The pain would mount until flesh and blood could stand no more, and he would mercifully lose consciousness. Next day it would begin all over again.

A banner of the Virgin Mary and St. Nicholas in the church and city of Sint-Niklaas, Flanders, Belgium

Faith in Christ gave Nicholas the strength to endure the torture of the Roman persecution.

That September, Diocletian ordered the torture of any Christian who refused to worship Roman gods. And he gave orders that soldiers should not wait for Christians to disobey, but track down every last one. Then, tired of the whole thing, he resigned the imperial purple and left the firestorm to his successors.

Maximian carried out the edict mercilessly in Italy. Galerius, now Augustus, unleashed a reign of terror throughout the entire East. The roll of martyrs increased everywhere except in Gaul or Britain, for Constantius alone refused to institute a bloodbath, contenting himself with burning down a few churches. But his realm was the only refuge. The historian Eusebius noted that "men were flogged till the flesh hung from their bones, or their flesh was scraped to the bone with shells; salt or vinegar was poured upon the wounds; the flesh was cut off bit by bit and fed to waiting animals; or, bound to crosses, men were eaten piecemeal by starved beasts. Some

From the Ukraine, a soldier's dream and remembrance, 1913

victims had their fingers pierced with sharp reeds under the nails; some had their eyes gouged out; some were suspended by a hand or a foot; some had molten lead poured down their throats; some were beheaded, or crucified or beaten to death with clubs; some were torn apart by being tied to the momentarily bent branches of trees."

This terrible persecution continued for eight long years. Though thousands recanted under the influence of terrible torture, most, like Bishop Nicholas, stood firm. As this resolve gradually impressed the pagan populace, more and more of them began to speak out against the most ferocious oppression in Roman history. In fact, many pagans risked their lives by hiding or protecting Christians.

By 311, Galerius had had enough. The most widespread persecution in Roman history had failed to force every knee to bow to Caesar and Roman gods. The people were outraged, the emperor's own guards were sullen about their role in this unrelenting bloodbath, and the Christians continued to choose torture or death rather than worship the emperor. *He*—God? What a laugh! Galerius was dying of a terminal illness and would soon be dead himself. His own wife had turned against his vindictive edict, imploring him to make peace with the all-powerful God of the Christians before it was too late. So Galerius finally caved in: he promulgated an edict of toleration, recognized Christianity as a "lawful religion," and contritely asked the Christians to pray for him in return for "our most gentle clemency."

What jubilation reigned in the Christian community! In spite of impossible odds, God had brought them through the furnace of persecution. Gradually, dungeon doors began to swing open, releasing what was left of those who had stood firm against hell itself. In one of those prisons, one morning, a guard descended into the bowels of the earth, unlocked an iron door, and informed a man young in years, but now aged by torture, mistreatment, privation, and separation from the world outside, that he was free.

Few would have recognized this frail man, attired in filthy rags, unkempt, unshaven, unbathed, as the stalwart bishop who had descended into those subterranean regions years before. Years that had seemed endless—without beginning, without end. The guard, who had learned to admire the prisoner's inner strength and rock-solid integrity, now unlocked the shackles and gently led Nicholas up the many damp steps, through foul air that gradually became pure, up and up and up until the blazing sun and deep blue Mediterranean sky so blinded him that he was at first unable to believe this was real. But it *was* real. In the street, he was approached by Christians who asked who he was; when informed, they praised God and assured him that his troubles were over.

Some weeks later, a ship sailed into Myra's harbor. Disembarking was a man so changed by all he had endured that at first his own people failed to recognize him. When someone finally

Porch window in St. Andrew's Parish Church in Surbiton shows St. Nicholas, protector of children. (Photo by Veronica Elks)

exclaimed, "It's our bishop! It's Nicholas himself come back to us! He's not dead after all!" people erupted out of every doorway and engulfed him in a tidal wave of tears, joy, thanksgiving, and love.

And the good bishop urged his people to give thanks to God.

Soon he was back on his accustomed rounds, and the rhythm of his old life gradually resumed.

When Nicholas returned from prison, inwardly strengthened and seasoned by all that he had endured, the "Boy Bishop" was a boy no longer. Somewhere in that crucible of seemingly unending anguish, he had achieved a level of insight, vision, wisdom, and greatness granted only to those who have been forged in fire. To the people of his time, if anyone deserved to be called a saint, it was he.

Detail from card "Nicholas of Myra" by Kris Meigs, Santa Rosa Beach, Florida, USA

Nicholas of Myra

So they came to him—all those who needed strength, courage, comfort, even those who were physically sick, and urged him to intercede with the Eternal on their behalf. They did so because there could no longer be any doubt that God and he walked hand in hand. He was famous now, not only among Christians, but among pagans as well.

Two years later, church properties throughout the empire were finally restored.

It didn't take Nicholas long to discover that the victory won against Caesar did not equate to victory over the Greco-Roman gods. Those gods had been venerated for millennia and showed not the slightest desire to leave. Fiercely did their priests and priestesses hold their ground. Certainly, this was true in Myra's magnificent temple of Artemis. Artemis (known to Romans as Diana), as a daughter of Zeus, was viewed as one of the most powerful of all the ancient gods. Artemis was, among other things, the goddess of seafarers. She was the one sailors prayed to for fair weather and successful sea voyages. She and Poseidon (Neptune).

Diana/ Artemis, the arch-enemy of St. Nicholas. This statue stands near the icon of St. Nicholas and some bones said to be his relics in the Antalya Museum in Turkey.

Artemis's temple in Myra was beautiful almost beyond belief, with extensive grounds, complete with many plants chosen for their ability to keep the earth fresh. There was a great inner court, surrounded by columns, altars, and statuary (with a large statue of the goddess). Nicholas had known for a long time that sooner or later he would be forced to battle with Artemis, who he considered to be leagued with the Dark Power. That war now raged, with no quarter given on either side. In the end, the prayers of Nicholas won out. Simeon Metaphrastes tells the story in these words: "As soon as the Saint began praying, the altar collapsed, and the statues of idols fell down, like leaves of a tree when a strong wind blows in autumn.

The demons who inhabited the place left, but protested to the Saint amidst their tears: 'You have been unjust to us. We did you no harm, and yet you send us away from our home. We had made this our home, while these misguided people adored us, and now where can we go?' And the Saint replied, 'Go to Hell's fire, which has been lit for you by the devil and his crew.' In this manner, all altars in the area were destroyed." Even the demons who ruled there found themselves powerless against Nicholas and his God, and fled, shrieking.

Impact of these Stories

The stories of Nicholas's nativity and early years quite likely came later after the evolution of the myth was already in motion. They helped to build a foundation under the myth by depicting his miraculous birth, how spiritual he was during his earliest years, and how predestined he appeared to be from birth to do great things for God. Even his name was significant ("People's Victor" rather than a victor chosen by a ruler or members of the clergy), for it would be the people who would elevate him to sainthood and keep his memory ever fresh.

King's College Cambridge (England) Chapel of Our Lady and St. Nicholas is likely the most famous church associated with St. Nicholas. The chapel has as its focus the great Anglican choral tradition, and the much-loved Festival of Nine Lessons and Carols is broadcast worldwide from here each Christmas Eve.

Unquestionably, however, it was the story of the Three Dowerless Daughters that made St. Nicholas a legend. It had everything going for it: three lovely young women threatened by a fate worse than death, a desperate father, and a wealthy young man who gave away his riches secretly and anonymously. The post-apostolic church was looking for role models, and Nicholas's selfless giving made him a natural. Through the centuries since then, this has remained the most beloved Nicholas story, transcending ages, transcending time. In fact, many consider it to be the genesis of all gift-giving. As for the three golden balls (symbols for sacks of gold), they form the most common image on St. Nicholas statues and art.

The early church leaders were also seeking for a Christian replacement to the Greco-Roman god of the sea, Poseidon/Neptune. Since the Mediterranean represented both their breadbasket and their fastest transportation system, and since seamen were notoriously superstitious about the sea and the weather, the story about St. Nicholas helping to control storms and mediating with God to bring the dead sailor back to life made him a natural replacement for Poseidon in the church. Pagan beliefs died hard, so it was essential that the proposed replacement figure be vivid, persuasive, likeable, and powerful. Nicholas qualified on all fronts, and his visit to the Holy Land added additional validity to his candidacy for sainthood.

Next came the bishop story. The early church, each generation strongly believing that Christ would return during their lifetime, didn't encourage marriage and family much, hence the attractiveness of someone like Nicholas, who dedicated his entire life to God's service. Also, in those troublesome times, the church community had a major

Likely the oldest representation of St. Nicholas in the Western world, St. Nicholas Church, Potter Heigham, Norfolk, England, 10th century

> **S**t. Nicholas was a Christian replacement for Poseidon as a protector of sailors.

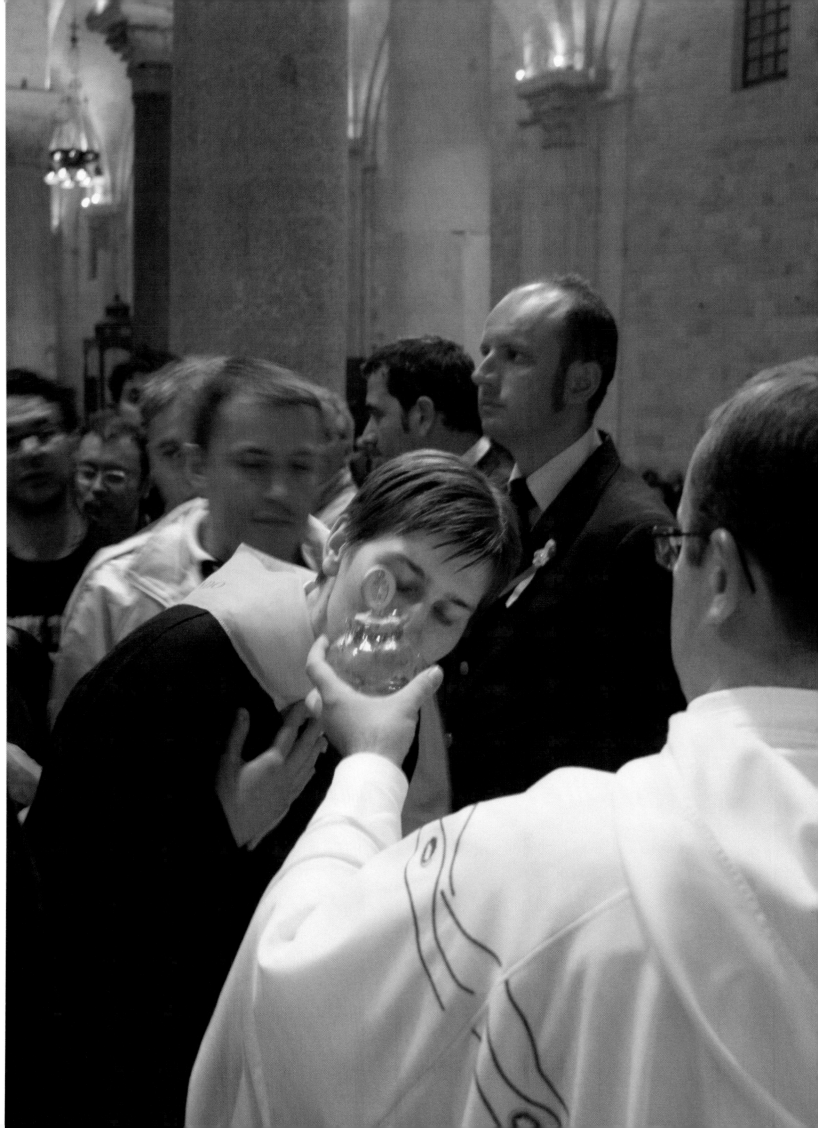

too. So did Maximinas Doza. Now there were six who claimed supremacy—and the empire spiraled into chaos. Maximian tried to dethrone Constantine; Constantine defeated him and kindly permitted him to commit suicide. When Galerius died in 311, full-scale war took place. Constantine led his army across the Alps, defeated one army at Turin, advanced on Rome, and on October 27, 312, Constantine cornered Maxentius at the Tiber.

According to Eusebius of Caesarea (historian and confidant of Constantine), on the afternoon before the battle, Constantine had a vision: he saw a flaming cross in the sky, along with three Greek words, *en toutoi nika* ("in this sign conquer"). That night, Constantine was commanded in a dream to have his soldiers mark an X with a line drawn through it and curled around the top (the symbol of Christ). When Constantine awakened next morning, he was so impressed by the dream that he immediately ordered the creation of a new standard to be carried into the forefront of the battle. That standard (carrying the initials of Christ interwoven with a cross) would henceforth be known as the *labarium*. As Maxentius's banner displayed his allegiance to the unconquerable Sun of Mithras, the battle took on an unexpected spiritual dimension. Since there were numerous Christians in Constantine's army, he certainly faced no opposition with *them*! Under this banner, Constantine drove Maxentius and thousands of his soldiers into the Tiber, where they drowned in their armor. Then Constantine entered Rome, now supreme ruler of the western part of the empire.

Next, Constantine met with Licinius to consolidate their Christian base. Their "Edict of Milan" (313) not only confirmed the edict by Galerius but extended toleration to *all* religions. They also ordered the return of all confiscated Christian property. Ten years after the Edict of Milan, Constantine (now the acknowledged defender of Christianity), with 130,000 men, met Licinius (the defender of paganism), with 160,000 men, at Adrianople, and again at Chrysopolis. Licinius was defeated, and Constantine thereby became undisputed master of the Roman world.

Classic icon of St. Nicholas

Seventeen long bloody years had passed before Constantine became monarch of the entire empire. During those long treks from battle to battle, he had thought a great deal about the city of Rome. Eventually, he concluded that it was too corrupt to be worth saving. Immediately after Chrysopolis, he implemented his momentous decision to move the capital of the empire from the Tiber to the Golden Horn, from ancient Rome to ancient Byzantium. It was a calculated decision. Once he cast his lot with the Christians, it made sense to move his capital to where Christians were strongest.

If you look at today's map, it's hard to understand Constantine's reasoning. But if you open your Bible to maps that detail the missionary journeys of the apostle Paul, you'll notice that the eastern Mediterranean was then the hub of early Christianity. By the time of St. Nicholas and Constantine, almost three centuries later, it was even more so. Throughout Asia Minor, a minimum of 25 percent professed Christianity. Powerful bishops ruled great sees such as Alexandria, Carthage, Jerusalem, Hippo, Caesarea, Damascus, Ephesus, Athens, and Byzantium.

Other cities known to students of Bible times were also Christian centers: cities like Thessalonica, Berea, Corinth, Phillippa, Thyatira, Pergamum, Miletus, Nicomedia, Colosse, Myra, Lystra, Philadelphia, Sardis, Laodecea, Memphis, Babylon, Capernaum, Neapolis, Gaza, Tyre, Sidon, Heliopolis, Petra, Thebes, Adrianopolis, Seleucia, and Derbe. These cities just happened to be the center of St. Nicholas's world.

Engraving of St. Nicholas Church, Moscow

Mosaic of St. Nicholas in St. Nicholas Greek-Catholic Church in Berlin, Germany

Belfry of S.t Ivan, with the Church of S.t Nicholas, in the Kremlin, at Moscow,

after a drawing by Camporesi.

This unusual chapel features St. Constantine with the Mothers' Union Banner of the stunning St. Nicholas Church, Blakeney, Norfolk, England.

Byzantium was already almost a thousand years old when Constantine decided to build "New Rome" there. The emperor chose wisely, for no site on earth could have surpassed it, situated as it was on the crossroads of the world, the place where Europe and Asia meet, where the West ends and the East begins.

In November of 324, Constantine the Great led a small army of aides, engineers, priests, etc., from the harbor of Byzantium out across the nearby hills. As they progressed, the foundation positions of the proposed new capital were duly marked. When some questioned why the site was so vast, Constantine answered, "I shall advance till He, the invisible God who marches before me, thinks proper to stop." Afterward, he summoned thousands of workmen to build the great city. And he issued orders that the finest and most acclaimed art in the empire should be requisitioned and sent to the new capital. Same for Christian relics. Great walls were constructed, as were palaces, homes, administrative buildings, squares, boulevards, and fountains. A magnificent hippodrome, seating 70,000, for the people's games was also constructed. The city was dedicated on May 11, 330. Within seven years, 50,000 people had moved in; by A.D. 400, 100,000; and by A.D. 500, almost a million. For over a thousand years it would remain the richest, most beautiful, and most civilized city in the world (Durant, *The Age of Faith*, 3–6).

But meanwhile, problems were mounting where the emperor least expected them. Though he had not openly converted to Christianity, he had all but married the Christian community in a political sense. Not because of childhood indoctrination, for his mother hadn't become a Christian until after Constantius divorced her. Nevertheless, Helena was a powerful force in her own right. After Chrysopolis, she became the imperial requisitioner of Christian relics, bringing them to the new Rome in the name of the emperor.

Constantine was profoundly impressed by the fortitude and courage evidenced by the Christians during the three persecutions during his lifetime. He was also impressed by other qualities evidenced by Christians, especially their integrity and strong sense of marriage and family. Perhaps the support of such a loyal hierarchical church might help him solidify his political power base.

Gradually, as he consolidated his power, he favored Christians more and more, and began curtailing the freedoms of pagan sects.

Statue of St. Nicholas ensconced at the Hussite Church of St. Nicholas in Prague, Czech Republic

He gave his sons an orthodox Christian education, and gave Christian leaders civil power to go along with their religious power.

What he hadn't counted on was the fall-out from terminating the periodic Christian persecutions. As long as they were suffering or dying for their faith, the church remained pure, but when they became dominant in the political arena, the church gradually succumbed to the blandishments the world had to offer and began to break up into snarling sects, each determined to injure or destroy the others.

Constantine was now dismayed to discover great cracks in the Christian community. First there were the Donatists, who believed only the certifiably pure—themselves—could be trusted to lead the church. Second was the rise of monasticism. As the result of the materialism generated by the church's transformation from a persecuted church to the dominant state-sanctioned church, many Christians concluded that only by withdrawing from the world could Christianity be saved. Third, and the most serious crack of all, was that represented by the philosophy of a tall, thin, melancholic mystic from Alexandria named Arius. Arius maintained that Christ was not a co-equal with God at all, but merely the first and highest of all created beings. Congregation after congregation split right down the middle on this issue, and each side attempted to destroy the other. Needless to say, the pagans were delighted to see the Christians destroying themselves without any outside help.

The loving saint with a loving child in a classic Dutch postcard for December 5

Constantine did not hear about the schism until 323, when he had just defeated Licinius and was looking forward to some well-deserved rest. As soon as he had digested the news, he wrote both Bishop Alexander and Arius, urging them to peaceably resolve their differences; but his letter accomplished nothing. Constantine was stunned by the speed at which Arianism spread, for soon the entire eastern Roman Empire was aflame with it. Even though he was not a theologian, he realized full well that if Christ was not perceived to be God, Christianity would crack wide open; and if that were permitted to happen, the church, instead of being

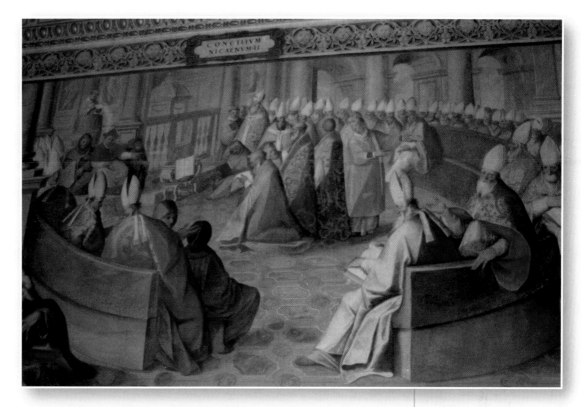

A mural of the Council of Nicaea in the Vatican Museum

an asset to him, would become a liability. That realization resulted in some of the darkest days of his life.

The Council of Nicaea

There have been two epic conclaves in the history of the Western world, two defining moments that have never been equaled at any time or any place.

The second was the showdown in 1551 between the twenty-year-old ruler of half of Europe and most of the Americas, Charles V. The host city was Worms, capital city of Hesse, near Heidelberg. In 436, Worms and the Burgundian kingdom had been destroyed by the Huns and Romans after they adopted Arianism. That event was later incorporated into the *Nibelungelied* and *Rosengarten*. The antagonist was until then an almost unknown Catholic monk named Martin Luther. On April 17, Luther stood alone facing a glittering Diet, composed of the emperor, six electors, and an awesome assembly of princes, nobles, prelates, and burghers. That event changed the world.

The first took place 1,226 years earlier, in 325. Constantine, although not a Christian by profession, decided to assume that role in order to preserve the empire. He summoned a great conclave of bishops from all across the Mediterranean to meet in Nicaea (Iznik in today's Turkey) near his capital, Nicomedia. Ironically, the primary purpose of the enclave was to deal with Arius, whose doctrine would later doom the first city of Worms.

The Chapel of St. Nicolas in Rome's French Church of St. Louis King of France

The Council was to meet in the emperor's palace in Nicaea of Bythinia, very close to the summer palace in Nicomedia. For days, ships had been arriving with the bishops and their entourages who came from as far away as Cordova, Spain.

The morning of that May 20 was one the participants never forgot: the deep blue sky of Bythinia, the grandeur of the sprawling palace and its great hall, the sight of famous bishops walking into the hall in all their episcopal glory. Here and there were figures who towered over their age: personages such as the bishop of Alexandria, the bishop of Antioch, the bishop of Jerusalem, the bishop of Nicomedia (Eusebius), the bishop of Cordova, and the bishop of Caesarea (another Eusebius). Also attending were the next generation of bishops, including Athanasius, destined to become bishop of Alexandria.

The opulence of the magnificent palace must have seemed almost surreal to Nicholas and his fellow bishops, so recently tortured and entombed in dungeons. Even more so when the brass trumpets announced the arrival of the emperor, resplendent in his imperial robes. He proceeded until he reached his throne (covered with gold leaf) on a raised dais, one half of the bishops positioned on either side of him. In his role as President, Constantine would coordinate the enclave's discussion during the rest of May, all of June, and finally conclude on July 25.

The emperor opened that first session with an earnest appeal to the bishops, urging them to make church unity their number one priority. Before long, Arius was permitted to make his case. He calmly declared that Christ was "a created being, not equal to the Father, and divine only by participation."

According to the Athenian monk Damaskinos, this is what took place as Arius was presenting his case:

> "The emperor was sitting on his throne, flanked by 159 bishops to his left and 159 to his right. Arian was presenting his views with great vigor and detail. As Saint Nicholas observed the scene, the bishops listened to Arius in complete silence and without interrupting this discourse. Outraged, and prompted by his saintly vigor, he left his seat and walked up to Arius, faced him squarely and slapped his face.
>
> At this, the assembly was shocked. Arius's supporters turned to the emperor, asking that he intervene and punish Nicholas. They said, 'Oh Just One, tell us, can it be fair that in your very presence someone should be permitted, without hindrance, to assault another? If he has anything to say in rebuttal, by all means let him have his say. But if he is not sufficiently learned to make a proper argument, then it were better if he remain in his seat, quietly, and listen to others who are prepared to state their case in words.'
>
> "Arius himself spoke directly to the emperor, 'Should anyone who has the temerity to hit me, in front of Your Majesty, remain unpunished?' Emperor Constantine replied, 'Indeed, there is a law which forbids anyone to lift his hand in violence in the presence of the emperor and it specifies that his hand be cut off. However, it is not up to me, in this Assembly, to act upon it. Instead, you, Your Holinesses, should make the decision in this case; I leave it to your judgment, whether and how this act is to be punished.'
>
> "The bishops conferred with each other, and when they came to a decision, they said to the emperor, 'Your Majesty, the bishop of Myra has acted wrongfully. We all saw it happen and attest to it. We therefore ask your permission to let us strip him of his clerical garments, shackle him, and place him under guard as a prisoner. In this way, he shall not be permitted to participate in the proceedings of the Council for the

Stained-glass image in the Anglican Church of St. Nicholas, Sturry, Kent, England

Below: Elaborate European postcard showing a bishop speaking to his people

Above: Colorful European card depicting the welcoming of a bishop into his cathedral

rest of our deliberations. Once the synod is completed, a final judgment in this case may be made.'

"As a result, that evening, Nicholas was made a prisoner in another wing of the Palace. He was placed in a jail-like room, without his bishop's mantle and shackled on hand and foot. However, during the night he was visited by Jesus [and His] Mother. They observed Saint Nicholas in his cell and said, 'Nicholas, why are you imprisoned?' And Saint Nicholas said, 'Because of my love for you.' First they freed him from his shackles. And then Jesus said, 'Take this!' and he gave him a volume of the Holy Scripture. Then [Mary] went away, returned, and brought him his bishop's garments, so that he might clothe himself with appropriate dignity. At peace, he studied the Holy Book through the night.

"The next morning, a jailer came to bring him bread, saw that Nicholas was no longer shackled, that he was clothed in the garments of his position, and that he was studying the Scriptures in his cell. Even his stole was in one hand, while he held the book with the other. News of this miraculous event was quickly brought to the emperor. He asked that Nicholas be freed, and when the two men met, the emperor asked the bishop's forgiveness" (Ebon, 34–35).

> The saint now is coming
> We all sing with cheer.
> A day of rejoicing
> His message is clear.
> We love you, St. Nicholas,
> Your praises we sing,
> Awaiting the good news
> This glad season brings.

It appears probable that the original account has been embellished. Quite possibly, the good bishop may have lost his composure and attacked Arius personally; however, the heavenly visitation section quite likely was added later for effect. In all probability, the fact that Nicholas's impulsive act weighed in on the emperor's side rather than on Arius's saved him. Secretly, Constantine may have enjoyed it, yet felt that the firebrand deserved a lesson for forgetting in whose presence he was sitting.

The issue of Arianism was debated loud and long during the Council, tempers getting frayed in the process. Constantine not only served as moderator, he entered into the discussions. All around the room were attendants of the emperor, as well as members of the Imperial Guard. The opposition had been given plenty of time to get ready for Arius. Clever questioning forced him to admit that if Christ were but a created creature, what was there to prevent him from veering out of virtue into vice? Pugnacious and clever Archdeacon Athanasius of Alexandria, a brilliant theologian and debater, pointed out that if Christ and the Holy Spirit were not one with the Father, then there was no alternative to polytheism.

The deliberations on the matter went through several stages before the final condemnation of Arius. In the end there was a small hard core of support for the Alexandrian position, and another of equal size for the Arian. The rest of the bishops, not being theologians, were strung out somewhere between. But few of them wished to force an outright break with their peers. Had the emperor not forced the issue there would have been no condemnation of Arius. Constantine was far-sighted enough to know that if the bishops adjourned without taking a position on the issue, then the conclave would have been for naught. The bishops, confronted with an intractable emperor, rather grudgingly came up with a statement of belief that left squirm-room for everyone, and put them all on record. This is how it read:

> *We believe in one God, the Father Almighty, maker of all things visible or invisible, and in one Lord Jesus Christ, the Son of God, begotten . . . not made, being of one essence (homoousion) with the Father . . . who for us men and our salvation came down and was made flesh, was made man, suffered, rose again the third day, ascended into heaven, and comes to judge the quick and the dead.*

Only five bishops—at the end, only two—refused to sign this statement of belief. Those two, with the "unrepentant Arius," were anathematized by the Council. The emperor made clear his position on the matter by exiling them. Also, Constantine issued an edict that ordered all Arian books to be burned and made concealment of his books a crime punishable by death. Arianism would continue to disrupt the church and the empire for many centuries to come.

Over time this simple statement of belief became known as the Nicene Creed. The mere fact that they signed it forced the church leaders to debate it, study it, tinker with it, until eventually they hammered it into a creed that would unify believers.

This was not all the Council accomplished. It was here they declared that all churches should observe Easter on the same day (date to be named each year by the bishop of Alexandria, and agreed upon by the bishop of Rome). Some maintain that the Council helped to define the biblical canon; others maintain

Near Bari is the city of Rutigliano, Italy, where the cathedral is dedicated to San Nicola. This statue adorns the church.

"The Madonna and Child with Saint John the Baptist and Saint Nicholas of Bari (The Ansidei Madonna)," **Raphael, 1505. St. Nicholas is on the right.**

SALVE·MATER·CHRISTI

The Ansidei Madonna - Raphael
National Gallery, London

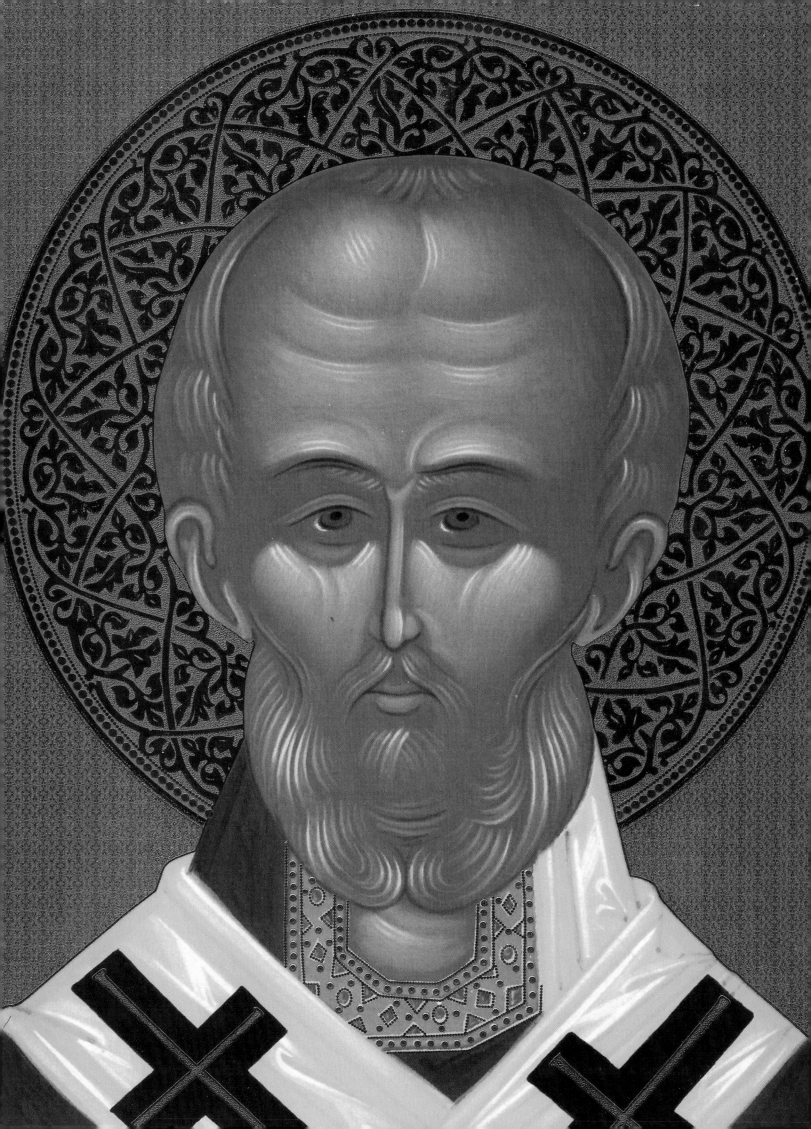

that there was already a consensus on it. The Nicene Creed would eventually result in the defeat of Arianism and victory of Ortho-dox Trinitarianism.

The Council also revealed that the emperor was not only supreme in secular matters, he was also supreme in matters that dealt with religion.

～

Constantine lived only twelve more years. At Easter of 337, there was an empire-wide celebration of the thirtieth anniversary of his becoming Caesar. But even as the celebrations continued, the emperor knew the sands of his life were running out. As the end drew near, he finally took the long-delayed step: he called for a priest to administer the sacrament of baptism to him. He had many sins to account for, including the executions of a wife, son, and nephew. But even so, he was a far bet-ter man than most rulers of his time.

The good bishop would outlive his liege-lord by only six years. By this time, his fame was already radi-ating in waves out of his native Lycia into the great East. It was his good fortune to be born in the right place at the right time, the end of the old Roman Empire and the beginning of the Byzantine Empire. Born at the end of the post-apostolic church and the beginning of the Orthodox and Catholic churches. Born at the end of the pagan world and the begin-ning of the Christian world. During his brief life-span, he would be a casualty of the last great per-secution of the Christians; he would see the rise of Donatism and the beginning of its long decline. He would experience the earliest stage of monasticism. And he would be one of the fiercest gladiators in the most pivotal war the Christian church has ever fought: Trinitarianism versus Arianism.

As we shall see, Nicholas will go on to become all things to all people, as each age reinvents him. The patron saint of practically everybody. A man who will refuse to stay dead. A man who will have immortality thrust upon him, whether he'd have wanted it or not. And, perhaps strangest of all, a man who, like the proverbial Wandering Jew, will wander through the centuries playing many parts in the great drama between the forces of Good and Evil.

According to Voragine's *Golden Legend*, ". . . when the Lord decided to take Nicholas to Him, the Saint prayed that he might send him his angels. With head still bowed in prayer, he saw them approaching. He recited the Psalm *'In te Domine sperari'* [In Thee, O Lord, have I trusted (Psalm 30 and 31)], and when he reached the words *'In manus tuas Domine commendo spiritum meum'* [Into thy hands, O Lord, I commend my spirit (v. 5)], he breathed his last, and at his passing, the heavenly choirs were heard. This was in the year of our Lord 343." . . . And the mists of Myra closed in around him.

Closing out this biographical section is a remarkable statement penned over 1,600 years later, after an examination of the St. Nicholas relics in Bari, Italy, by Dr. Luigi Martino, Professor of Anatomy at the University of Bari, and Dr. Alfredo Ruggieri, assistant to Prof. Martino. During 1953 restoration work at the St. Nicholas Basilica in Bari, a commission was set up by the pope and Enrico Nicodemo, Roman Catholic archbishop of Bari, for the purpose of studying the relics in order to give them canonical recognition. Following are some of their findings:

"The sacred Relics were found in a monolithic reliquary of hard rock. Since the period of their deposition in 1089 the reliquary had been covered with a succession of stone slabs. The Relics in the reliquary were floating in a transparent, colorless, and odorless liquid, which was almost 300 centimeters deep. The examination of the liquid by the Institute of Chemistry and Hygienics at the University of Bari showed that it was clear water, 'free from salt and devoid of micro organisms.' The inquiry proved that this liquid came from the marrow of spongy bones.

This fact constitutes the scientific confirmation of the myrrh-gushing of the St. Nicholas Relics. . . .

The third historical removal occurred on the night of May 7–8, 1957, with the goal of a new recognition, measurement, and anatomical and anthropological study before the final deposition in the reliquary, after the end of the restoration work. . . .

The results of the anthropometrical-anthropological examination by Prof. Martino were impressive. 'All the bones,' he writes, 'belonged to one and the same individual and in particular to a man who was about 1.67 meters tall, was nourished chiefly with vegetable products and died aged over 70. This individual belonged to the white Indo-European race. . . .

Statue of St. Nicholas in the Asidale College Chapel in Ghana, West Africa. The college is run by the Anglicans, and alumni of the school are called, "Santaclausians." St. Nicholas Seminary is just minutes away.

The condition of certain bones showed further that the individual to whom they belonged must have suffered a good deal under the particularly adverse circumstances of his way of life, which left marks on the remainder of his life. The crooked spondyloarthritis and the general endo-cranial hyperostosis, which were detected on the corresponding bones, must have been inherited from some damp jail, where he would have passed several years of his life and especially at an advanced age.'

The re-creation of his face in the form of a sketch that was made by the same professor, using the method of hyperskeletal refashioning of the tender parts of the head, yielded equally spectacular results. 'The countenance that was re-created in this way,' note the Dominicans, 'reveals a person who was ascetical, noble, with harmonious proportions, with a lofty and broad forehead, with large eyes—gentle deep-set—sweet and austere at the same time, the eyes of a man who was pensive and troubled.'

The relevant sketches which Prof. Martino published demonstrate that the passage of time did not dull the memory of the basic characteristics of St. Nicholas's countenance, and especially as the Orthodox iconographic tradition preserved them (large forehead, closely parted beard, somewhat pronounced zygomatic bones, baldheaded). Above all, they are in agreement with the oldest known portrayals of the Saint: that of Santa Maria Antiqua in Rome (8th or 9th century) and that of the chapel of St. Isidore, in the Church of San Marco in Venice (a mosaic of the 12th century)" (Markou, 20–1).

Tomb of San Nicola, resting place of the relics of St. Nicholas and place of pilgrimage, Bari, Italy

Many stories of St. Nicholas connect him with Emperor Constantine.

The Nicholas and Constantine Stories

Many stories of St. Nicholas tied him to the emperor in one way or another. Following are some of the more significant ones.

The Three Generals (or Three Princes)

Undoubtedly, this is the longest of all the St. Nicholas stories. Note the repetition of threes; St. Nicholas mythology is replete with triplets (symbolic of his earnest defense of the Trinity). This particular account is the oldest of the Nicholas miracle accounts.

The time frame is during the reign of the Emperor Constantine, both he and Bishop Nicholas growing old. Constantine was constantly having to put down rebellions here and there across the vast empire. This particular revolt occurred in Phrygia, southeast of Byzantium (Constantinople). Constantine sent three of his most trusted generals, Ursos, Nepotianos, and Herpylion, to quell the outbreak. Storms forced the expeditionary forces to seek refuge in Port Andriaki and Myra. With time on their hands, arguments with the tradesmen led to fighting, looting, and general destruction.

The generals, meanwhile, relaxing back at the harbor, were blissfully unaware of the commotion farther inland.

Unaware, that is, until Bishop Nicholas burst into their midst, demanding to know under what authority their soldiers were permitted to loot peaceful villages.

"Looting? Where? How could it have happened?"

The great colonnade at the Vatican with St. Nicholas of Bari among those guarding St. Peter's basilica. St. Nicholas is on the right.

Antique postcard: A classic Russian image of Bishop Nicholas

Ко крсно име слави оном и помаже!

Great window in the Roman Catholic Church in Bethlehem, Israel/Palestine

The bishop was stern. "*You* are to blame, for you have permitted your soldiers to go on this rampage."

The generals rushed to Myra's public market. Upset by their troops's lack of discipline, they had some of them flogged, and shouted to restore order. While the townspeople and the soldiers joined forces to repair the damage, Nicholas invited the three generals to join him for refreshments in the Cathedral of Myra. Then, after advising and blessing them, he walked with them down to their ships.

The second part took place before all the soldiers had returned to their ships. Only minutes after leaving the princely generals, the bishop heard the sound of weeping. The cause was not difficult to find. At that time, the provincial prefect was a man named Eustathios, widely known to be so corrupt that he was willing to sentence to death and execute innocent people if a bribe was high enough. Now three innocent people were about to be beheaded in the center of town.

Clearly, there was not a moment to be lost! Nicholas and the three generals reached the execution just in time. Nicholas rushed up to the executioner and ripped the sword out of his hand. Angry and exhausted, he untied the ropes that bound the victims and set them free. News of the event spread like wildfire through Myra and Andriaki, and people streamed toward the execution square from all directions.

Alarmed by all the commotion, Prefect Eustathios mounted his horse and rode toward the square. Seeing him, the bishop stopped his horse and castigated him for his corrupt acts; then he turned to the three generals and announced that he was going to personally inform the emperor of his prefect's unworthiness. At that, Eustathios was "seized by fear" and fell on his knees to beg forgiveness and confess the error of his ways. Forgiveness was granted, and all returned whence they had come.

Following this, the three generals led their troops into Phrygia, successfully crushed the revolt, and returned in triumph to Constantinople. Highly pleased, the emperor rewarded them with rich gifts and promoted them to even higher rank.

The third part of the story has to do with the aftermath. The adulation showered on the three victors aroused so much envy among their rivals that some of them resorted to lying

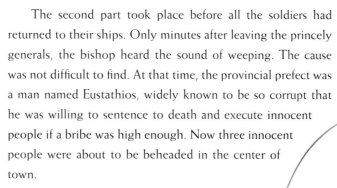

Nicholas miraculously saved three generals from the executioner.

The Italianate Anglican Church of St. Mary and St. Nicholas, Wilton, near Salisbury, England, features this window transformed from a "Fatherly God" to St. Nicholas.

Icon depicting scenes from the life of St. Nicholas

to Evlavios, the imperial Chancellor. Instead of subduing the revolt, they told him the generals had enriched themselves and encouraged their own soldiers to join the revolt. They did this so that they might rule over the region themselves! And just to make sure Evlavios was firmly in their camp, they bribed him with a large sum of money.

But Evlavios had not been born yesterday. He sent couriers into Phrygia to find out whether or not the story was true. As time passed, the rivals became more and more apprehensive. So much so that they gave the Chancellor more and more gold, urging him to put the generals to death quickly lest the rebellious Taiphalis raid the jail and set the generals free.

Evlavios was caught in his own mesh: he neither wished to be personally responsible for the death of the three generals nor wished to repay any of the bribe money. So he went to the emperor and told him that the three generals were guilty of treason and were now awaiting their fate in prison. "What should be done with them?"

All his life, Constantine was known for his quick decisions. Assuming that his chancellor's intelligence reports were correct, he ordered the accused to be executed the following day.

The generals were stunned, for they considered themselves to be among the emperor's most faithful and trusted commanders. And now, suddenly, they were condemned to death without official accusation or explanation. It made no sense. "How did we offend either God or emperor," they wondered, "that we should be treated this way?"

It was Nepotianos who, realizing that no human power could save them, finally thought of St. Nicholas. He urged his associates to plead with God and St. Nicholas to save them, just as the bishop saved the lives of the three innocent men. So they knelt down and prayed all night.

Shortly before dawn, the emperor dreamed that a stately figure stood before him and said, "Arise, Emperor—rise quickly! You must free three innocent men

Opposite: A Byzantine icon image; one of the most popular of St. Nicholas

Below: Small Orthodox church of St. Nicholas in the busy streets of Old City Jerusalem

whom you have condemned to death! If you do not free them, God will involve you in a war that will cause your death."

Constantine, still not sure that this wasn't just a dream, said, "Who are *you* to threaten me, and how did you manage to break into the palace in the middle of the night?"

Nicholas said, "I am bishop of Myra, and God has sent me to tell you that those three men must be freed without delay!"

Neither was the Chancellor spared. In his case, the apparition spoke with all the subtlety of an Old Testament prophet: "Evlavios, you who appear to have lost your mind, tell me why you so lowered yourself and your high office that you permitted yourself to be bribed! Furthermore, why have you permitted such a thing to happen to three innocent men! Free them immediately, or I'll ask God to take your life!"

Evlavios guiltily asked the visitor who he was. The bishop

German postcard depicting a powerful St. Nicholas

identified himself, after which the Chancellor awoke, confused, apprehensive, and in a quandary. Then there was a loud knock on his door, and an imperial messenger rushed in and ordered, "Get dressed immediately—and hurry! The emperor has summoned you!"

The Chancellor did so, and was soon with the emperor. The two then compared dreams. It was decided to immediately summon the generals to the palace.

When they arrived, haggard from worry and lack of sleep, Constantine demanded that they tell him what magic they had used on him and the Chancellor to awaken them in the middle of the night with the same dream.

The generals looked at one another apprehensively. Filled with fear, they were incapable of speech. Finally, the emperor took mercy on them and said in a more kindly manner, "Go ahead, you can answer without being afraid. I'm your friend as well as emperor."

Finally, the whole story came out, and Constantine was silent for a time, pondering what had taken place, and what measures should be taken to rectify things. He then turned to the three and pronounced them free. He had brought in a gold-covered Bible manuscript, a gold incense vessel, and two gold-plated candlesticks. These they must take to St. Nicholas and tell him that the emperor had obeyed him, but please "don't threaten him anymore!"

The three generals then gave away all their rich possessions, became monks, and, as the emperor had ordered, presented the rich gifts to Bishop Nicholas, bowed low to the ground, and offered their heartfelt gratitude. But the bishop broke in kindly, raised them to their feet, and told them that no gratitude was due him, but rather to the God who had so miraculously saved them (adapted from Markou, 20–1).

The Great Famine (or Grainships 7)

As Voragine tells the story,

"There was a great famine in the region where Bishop Nicholas lived, so that finally there was no food left for anyone to eat. Now the man of God learned that some merchant ships loaded with corn were moored in the port harbor. Immediately, the bishop set out for the port area. There he asked the sailors and their leaders to come to the aid of the starving city by each sharing a little: say a hundred measures of corn from each vessel. The sailors responded that they really wished they could do just that, but the grain had been carefully measured and weighed in Alexandria; if any were missing when they arrived to unload at the imperial granaries, their lives might be forfeit. The saint responded, 'Do as I tell you, and I promise, through the power of God, that there will not be any grain missing when you reach the emperor's granaries.' Somewhat fearfully, they acceded to his request. Sure enough, arriving at the capital, the emperor's steward found that not a measure of corn was missing. They told everyone of this miracle, and praised and glorified God for his servant Nicholas. As for the corn they had given him, Nicholas distributed it to everyone according to their need, and miraculously provided not only enough food for two whole years, but grain for sowing as well."

The Charter or Praxis de Tributo 8

According to this story, Nicholas journeys to Constantinople (a little over 500 miles by land, but probably twice that far

---

In a story reminiscent of the biblical miracle of the loaves and the fishes, Nicholas multiplied grain during a famine.

The Troparion of Saint Nicholas

The truth of your dealings,
our Father and Bishop Nicholas,
showed you to your flock as a standard
    of faith,
as the image of gentleness,
and as a teacher of self-discipline.
By lowliness you attained to the heights,
by poverty to great riches.
Therefore, we beseech you,
pray to Christ our God for the salvation
    of our souls.
In Myra, thou, O Saint,
didst show thyself a priest,
for thou didst fulfil the Gospel of Christ,
give thy soul for thy people,
and save the innocent from death;
wherefore thou art hallowed as one
    well-learned in the Grace of God.

—From the Orthodox tradition

SAINT NICHOLAS

BISHOP OF MYRA   DEC. 6   AD 326
THE PATRON SAINT OF CHILDREN, MERCHANTS
AND SAILORS.

Elaborately vested St. Nicolas in a classic French-style print

by sea) to see the emperor about granting a charter of liberties to the citizens of Myra. After receiving it, St. Nicholas ungraciously heaves it into the sea. (We never learn how or where this act takes place.) Apparently, word gets back to Constantine about the latest act by that firebrand bishop of Myra. Constantine sends guards to St. Nicholas and demands an accounting. Nicholas calmly tells them that the Charter had already been delivered to the citizens of Myra. Not believing that tale for a minute, Constantine sends a delegation to Myra to find out (by ship, this round trip would probably have taken a number of weeks). The delegation discovers that the charter had washed up on the Myra shore the very day it had been signed in the capital.

The Goldpiece 33

A pauper grieves because St. Nicholas Day is soon to come, and he is so poor he has nothing to offer him. While asleep, he dreams that a venerable old man pulls out a goldpiece. On awakening, there before him is the piece of gold! The story of this miracle quickly spreads, even reaching the ears of the emperor, who summons the pauper to the palace and exchanges the pauper's one miraculous goldpiece for 24 others. These the pauper joyfully gives to St. Nicholas.

Impact of these Stories

In the story of The Three Generals, Nicholas is portrayed as an equal to the emperor himself. Furthermore, God Himself listens to the bishop's urgings. Perhaps most significant of all, Nicholas is portrayed as being at least "semi-omniscient," a quality that later on would be translated as St. Nicholas/Santa Claus knowing who is "naughty" and who is "nice."

In The Great Famine, Nicholas is portrayed as one God works miracles for. From this story the earliest iconographic symbol of St. Nicholas was born: three loaves of bread. "Saint Nicholas loaves" became such a standard symbol that, as late as the seventeenth century, Mediterranean sailors refused to leave harbor without such loaves to throw overboard and calm the waters in case they encountered a storm.

Sources for this chapter: Durant, *Caesar and Christ*, 639–68; Durant, *The Age of Faith*, 3–10; *Encyclopedia Britannica*, vols. 19, 505; 23, 793; Jones, 9, 18, 19, 27, 32–3, 35, 38, 42, 63, 70, 82, 94, 298–9; Maarkou, *Concerning the Relics of St. Nicholas*, 20–1; Voragine, n.p.

CHAPTER 3

Constantinople and the Arabian Whirlwind

The good bishop was dead. But to rephrase an Emily Dickinson poem about the power of spoken words, we may observe that

St. Nicholas was dead
When he took his last breath,
Some say.

I say he just
Began to live
That day.

Constantine's successors shared his great dream. Constantinople (the New Byzantium, the New Rome) was destined to become the greatest city in the world. The Byzantine Empire's Golden Age would be the reign of Justinian (527–565) and his beautiful wife, Theodora. Justinian could afford to breathe easy, for forty miles of great walls (some two hundred feet thick!), stretching from the Sea of Marmara to the Black Sea, now made Constantinople close to impregnable. Well over a million people now lived within those walls. Justinian was fortunate to have Belisarius as his general, one of the greatest generals this world has ever known. With him at the helm, the empire vastly expanded: all of northern Africa was recaptured from the Vandals, as was southern Spain; the Ostrogoths were defeated in Italy as well. Justinian is also remembered for his revision of the legal system, which became known as The Code of Justinian. It lasted for almost a thousand years in the Byzantine Empire and lives on in modern jurisprudence throughout the world.

Justinian is also responsible for the construction of one of the most beautiful buildings ever built, the *Hagia Sophia*. Ten thousand workmen were needed, and an astronomical $134,000,000,

Vincenzo Catalano creates old archive images of scenes from the life of San Nicola affixing them to leather backing. Here is a depiction of the death of our saint. From the Rosenthal Canterbury Collection.

which just about drained the imperial treasury. On December 26, 537, the emperor and patriarch of Constantinople led the inaugural procession into the great cathedral. Filled with awe and joy, Justinian lifted his hands and cried out "Glory be to God who has thought me worthy to accomplish so great a work! O Solomon! I have vanquished you!" (Durant, *The Age of Faith*, 3–110, 426).

Justinian's reign was the peak. Never again would Constantinople rule over so vast an area. After Justinian died, the vast empire contracted again. St. Nicholas was celebrated as the great city's patron saint until the iconoclastic purges almost tore Christianity apart. And then again when iconography was restored.

Prior to Constantine, because of the Second Commandment admonition, church fathers kept visual imagery to a minimum. However, Helena, Constantine's mother, led out in finding, identifying, and authenticating the sites associated with Christ, the Apostles, and early church leaders and martyrs; the emperor then made them into pilgrimage destinations for Christians everywhere (Willis, interview).

An explosion of iconography followed. In Greek Christianity, especially, these sacred images could be found everywhere one went. Traffic in holy relics abounded, too.

Early in the eighth century, Leo III, the new Byzantine Emperor, became very concerned about these excesses. It seemed to him that the pagans were conquering Christianity. Consequently, he called a great council of bishops and senators to discuss the issue. Out of that came his imperial edict of 726, requiring the complete removal of icons from the churches, even representations of Christ and the Virgin. And church murals were to be covered with plaster.

The edict was greeted with empire-wide rage. Soldiers trying to enforce the laws were attacked by furious worshipers who felt their churches were being desecrated. Even Pope Gregory II and the patriarch of Constantinople opposed it.

In the end, the pope withdrew the papacy from the eastern Roman Empire over the issue. Thereafter, the bishop of Rome ruled the churches of the west and the patriarch of Constantinople the churches of the east. That historic schism continues to this very day.

Painting by Nykola Sudbury, Ontario, Canada, 2004

As fate would have it, the persecuted clergy fled and spread all across Europe, taking St. Nicholas with them. In 972, Germany's Emperor Otto II married the Byzantine Princess Theophano. She introduced St. Nicholas to the imperial court there. But an even more significant marriage (in terms of impact on the culture) was that of Theophano's cousin, Byzantine Princess Anna, who married Vladmir, Grand Duke of Kiev (972–1015). Vladmir supposedly gave up five wives and 800 concubines when he married her.

Then Vladmir ordered the entire population of Kiev to walk into the Dnieper River and be baptized en masse. As a result, all Russia eventually became Orthodox, and Nicholas its patron saint.

The Arabian Whirlwind

In 570, far to the east, Mohammed was born into a poor family in the desert. This unlettered child would grow up to write one of the world's most significant books, *The Koran*. Since he was a descendant of Abraham and Hagar, Mohammed felt himself to be heir to both Jewish and Christian traditions and thought. Both were incorporated into *The Koran*. The new faith spread like fire in a tinder-dry forest. The Arabians, led by great tacticians and mounted on some of the world's fastest horses, then set out to conquer the Mediterranean world. Saracen fleets attacked by sea as horsemen attacked by land. "There is no god but Allah, and Mohammed is His Prophet," rang out everywhere, and cities that had been Christian since apostolic times now turned Muslim. Unlike the Byzantines and other Christian rulers, the Arabs evidenced toleration to all, regardless of their faiths, and this fact not only made Arabian victories easier but also made their reign more permanent. Almost overnight, the great Christian East became the great Muslim East; the Mediterranean an Arab lake, and the powerful sees of Alexandria, Antioch, and Jerusalem were no more.

Damascus became one of the world's greatest cities under the Arabs, and Baghdad, by the tenth century, rivaled Constantinople, as one of the two largest and richest cities in the world. Their culture proved superior to that then found in most of the Western

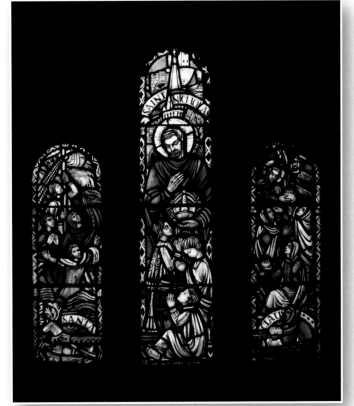

Unique window of St. Nicholas and Santa Claus in the children's chapel at Carrickfergus Parish Church of Ireland

world, their universities renowned everywhere; and as for their architecture, one has only to look at The Alhambra in Spain to appreciate its lyrical beauty.

So here we have the eastern Roman Empire, shrunken again, but amazingly, still alive. The year 1000 arrives, and the world does not come to an end, neither does Christ return. In 1036, the Normans invaded Italy. The bravest and wiliest of all the Norse leaders was Robert Guiscard, who had pretensions of making himself the mightiest monarch in Europe. He almost succeeded, defeating the Byzantines twice. In 1071, he conquered Bari, on Italy's south coast.

The Stories Continue

Thanks to the story of the three dowerless sisters, Christians were now honoring St. Nicholas by imitation, giving presents to those who were in need. It is very likely that the later practice of hanging up stockings at Christmas stems from the stocking-like sacks the gold was in and the fact that the third sack landed in or on a stocking hung up to dry by the fireplace. The story also reminded Christians of Christ's injunction to give secretly (Matt. 6:3).

St. Nicholas was dead, but you'd never have known it by the stories. New Nicholas stories began to surface and become part of the oral Christian tradition. Some were set during Nicholas's lifetime, but most would be set later.

The miracle of the return of the captive child. This image is from the base of the main image that is processed through the streets of Bari. The unique image shows Nicholas as vested in both Western and Eastern Christian apparel, as indeed the ministry of the shrine is ecumenical and welcomes participation by all Christian churches.

Members of the post-apostolic church took literally Christ's promise in John 14:12–13 (NLT): "The truth is, anyone who believes in me will do the same works I have done, and even greater works, because I am going to be with the Father. You can ask for anything in my name, and I will do it." Because of such promises, they believed that St. Nicholas would intercede for them if they only asked him.

Power over Fire or Boiled Infant 66

St. Nicholas was perceived as one to turn to where fire danger was concerned. In this particular account, an irresponsible mother living in Patara very badly wants to rush over to the cathedral so that she can see the installation of Nicholas as bishop. Unfortunately, she has a baby and cannot take it along.

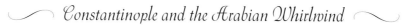
Helping the falsely accused, St. Nicholas the Wonderworker as shown in stained glass at St. Nicholas Church, Warwick, England.

As she is bathing that baby in a tub of hot water placed over a fire, she decides to leave the baby there and go to the service anyhow. After the service, she returns only to find that the water in the tub is now boiling, but her baby has been miraculously preserved from death by St. Nicholas, and is happily playing away, oblivious to the temperature.

After the bishop was buried, stories about the burial site began to surface.

The Tomb of Nicholas or Myrrh 18

According to this story, after Nicholas died and was buried in a marble tomb, a fountain of oil streamed out from his head and a spring of water flowed from his feet. This holy water (very much like myrrh) was poured into bottles and made available to those who were afflicted by diseases. Many were healed as a result.

Some time later, the man who had followed Nicholas as bishop became embroiled in church politics. Tempers flared, and the poor bishop was unable to satisfy either side. In the end, the warring parties ungraciously threw him out. That very day, the holy water ceased to flow. As day followed day and those who were ill were turned away without the myrrh they came for, more and more of them began to say, "St. Nicholas is angry at us because we threw out his successor for no good reason!" And they turned on those who had expelled their bishop. It didn't take long for their message to get through. The good bishop was recalled to his post, and immediately the holy water began flowing again.

Why St. Nicholas's body did not decay is indeed a mystery, though he certainly is not unique in that respect. Throughout history, this phenomenon has occurred now and then. Such a saint is called a myroblyte. As for why it occurred with St. Nicholas, Christina Hole theorizes that it was because of his great holiness that his body remained uncorrupted and gave forth the sweet-smelling essence known as "the manna of St. Nicholas," also known as "balm," "balsam," and "unguent" (Hole, 1).

A number of stories have to do with attempts to outwit St. Nicholas (such as this one):

Nicholas's body did not decay afer death, and it produced holy water.

The Two Golden Goblets or Substituted Cup 62

A nobleman prays, asking St. Nicholas for a son, promising the saint a golden goblet if his prayer were answered. A son is born to him, and the nobleman has a golden goblet made—but he likes it so much he has another made of equal value for the saint. During the voyage to Myra, the son falls overboard and disappears while trying to fill the first goblet made with water. In sorrow, the father continues to Myra and lays down the second goblet at the altar. It falls from the altar as though repulsed. The second time, the goblet is thrown even farther away. Then all present stare in amazement as the child arrives safe and sound, carrying the first goblet. He tells them of St. Nicholas's care and protection. The joyful father then offers *both* goblets, and they are accepted.

Many of the St. Nicholas stories have to do with those intrepid souls who ventured out every day on the waters of the Great Sea. The following narrative is typical of these.

Saving People at Sea or Mariners 6

In this story, an eastern Mediterranean ship runs into a great storm. The waves reach such towering heights that the mariners despair at ever seeing their loved ones again. Finally, one of them manages to be heard above the tempest and suggests that they pray to St. Nicholas, urging him to come to their rescue quickly, else they'd all be dead men. Immediately, they all begin to pray for that aid. Suddenly, a figure appears out of the storm, a figure that looks like St. Nicholas. His words are few and to the point: "You have called me—and here I am." Then, not content with mere words, he joins the crew in their frantic efforts to salvage their sails, secure their cables, and save their tackle. Then, as suddenly as he had appeared, he disappears. Just as suddenly, the storm abates.

Some time later, having made it safely to port, the sailors stream into a church in order to express their gratitude. Inside, lo and behold, there is Bishop Nicholas. When they effusively thank him for saving their lives, he gently reproves them, telling

The cherubim hold the miraculous manna in the traditional bottles found in Bari, Italy. The image is from the processional statue of San Nicola di Bari.

them that all thanks should be directed to God, for it was *He* who had delivered them!

Similar storm stories include *Father John 27, Monk John 28,* and *Demetrios 29.* In them, after having been summoned, St. Nicholas appears in time to save the mariners. St. Nicholas is one of the few saints who is said to go almost anywhere instantly, due to a magical robe that he wears (also, he has thaumaturgic powers: able to be in more than one place at once). He is also given the power to walk on water. We can see those thaumaturgic powers at work when St. Nicholas and Santa Claus deliver presents all around the world in only hours.

The following story is one of a number dealing with St. Nicholas's warfare with the Roman gods:

Diana and the Burning Oil or Firebomb 5

It is not known whether this story preceded or followed the invention of Greek fire by the Byzantine engineer Kallnikos in 678. Greek fire would revolutionize warfare almost as much as gunpowder 650 years later. It was originally packed in clay jars and hurled onto enemy ships where they would break, then explode. The Byzantine emperors kept its ingredients a military secret for several hundred years. In 941, it saved Constantinople from being captured by an immense invading army of Russians; they jumped into the sea fully armored rather than face it. After that close call, contemporaries began calling Constantinople the "God-guarded City."

Danish sailors at the St. Nicholas Anglican Cathedral exhibition in Newcastle upon Tyne, England

Pilgrims flocked to Myra from all directions. Just before boarding a ship, one group of Lycian pilgrims was accosted by a malignant demon who once served the goddess Artemis. Now, out to get revenge, and masquerading as a woman, the demon asked them if they would take a certain jar with them to the tomb of the saint and fill it with holy oil for her.

In the middle of the second night at sea, St. Nicholas appeared and directed them to cast the jar into the sea. Early in the morning they did so. Instantly, the sky was engulfed in an explosion of fire, the waters began to convulse, booming like hell broken loose, with a tremor like an earthquake, all accompanied by a terrible stench. The huge waves that resulted crippled the ship. It began to sink. But St. Nicholas had not

Artist's rendition of the Bari church

SAN NICOLA - BARI

forgotten them. He appeared before them, calmed the storm, and the pilgrims were able to proceed to Myra.

The Arab-related Stories

After the Muslim invasion of the Mediterranean, life was never the same, *especially* for those who dwelt in coastal areas. For over a thousand years warfare between Muslims and Christians was almost continuous. The stories reflect that.

A number of the stories have to do with the Lycian coast during the years 824–954, when the Arabs controlled Crete. For 130 years the nearby Asia Minor cities were never safe from attacks from that quarter. Of this period Jones writes that "Each spring Crete vomited out like a monstrous war machine fleets of armored ships with black sails of marvelous speed. Cruising their *mare nostrum*, the freebooters burned cities and decimated towns before imperial forces could arrive. 'Only hours sufficed for these remarkable corsairs, of agility, audacity, incomparable precision, to transform a flourishing Byzantine city into smoking ruins.' The goods and slaves were marketed in the bazaars of the Asian and African coasts" (Jones, 74–75). Quite naturally, parents in Lycian cities felt utterly helpless to defend their families during this horrendous period. Since St. Nicholas was viewed as the premier defendant against the Arabs, whenever trouble from that quarter arrived, his was the first name to be invoked. Case in point, the following several stories:

St Michael's Church in Old City Bari, Italy, is where the relics were first taken when they arrived from Turkey in 1087.

Priest From Mytilene

It was St. Nicholas's feast day in Myra. A certain priest felt convicted to make a pilgrimage there. As he neared the city, he mingled with the crowd of pilgrims. After reaching the shrine of St. Nicholas, the priest heard some commotion outside. Suddenly, a man ran in, shouting, "Run for your lives! Cretan Arabs have landed—and they're heading this way!" Immediately, everyone in the sanctuary made a rush for the door. Graciously, the priest let the others go first. By the time he reached the doorway, it was too late.

The glorious St. Mark's Basilica in Venice has several images of St. Nicholas, including this stunning mosaic on the great west front.

The Cretans were looking for slaves, women, children, and booty. All others they considered useless, and hence better off dead. First in line to be dispatched by the executioner was the priest. St. Nicholas was there, but invisible to all except for the priests. Just as the sword was descending, the invisible hand of St. Nicholas wrenched the sword out of the executioner's hand and set the priest free.

Basileos 22

This story was so popular that it is found in many variant texts, with different lead characters and settings. The following text was unearthed by Ebon:

Mosaic of St. Nicholas in the Anglican Cathedral of St. Mary the Virgin and St. Nicholas, Seoul, South Korea; shown as a prayer card from the St. Nicholas Society

Some years after the death of Saint Nicholas, the townspeople of Myra were celebrating his memory on the eve of his nameday, December 6, with eating, drinking, and a generally festive air. Unarmed and unaware of events around them, the townspeople did not realize that a band of Arab pirates from Crete had landed on their shore and was making its way in to Myra. The pirates even managed to get into the Church of Saint Nicholas itself to collect booty in the form of chalices, altar decorations, and bejeweled icons. As they left town, they took along the son of a local peasant, Basileos, as a slave.

When the pirates returned to their home island, the emir of Crete selected young Basileos as his personal cupbearer. But, back in Myra, his broken-hearted parents were inconsolable. It was terribly hard for them, a year later, to again celebrate Dec. 6, but they eventually did so quietly at home.

Suddenly, the dogs began to bark fiercely. The father, ever so cautiously, opened the front door, and there was a ghost-like-figure standing there: Basileos, dressed in an Arab tunic, holding a full goblet of wine in his hand, staring unseeingly into space.

Finally, Basileos, realizing he was home at last, told everyone how, while he was carrying a cup of wine to the emir, he had felt himself picked up by an invisible force. St. Nicholas appeared in mid-air to give him courage, then accompanied him to Myra. Then the entire city rejoiced! (Ebon, 50–52).

The story became a popular miracle play in the twelfth and thirteenth centuries. It has been adapted in many different settings. Some of them are *Adeodatus 75*, *Son of Gertron 46*, *The Eubuan Laborer 23*, *The Sicilian Priest 24*, and *The Catanian Images 25*.

Other such stories include "Joseph the Hymnographer," "Peter the Scholar," and "The Cretan Boys." Interestingly enough, St. Nicholas did not exclude the Arabs from his services, as a number of stories evidence.

St. Nicholas came to the rescue of all who called on him.

The Lone Sailor 30

This particular story has to do with an Egyptian Arab who ventured far out to sea one day in his fishing boat. Suddenly, a terrible storm blew in, and the little boat was tossed here and there as though it were but a chip of wood. Terrified, the fisherman invoked his gods, telling them that if they didn't quickly quell the storm, his boat would certainly sink. But these prayers were to no avail: the storm just got worse. Finally, as the boat was beginning to founder, the fisherman gave up on his gods and turned to St. Nicholas, figuring he had little to lose by changing allegiance. In his desperate prayer, he promised that if the saint would come to his rescue he would turn Christian. The boat sank, but not before a figure swooped down and lifted him out of the boat, then bore him off to Attalia. Once on shore, his rescuer vanished, but later on the fisherman confirmed the identity of his rescuer by matching him to the picture on a St. Nicholas icon.

The Saracen Trader 32

A Saracen trader was returning from a grueling but successful expedition to the Orient. How good it felt to finally be nearing home after such a long time on the trail! And the goods he was returning with would make him a rich man at the marketplace.

Then a wind came up. He wasn't apprehensive until it began to increase in intensity. Now he really began to worry, for he was traversing a dangerous mountain pass, where one misstep on the slippery rocks could be fatal. As the storm closed in, he could no longer even see the caravan behind him. His worst fears were realized when the camels behind him panicked and plunged off the trail into a deep abyss. The trader, having heard that St. Nicholas would come to the rescue of those who called upon him, concluded that he'd never need such assistance more than he did now, so he prayed to him.

Some time later, after the storm had abated, the ruined trader sorrowfully continued down the trail. Twelve miles farther on, as he came around a bend, what a sight met his eyes: his entire caravan (riders, camels, and goods) were there waiting for him!

When he reached his home in Seleucia, in gratitude the trader purchased an expensive golden icon of St. Nicholas and presented it to his city as a token of his deep appreciation.

Each June the people of Siggiewi, Malta have a three-day festa in honor of St. Nicholas, their patron saint. This is the statue in the parish church.

CHAPTER 4

St. Nicholas Comes West

The Crusades: Flawed Fervor

In recent years, there has been a collective wave of public revulsion about the Crusades and what they accomplished, just as with Columbus some centuries later. Both events have been so muddied by revisionists and deconstructionists that objectivity has been in mighty short supply. The truth of the matter is that nothing is ever as simple as we try to make it, for life is incredibly complex. Contemporary students often express shock that Crusaders were violent, jealous of one another, vindictive, avaricious, revengeful, unscrupulous, and intolerant—all traits every generation shares. But the Crusaders were also sincere, faithful, self-sacrificing, empathetic, devoted to God, and willing to risk everything they owned in a cause they firmly believed to be a righteous one. Untold thousands paid the supreme sacrifice (losing possessions, relationships, and life itself) because of their beliefs.

Coming near the half-way point of the last two millennia, the Crusades had a seismic effect on Mediterranean history. Why they occurred no one really knows, but there were a number of probable causes: the apocalyptic fervor associated with the thousand-year turn, the capture of Jerusalem by the Seljuk Turks, the fear that the Byzantine Empire would fall, the desire to expand commerce eastward, wanderlust, desire for fame and fortune, and Pope Urban II's desire to make Rome once more the capital of the Christian world.

So Urban took his challenge to the people in 1095, urging them to save the Holy Land from the Turks. *Dieulivolt*—"God wills it!" became the battle cry, and the Cross their symbol. Serfs were allowed to leave the soil, debtors were offered a moratorium on interest, prisoners were freed, and nobles were promised protection from usurpers who might invade their lands while they were gone.

During the First Crusade, Antioch and Jerusalem were conquered, and thousands were slaughtered. The Second Crusade in

1147 fared much worse: barely one in ten crusaders survived. The Third Crusade in 1189 resulted in the loss of most of the crusaders before they even got to the Holy Land. And what moved all Europe to wonderment was that in the many battles and negotiations, infidels like Saladin proved far more worthy of admiration and emulation than their own Christian leaders. But even that paled in comparison to the disaster of the Fourth Crusade of 1202. Instead of attacking their Arab enemies, the Crusaders turned on their Christian hosts and laid Constantinople waste, treating it and its people worse than the Vandals and Goths ever treated Rome! Libraries of irreplaceable manuscripts were torched. The Byzantine Empire never fully recovered. In 1212, there came the Children's Crusades: 30,000 left, and only a precious few returned in the first; 20,000 left in the second, and at the end almost all of the children were either dead or had been sold as slaves. In 1217 came the Fifth Crusade, in 1228 the Sixth. The Seventh and Eighth fizzled out as well. By 1270, it was all over.

So what were the results? Well, the Christians lost Jerusalem again, they all but destroyed their Christian allies in Constantinople, the Arabs were now intolerant of all dissent, thousands of serfs refused to return to their bondage, many nobles were wrecked financially, and the church had greatly suffered as well. "Mohammed," jested the skeptics, "had proved stronger than Christ." The net result was to discredit religion and to accelerate the secularization of Europe.

As for St. Nicholas, his story is intertwined with the story of the age.

A regal Nicholas in the classic vestments of an Orthodox prelate

The Normans, Hastings, and the Bari Abduction

Everywhere at once the Norman Vikings were on the attack: out to change the world. On the northern coast of France, Duke William's men were preparing for one of the most audacious attacks in history: invading England. Throughout the spring and summer of 1066, all the seaports of Normandy, Piccardy, and Brittany rang with the busy sound of preparation. After a very long wait, the wind changed, and the duke's great fleet set sail. Before they could get across the English Channel, a violent storm blew up out of nowhere, many of the vessels were wrecked, and the entire coast of Normandy was strewn with the bodies of the drowned. The

St. Nicholas with Mary and the Christ Child, clutching the three gold balls and riding the waves of a turbulent sea (Susak, Croatia)

Painting of San Nikola commanding the sea by Italian artist Orofrio Bramante, 1976.
The Chapter Room of the Dominican Fathers in Bari, Italy

superstitious mariners urged the duke to call it quits, but the duke, in this last resort, called in the patron saint of mariners himself, St. Nicholas. He also vowed to St. Nicholas that if victory over King Harold were granted him, he would erect an abbey on English soil. That very night, the wind changed, the waters calmed, and the remnants of the fleet sailed again. That showdown with Harold, the Battle of Hastings, was considered by Sir Edward Creasy (Creasy, 93–108) to be one of the fifteen most pivotal battles in world history. After his great victory, the Duke (now surnamed "William the Conqueror"), remembering his promise to St. Nicholas, constructed "Battle Abbey" in gratitude (Jones, 227; Robinson, 100–110).

Just before the Crusades began, an event of far-reaching significance took place. As the power of Constantinople waned, marauders attacked outlying provinces at will. When the living feared so much for their lives, they had little energy left for worrying about the dead. What then was likely to happen to the revered grave of St. Nicholas?

Until another Norman invader, Duke Robert Guiscard, conquered Bari (after a three-year siege), the city had been the seat of the Byzantine governors. Shorn of that eminence, Barians felt themselves greatly reduced in importance. So much so that a group of their merchants got together to discuss remedies. One of them apparently sighed, "If *only* we had a saint!" For, in those days, owning a saint, or a part of him or her, meant instant status in the Christian community. But alas! Bari didn't even own part of a saint. So they

William the Conqueror built an abbey in honor of St. Nicholas after the Batttle of Hastings.

83

began pooling their saint-related knowledge. Raising a saint from birth was too time-consuming, as well as being improbable; what they needed was a sure-thing. Whose bones were out there in a relatively unprotected state? It wouldn't do to go after a saint who had powerful protectors or avengers. And it wouldn't do to get the pope riled up. That pretty much ruled out the West.

But that left the East. That was a good thing, for most of the early saints and church fathers were buried there. Had the Byzantine emperors been strong right then, the East also would have been off limits to all but the foolhardy. But the Byzantine emperors were so weak that the Arabs were already digging up relics and disposing of them as they saw fit. Somebody in the group mentioned St. Nicholas, and it was as though there was spontaneous combustion in the room. The very person! One that they revered already, one whose roots went back to post-apostolic times, one who had been at the Council of Nicaea, one who had been associated with Constantine.

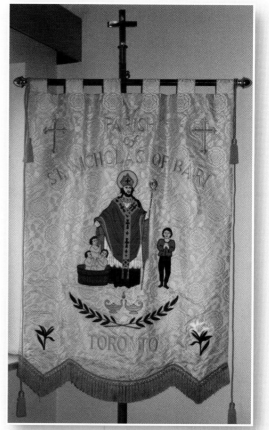

Processional banner from St. Nicholas of Bari Roman Catholic Church in Toronto, Canada

An exquisite hand-painted manna bottle that stores a sample of the myrrh flowing from the tomb of St. Nicholas in Bari

They decided to act immediately. Before long their crew of 70 (62 were Barians) was in Ephesus, trading goods. One day one of their group came running in with dramatic news: Those perpetual thorns in their sides, the Venetians, not only planned to abduct St. Nicholas's bones themselves, but they had already left the Ephesus harbor, armed with iron instruments to help them break through the floor and into the tomb. There was not a second to lose! Quickly disposing of their merchandise at any price they could get, they put out to sea under full sail. Arriving in Myra, they noted with joy that they had beaten the Venetians in. They didn't feel a bit sorry for them: after all, Venice already had St. Mark—so it didn't need to grab St. Nicholas, too! Dividing their group in two, 23 stayed on board to guard against a Turkish attack, and the other 47 proceeded

SAGRA DI SAN NICOLA

The "sagrada"—the colorful schedule of the May celebration in Bari, Italy, and set out in this elegant program

to the tomb. According to Nicephorus (a Benedectine monk), this is what happened. A similar account was chronicled by John, Archdeacon of the Bari Cathedral. Both stories read like a Keystone Cops script.

Once at the tomb, they asked the monks who protected the tomb where the body of St. Nicholas lay. Assuming they were there to show reverence to the saint, they gladly showed them where the body was. But then the monks, noting the size of the growing crowd, grew apprehensive. They now questioned the visitors sharply as to their intentions, saying, "You haven't planned to carry off the remnants of the holy saint to your own region, have you? If you have, we'll fight to the death to keep that from happening."

The Barian's responses proving devious, the monks began to grow angry.

Humility and honesty having failed, the Barians told the monks a whopping lie: that the pope and all his archbishops and bishops had demanded that they journey to Myra and bring the body of St. Nicholas back to Bari. In fact, the saint had appeared in a dream to the pope himself, urging him to rescue his bones in all haste.

Seeing that the monks didn't believe a word of it, they used force, and shouldering the monks aside, forced their way into the tomb. At this, the monks began to weep, and several began to creep away so as to bring reinforcements in from the town. The Barians put a quick stop to that by placing a guard around them.

The shrine in Rome's Church of San Nicola di Bari, Prefretti, near the Via Del Corso

One of the raiders, Matthew by name, now raised a huge mallet, and hammered with great force on the tomb cover on the floor until he had shattered it. Underneath, a second cover was discovered. Matthew then beat on it until he had shattered it as well.

"And immediately such an odor was wafted up . . . that they seemed to be standing in Paradise."

At that, Matthew, fully clothed, descended into the sacred tomb. Beholding the sacred remains "glowing like coals of fire, fragrant above all fragrance," he picked them up and kissed them endlessly before handing them up to Grimaldus and Lupus, the two Barian priests.

Meanwhile, the watching monks broke down in despair, but it was in vain. The armed abductors quickly hustled the Relics down to their ship.

The treasury at the basilica in Bari features icons, statues, reliquaries and paintings, as well as the famous painted bottles for the manna of St. Nicholas. "Manna of St. Nicholas" is pure water that forms in St. Nicholas's tomb.

By this time, the inhabitants of the city were hurrying down to the harbor. Here they pled with the Barians to have mercy on them, they who had so faithfully watched over the saint for over 700 years! And they waded into the water and tried to grasp any part of the ship they could hold on to. Alas! It was to no avail. The Barians placed the holy remains in a small wooden chest and sailed out of the harbor. And they certainly had no desire to be stopped by the Venetian ship at this juncture!

A storm forced the ship to pull into the harbor of Majesta. It was there that they realized some of the expedition had already proven faithless and were hoarding portions of the Relics. The captain refused to set sail until the ship had been searched top to bottom and the Relics recovered.

Finally, after a long voyage, they arrived home. Runners were sent ahead into the city with the good news. By the time the ship drew into the harbor of Bari, on May 9, 1087, practically the entire city was at the dock waiting for them.

Almost immediately there was trouble. Who would have custody of the precious Relics? Some wanted to take them to the Cathedral at once, so word was rushed to Archbishop Ursus. But Ursus was visiting in another town, Canusiam [Canosa], so the mariners entrusted their temporary custody to Elias, Abbott of the Monastery of St. Benedict. But they didn't trust the Abbott either, so they posted guards at the gates lest someone spirit the Relics away from *them!*

When Ursus rushed back to Bari to claim the Relics, the sailors and townspeople met him, teeth bared. The archbishop, unwilling to give in, decided to return later and take possession by force. In subsequent fighting, four died (two from each side).

A large crowd of citizens now rescued the Relics from the monastery, singing *Kyrie Eleison* all the while, and they brought them to the royal praetorium and placed them in the altar of St. Eustratius (the great martyr). And a large guard was posted to make sure the Relics stayed *there.*

Then there came sick and lame people from all over the city; within 24 hours, forty-seven had been cured . . . and they kept coming. (Cioffari, *Saint Nicholas*, 53–68).

What a document!

Jones maintains that there was ample reason to rush to completion this account by Nicephorus (probably within a week after

The arrival in Amsterdam is a great national event with tens of thousands filling the streets on the Damrak to welcome Sint and many Piets.

The saint makes his way through the streets of Bari over a period of seven days during the festival each May. Here San Nicola is on his way to the main shopping district.

May 9, 1087): "The party that at that moment possessed the relics, that is the Byzantine burghers, the crews that performed the feat, and the Greek aristocracy, were rushing into circulation that which would confirm their claim and their plans."

Then we have the opposite party that was headed by Guiscard's chosen prelate, Archbishop Ursus. Had Ursus only known, he would have been there to meet the boat and awe the sailors into surrendering their precious burden. Instead, he was off on one of his many jaunts, and would spend the rest of his life regretting it. Here he was, building church after church, in order to shore up his reputation as an up-and-comer. Of this, Jones chortles, "It is one of the piquancies of true history, unmatched in legend, that the ambitious Ursus was caught absent from his post of duty at the most important moment of his life" (Jones, 194). Interestingly enough, it took only two years for Ursus to lose his archbishopric to Abbott Elias!

Both sides were careful not to use the word "abduction" to define the act; rather the word "translation" implied a higher power than the merchants/mariners was involved. But once translated, there was definitely very little peace in Bari. Possession being nine-tenths of the law, the citizens now had no intention of losing the fruits of all their labors. And the archbishop, his future prestige dependent on how he handled all this, and where the relics ended up, was openly angry about being squeezed out of the action. In the end, the deadlock had to be solved by a neutral, the Benedictine Abbot Elias. Had there been a strong pope in power, and had Ursus been on the job when the ship landed, chances are that the St. Nicholas relics would have been housed in the Cathedral, but since that was not so, the basilica and tomb would be erected separately, all sides contributing.

Pope Urban II consecrated the altar on May 9, 1089 (thereafter May 9 would be celebrated as St. Nicholas Translation Day across the Mediterranean). At this dedication, probably the first public appeal to Christian men to rally in defense of holy places in Palestine was made at the opening of the crypt. Urban it was, by the way, who first promoted St. Nicholas as the church's only ecumenical figure with the power to unite East and West.

> The father poor, the three young girls,
> Young men to life restored.
> Sailors can rest, the sea is blessed,
> Your miracles record.
>
> In prison dark, your faith was strong;
> Help those who suffer wrong,
> We heed your words, the gospel call,
> To hail Christ, Lord of all.
>
> As Bari's pilgrims make their way
> To sing of your great name,
> The wonder myrrh of Myra still
> Proclaims your loving fame.
>
> —J M Rosenthal, 2002

91

On Pentecost Sunday, 1137, Pope Innocent II presided over a magnificent service at the basilica in the presence of the Emperor Lothar II and many German princes. Three generations later, Chancellor Conrad of Hildesheim consecrated the completed facility on June 22, 1197. Also attending were five archbishops, twenty-eight bishops, and many clergy.

Many Crusaders came here before leaving for the Holy Land. Before leaving for the East in 1096, almost all the great knights of the First Crusade came here to receive the blessing of St. Nicholas. Other Crusaders who came here include the fiery Peter the Hermit of the First Crusade, Hugh of Vermandois (brother of the King of France), Robert of Normandy, Robert of Flanders, Stephen of Blois, Bohemond, and Tancred. Eric the Good of Denmark, St. Anselm of Aosta, St. Godfrey of Amiens, St. John of Matera, St. Brigid of Sweden, came, along with Popes Pasquelle II and Callisto II. King Roger II of the Two Sicilies came here several times, as did King William II the Good, King Aloysius of Hungary, King Alphonse the Great, and Ferrante of Aragon. And those were just during the medieval period (Cioffari, *The Basilica of Saint Nicholas*, 57–58; Jones, 216).

A silver bust of San Nicola di Bari in the basilica

It would take over a century to build the basilica, one of the most imposing and majestic churches in southern Italy, as well as one of the finest examples of Romanesque architecture in the world. According to art historians, it became the prototype of Apulian Romanesque for a great number of churches and cathedrals. Through the centuries, the basilica became one of the most important pilgrimage sites in the world, along with Rome and St. James of Compostela; as popular as St. Martin of Tours. To this day it remains a place of prayer for unity of all Christians. Although the basilica is Roman Catholic, an Orthodox chapel is maintained in the Crypt. The Anglican Church maintains close ties as well.

The good bishop's Relics are well-traveled. Thirteen years after being beat in the race to Myra, the Venetians returned, scooped up the rest of the bones (apparently, about 25%), carried them to

the City of Gondalas, and advertised far and wide that St. Nicholas was *there*. One of the popes sold St. Nicholas's right hand to Gican, ruler of Vlachia for 3,000 florins. Supposedly, it today resides in the Church of St. George in Bucharest. We say "supposedly," as the Holy Monastery of St. Irene Chrysovalantou in Lykovrsi, Attica, also claims it has Nicholas's right hand. A finger of St. Nicholas resides in the church of St. Nicolas de Port in Lorraine. The Museum of Antalya in Turkey houses two bones of St. Nicholas that had apparently escaped attention by prior "translation" expeditions, but their authenticity is questioned by experts. Major relics are also housed in the St. Nicholas Orthodox Church in Flushing, New York, an ecumenical gift from the city of Bari.

The Dominican Fathers in procession in Bari, Italy, with the famed painting from the shrine church

Most Popular Non-biblical Saint in Christendom

According to McKnight, not until his remains were transferred to Bari did the cult of St. Nicholas really explode in the West. From that time on, St. Nicholas rode the crest, by 1400 becoming the most popular non-biblical saint in Christendom. In fact, St. Nicholas is often depicted walking hand-in-hand with the Virgin Mary. But why is it that he would be taken to so many hearts? Some feel it is because so many religious figures appear to have espoused the Old Testament letter of the law as opposed to the spirit of the law in the New Testament. Even the church, during the medieval period, tended to stick to the letter, thus God was often perceived

Images on the walls of St Nicholas Church in Myra/Demre. Officials are working to restore the great church.

as being a stern, severe judge. Consequently, suffering humanity began to seek out more approachable figures, above all, Mary, as intercessor and companion. But of all the non-biblical saints, St. Nicholas was considered the most approachable, the one to turn to when in distress or trouble. Again and again, St. Nicholas is referred to as the most human of all the saints. And it is after the translation to Bari that this occurs: that St. Nicholas sheds much of his earlier severity and thereafter is generally depicted as a compassionate and generous benefactor.

One of the unanswered questions related to the abduction has to do with the unnatural silence out of Constantinople, for St. Nicholas's tomb in Myra was one of the most popular pilgrimage sites in the empire. The emperor had even declared his interest in bringing the Relics to Constantinople. But Jones notes that the situation was far more complex than it might appear. On the surface, Byzantium should have been greatly shamed by the abduction. As father-protector of the Greek Communion and the Aegean Isles, as author of the cult of St. Nicholas, as avowed enemy of the Normans, as leader of the ancient Orthodox split with the Roman Church, Byzantium should have professed her outrage at this violation of its territory and chief saint, and perhaps even sent ships to reclaim the Relics. "But the politics of the 1080s were not simple. Even the emperors and patriarchs rejoiced that N had found safe haven outside the now-Turkish world" (Jones, 197).

Exterior view of the Myra/Demre church

Sometime during the eleventh and twelfth centuries, all the legends of St. Nicholas having to do with his giving nature began to register in people's minds and bear fruit. Especially his tendency to give in secret without thought of recognition or reward. So, here and there throughout Europe, people began giving gifts in the name of St. Nicholas. Nuns in France began the practice of surreptitiously leaving gifts for children at houses in the poorer parts of town on St. Nicholas Eve or St. Nicholas Day. Some were left in packages, others in stockings. Often included were good things to eat—such as fruits and nuts, or even oranges from Spain (a great luxury in those days).

harmonia mundi

LEGENDS OF ST. NICHOLAS • ANONYMOUS 4   HMU 907232

harmonia mundi

LEGENDS OF St Nicholas

Medieval Chant and Polyphony

Anonymous 4

PRODUCTION USA
907232

Modern recording of medieval chant and polyphony telling the legends of St. Nicholas. The image on the cover is from the Book of Hours of the Duke of Berry, 1410.

The custom then spread like wildfire across Europe, gifts given now by rich and poor alike. In Oxford, by 1214, it was already a St. Nicholas Day custom to give bread, fish, and drink to the poorest children of the city. Some believed that St. Nicholas flew through the skies, looking for people who needed his help. When surprise gifts were given at celebrations and festivals, people began saying that they were gifts left by St. Nicholas.

Reginold and the New Wave of Music

Shortly before the arrival in Germany of the Empress Theofano from Constantinople, the ground for St. Nicholas had already been softened up by the leading musician of his age, Reginold of Eichstätt. Charlemagne had tried to freeze liturgy into an undeviating mold. After his death, however, choirmasters began to innovate. *Historia* was a tenth-century term for the entire liturgy of anthems, responses, lections, and prayers for saints' days. Reginold, literate in Latin, Greek, and Hebrew, decided to create a *historia* of St. Nicholas (which earned him a bishopric). Why, Jones attempts to explain:

> "The historia was artistically exceptional. Like a catchy new tune, it seems to have swept the world. Historia denotes both words and music, but since the words (which have come down to us) do not seem distinguished, indeed are largely copied from John the Deacon, the distinction seems to have lain in the melodies. Unfortunately neumes, the only form of musical notation at the time, are a very loose and ambiguous record, and musicologists have not yet successfully transposed the N liturgy into modern notation. We must accept the inference from other evidence that there was something new, exciting, and disturbing to traditionalists about Reginold's composition. It suggests youth or adolescence, the 'Rock liturgy' of his age. . . . Reginold could possibly have composed 'new music' for his new historia.

Episodes referred to in the *historia* include stories known as *Stratilates 3, Artemis 4, Firebomb 5, Mariner 6, Grainships 7, Parentage 10, Lactation 11, Three Daughters 13, Bishop 14, and Myrrh 18.*

We don't know how much borrowing Reginold did from the Eastern Church, but we assume it was considerable. What we *do* know is that he was the leading composer of music in the tenth century. And it was his plainchant melodies that swept the continent. While he wrote *historias* of other saints, his St. Nicholas *historia* not only spread the cult of the saint but the popularity of the liturgical form as well. Both *The Cross Legend 41* and *The Bari Widow 73* stories have to do with the popularity of the St. Nicholas liturgy. Jones notes that so popular did the St. Nicholas music become that "As in the Greek world, the eleventh-century Latin world whistled his name."

Other St. Nicholas-related music followed. Jones declares that "Perhaps

Stained-glass window, St. Mary's Church at Lambeth Palace, London, England

N's good fortune in musician friends resulted from his uncomplicated worldliness, which attracted adventurous youth. The eleventh century is filled with new music of an awakening world, and N was singing and sung about" (Jones, 112–113, this section). Tristran Coffin maintains that over 527 Latin hymns have been composed in St. Nicholas's honor (Coffin, 80).

Father of Modern Drama

The earliest form of drama that we know, we call "The Saint Play" or "The Miracle Play." Its subject matter dealt with the lives, martyrdoms, and miracles of a given saint, and was always accompanied by music. The only two saints generally excluded from these plays were St. Paul and the Virgin Mary. At the very beginning—the genesis itself—of such drama are the plays having to do with St. Nicholas (most written during the three centuries beginning around 1150).

Why were they so popular? Perhaps because even then audiences thrilled to vicarious adventure and violence. They could salve their consciences for having reveled so thoroughly in melodrama and escapism by rationalizing that it did have an overriding spiritual theme to it. Since they didn't have to tie them to biblical restraints, they were free to venture out into sensationalism. Their subject matter was most familiar to their audiences: dishonest innkeepers and their wives taking advantage of, or attacking, their guests; robbers breaking into homes; families struggling with extreme poverty, etc. And unlike church drama, in these miracle plays they were permitted to stray into humor.

What would it have been like to attend such a miracle play? Ebon obliges with a depiction of a medieval dramatic performance of *Iconia 34* (or *Vandal Icon*). This is the first St. Nicholas story to be set in Africa.

> "You are mingling with a festive, excitedly chattering crowd in a provincial French or Italian town. The year is, let us say, 1236; the date, December 5. It is late afternoon. All around the marketplace are food vendors. There has been some drinking in the city's taverns. By now, some of the men are as unruly as the children that are part of the throng moving toward the central marketplace. There will be something new to see and hear before the sun goes down: a play about a miraculous picture of Saint Nicholas.

The St. Nicholas character was the star of comical miracle plays.

Giant St. Nicholas featured in the "The Play of St Nicholas," produced by King Alfred College, Winchester, England

98

La Légende de saint Nicolas

. . . Le premier dit : « J'ai bien dormi,
— Et moi, dit le second, aussi. »
Et le troisième répondit :
« Je croyais être en Paradis. »

"It is a lively, at times raucous play, involving invaders, bandits, robbery, and violence. But in the end, Christian virtue wins out, and the villains turn honest, contrite, and faithful. The play was probably conceived as a pious but dramatic legend by someone who lived in what is today the Italian region of Calabria when it was part of the Byzantine Empire.

"The villain of the play is a Vandal chieftain, Barbarus. . . . This particular Vandal chieftain has looted many towns in Calabria and taken local citizens prisoners. He is worried that his treasures might, in turn, be taken from him by dubious friends or open foes.

"Barbarus is told that one of his looted treasures is a magical portrait of Saint Nicholas. He learns from a prisoner that the picture, or icon, will guarantee luck and wealth to its owner, as long as it remains in his possession. Barbarus is, of course, delighted to hear this good news. He assumes that the icon will transfer its strength to any possessor, whether ownership is legitimate or by robbery.

"Greedy, simple-minded Barbarus, portrayed on the stage as a cunning boor who is partly fearsome and partly ridiculous, decides to turn the holy icon into a magical watch dog for his accumulated loot. But while Barbarus goes off to celebrate his now-safeguarded gains, his loot in turn is looted.

"The audience in the marketplace roars with laughter as the boorish, drunken chieftain displays shock, confusion, and anger when he discovers that most of his treasure has disappeared. But the Saint Nicholas icon is still there. Barbarus, who only knows violent punishment, decides to treat Saint Nicholas as he would one of his own soldiers who may fail in guard duty: he threatens to give him a good thrashing unless he sees to it, miraculous or otherwise, that the ill-gotten treasures are returned.

"If you see yourself as a member of the audience, you can feel its excitement as the plot thickens: the holy icon has taken on human, indeed superhuman, characteristics; it is like an actor on the stage. Can Saint Nicholas permit his holy image to be mistreated, cursed, 'beaten,' damaged in demeaning ways by the piratical unbeliever?

"Now the scene changes. The bandits are assembled. With much shouting and arguing, they are about to divide the remaining loot among themselves. But just as they are about to lay hands on the loot, Saint Nicholas appears before them as a vivid apparition. Angered, he subdues them with his magnificence. He threatens to take them all before the town's judges unless they immediately return all stolen goods to their rightful owners. His appearance sobers and frightens the thieves. If they do not obey him, Nicholas threatens, they will all wind up with a rope around their necks. The thieves, contrite, return the loot.

"But Barbarus is even more deeply impressed. In the closing scene of the play, the Vandal invader kisses the icon of the saint. On his return to North Africa, he sees to it that all members of his household become Christians. Finally, he builds a chapel dedicated to the holy man whose apparition forced him to change his ways. And that, the stage play states in closing, is how Saint Nicholas became famous even in Africa.

"There is a wickedly impious note in this play, in line with the raucous nature of other public dramas of the period. The very idea that an icon of the saint could be threatened with a beating is hardly in line with the traditional awe that surrounds the stories, paintings, and plays that have Saint Nicholas as a central character. True, the 'happy endings' makes everything all right and furnishes an excuse for some of the rowdyism in the first two-thirds of the play. Violence, with some sort of 'redeeming social value'—to use a contemporary expression—was as much a part of the late Middle

One medieval play explains how St. Nicholas became famous in Africa.

This is an example of the traditional wax icon images sold in the street markets to pilgrims and tourists in Myra.

Ages as it had been in antiquity and remains in today's motion picture and television shows, not to mention the miracle-cum-morality play's successors on our own theatrical stages" (Ebon, 66–7).

McKnight maintains that "These little St. Nicholas plays have genuine significance in the early history of the modern drama. At a time when the classical drama was dead . . . , by one of the strange ironies of life, under the auspices of the church, which had been hostile in its attitude toward earlier drama, there was created, seemingly without being realized, the germ from which developed the modern drama. The St. Nicholas plays go back to an early stage in the new dramatic development. Little dramatic scenes from scriptural story began to find a place in the liturgy of the church as early as the tenth century. St. Nicholas plays are not much later, and are the earliest ones handling scenes drawn from outside the biblical story. St. Nicholas may almost be regarded as the patron saint of the modern drama, since he seems to have watched over its birth" (McKnight, 90–91).

The Stories Continue

Sometimes St. Nicholas protects both the victims and the perpetrators (in the same story!).

Dazed Thieves 69

During a local war, the wife of a prefect hid two sacks of valuable goods in the balcony of the local St. Nicholas church. Two boys hunting for birds' nests in the church found the sacks. They determined to return that night when no one would be around to see them. That night, they hauled off the two sacks but got lost in the woods. When they finally *did* find their way out, lo and behold, directly ahead of them, there was the church! Again they tried to find their way home, again they got lost and ended up at the church. At dawn, having once again returned to the church, they resignedly dropped the sacks in the churchyard and ran, this time finding their homes. A neighbor caught them trying to wash away the grime accumulated during the night and made them confess.

St. Mary and St. Nicholas Church, Littlemore, Oxford, where John Cardinal Newman once served as an Anglican priest

103

The prefect and his wife recovered their property and fervently thanked St. Nicholas for his protection.

A number of stories have to do with St. Nicholas's protection of Crusaders. Following are two of them:

Imprisoned in Gaza

One Crusader, Cunon de Richecourt, was taken prisoner in Gaza (1240). He prayed continually to Saint Nicholas, urging him to help release him. On St. Nicholas Eve, 1244, his prison door suddenly opened; next thing he knew, he was standing in his chains in front of the front door of the Church of Saint Nicolas de Port in Lorraine, France. In gratitude for his deliverance, the Lord of Richecourt funded a torchlight procession to take place every December 5 between 8:00 A.M. and 9:00 P.M., promising to be present for it every St. Nicholas Eve for the rest of his life.

Black Falcon

This is one Crusader story that almost ran away with Charles Jones. Initially, he just couldn't believe it, it seemed too far-fetched to be true. But then, the more he researched it the more convinced he became that it was historically accurate: Two larger-than-life superheroes, Fulk Nerra and his son Geoffrey Martel, "the Hammer," founders of the House of Anjou that filled so many thrones of Europe.

Fulk Nerra (the "Black Falcon") was described by Le Moy as "A strange and complex figure, indefatigable, athirst for vengeance, brutal in moments of reprisal, quick to remorse, hurrying to Palestine, making his own servants beat him, and despite those penances always the bandit, builder of castles and churches, including some marvels, feared and adored by all, uniting in his person all contrasts."

Fulk started out with a piece of land about fifty miles square. He had no pushover neighbors: to his north was Normandy and Maine, to the east, Chartres and Blois, to the south, Poitou, and to the west, the kingdom of Britanny. But in 53 years of rule, friend and foe alike trembled at his coming. By the time his son Geoffrey died, Anjou held the balance of power in all of France. It was even said that William the Conqueror attacked England rather than face the Anjous. When Fulk's first wife, Elizabeth of Vendôme, failed to produce a son, he had her put to death. Same treatment to Hugh of Beauvais, the favorite of King Robert Capet: Fulk and his knights slew him right in front of the king himself! But Fulk was always sorry after his rampages, hence his

Crusaders and kings appealed to St. Nicholas for protection.

Clockwise from top: Heiliger Nikolaus on an Austrian holiday stamp and postmark from one of the many villages and cities called St. Nikolaus; Swiss stamps featuring the great iffelen miters of Küssnacht am Rigi, Switzerland; French lottery ticket complete with St. Nicholas; First-Day Cover from St. Nicolas de Port, France

trips to the Holy Land in penance. After his wife died and he burned down Angers, Fulk became terrified that he was headed straight for Hell. Hence his leaving for Palestine. His second trip was caused by the killing of Hugh of Beauvais. It was during Hugh's pilgrimage there that the Caliph Hakim destroyed the Church of the Holy Sepulcher in Jerusalem and helped to bring on the Crusades by that act of desecration. Fulk had journeyed to Palestine alone, and somehow survived to return. On another trip, Fulk traveled to Palestine with Duke Robert (*le Diable*) of Normandy, father of William the Conqueror.

A gentle Bishop Nicholas with a doll and a donkey on this French postcard

On one of these trips, off the Antiochene coast, the ship Fulk was in was engulfed by a terrific storm. Each man aboard, anticipating death, invoked his favorite saint. Since Fulk heard the name of Nicholas being invoked all around him, he fell on his knees, promising St. Nicholas that if he'd only spare his life, he'd build a church in honor of him when he returned to France. The storm died down, and, not long after, Hugh left for home, stopping on the way to visit the pope. After returning to France, he decided to build a monastery in honor of St. Nicholas. It was this monastery that began the cult of St. Nicholas in western France.

In his later years, his son by his second wife, Adela Geoffrey, revolted against him. The old man not only defeated his son, he forced him to carry a saddle on his back for a number of days, finally collapsing on it in exhaustion. Fulk rose up and kicked his prostrate son, exclaiming, *Victus es tandem, victus!* ['You're still beaten'! Beaten!']. The son calmed his father down by saying that no one else on earth could vanquish him but his father.

Once again Fulk journeyed to far-off Jerusalem, where he commanded two servants to drag him naked, in the sight of the Turks, to the Holy Sepulcher, scourging him all the way, while he cried out, "Lord, receive the wretched Fulk, Thy perfidious scoundrel; look to my repentant soul, O Lord Jesus Christ." The mercurial count died returning from this last trip to Jerusalem. Afterward, the St. Nicholas Abbey remained a powerful cultural force for centuries (Jones, 99–107, 148, 160).

Notice the elaborate vestments on this French card, "Hail St. Nicholas."

Monk of Eynsham 72

A Cluniac monk of noble blood, Odo, became Pope Urban II. He had a tough time of it, as when he became pope, Rome and the Lateran were still controlled by Clement III, the Antipope. In 1089, he consecrated Abbot Elias as the new archbishop of Bari, and also declared May 9 (Nicholas Translation Day) a feast day for all Christendom. The battle cry, "God wills

it!" he would use to launch the Crusades; he had first encountered it in Nicephorus's account of the Translation from Myra to
Bari, of St. Nicholas's bones.

In 1095, he journeyed to Angers in order to rededicate the
sanctuary in Count Fulk's St. Nicholas Abbey. He decreed the
monastery's perpetual possession of all its holdings. Everywhere
he went, Urban invoked the magic of St. Nicholas as the bridge
between East and West.

In 1098, Urban called a council to meet at Bari. Among
those attending was Anselm, archbishop of Canterbury. Earlier
on, while Abbot of Bec, Anselm had written a long and effusive
prayer to St. Nicholas. In that prayer, he portrayed St. Nicholas
as a spiritual guide through Hell and Purgatory. He gave a copy
to Urban. It is said that Adam, an English chaplain and biographer, wrote the account of Eadmond, a monk of the Abbey
of Eynsham, who was entranced
for forty hours (Good Friday
Vespers to Easter Lauds in 1196).
Modern scholarship reveals that
the visionary was most likely
Edmund Rich, later archbishop
of Canterbury.

The account of this eschato-
logical vision went on to become
one of the most famous and
influential medieval works of the
genre. In fact, many believe it was
a model for Dante. Like Dante's,
Edmund's vision takes place at
Eastertide, involves a contest for
souls, and the theme is *one little
tear*. Jones describes the action
in these words: "Though pilgrim
and guide first travel through a
schematized Hell, the center of
interest is Purgatory, a hill as in
Dante. In the journey through
it the redeemed have their bur-
dens lightened. The therapy is
homeopathic. Specific clerics
and even a pope are punished. The transition from misery to
health is gradual, and during it the greatest suffering results
from uncertainty of salvation. Periods of purgation are fixed
periods of time, though the periods are shorter than Dante's.
There are the same nightly rests.

The guide, equivalent with Virgil, is N, who leads Edmund
not only through Hell and Purgatory but Paradise as well. . . .

**An elderly
woman rests
from the rigors
of pilgrimage in
Bari; thousands
gather to honor
St. Nicholas
each May from
all over Italy,
Europe, and the
globe.**

**St. Nicholas
postcards**

Gruss vom Nikolo

Gruss vom Nicolo.

Bonne Fête

Heureux Noël

St. NICOLAS

Vive St. Nicolas

Kese St. Niklaas

Sinterklaas rijdt op de daken

Groeten van St. Nicolaas.

Groeten van St. Nicolaas.

The icon of the Miracle of the Grain in St. Nicholas Chapel (Byzantine Catholic), Greek Catholic Union of the U.S.A., 5400 Tuscarawas Road, Beaver, Pennsylvania 15009

According to Matthew Paris, ten years after the Eynshan vision, Thurcill of Essex had a vision in which Saint Julian was guide; in that instance N was an overseer of Purgatory, not wholly unlike the Cato figure of Dante" (Jones, 238–9).

Might Chaucer also have been influenced by the St. Nicholas stories?

The Bari Widow

This tale is thought by some to have inspired Chaucer's *Troilus and Criseyde*, possibly even "The Miller's Tale" and "The Prioress's Tale" of his *Canterbury Tales*. The male protagonist is said by some to be modeled on Reginold of Eichstätt, not yet a bishop at this time. Jones feels it was composed somewhere around 1150.

It begins with "There was a man of noble birth and handsome features," who lived in Bari not too long after the St. Nicholas Translation. This clerk ran a school in that city. "In that same city lived a widow preeminently endowed in mind, though even richer in wealth and loveliness. In either grace she was so surpassing that by a look she could have enticed a stony Demosthenes to the nuptial bed or aroused passion in the most chaste Lucrece." But this widow was both chaste and true, and she venerated all the saints—but St. Nicholas most of all. In fact, she frequently held vigils next to the saint's tomb.

Well, it took but one look for the clerk (cleric) to be "stricken to the marrow." He was in anguish and torment from continually desiring her. And the more he tried to smother the flame the more it grew. By that time, even his face

A banner in St. Nicholas Parish Church, Chiswick, London, England

had become distorted by his continual lustful thoughts. Finally, he gave up and confessed his love to the beautiful widow, only to be rejected.

At a dinner party the widow held annually on St. Nicholas Day, she berated the clerks for their failure to compose "a single responsory or prose suitable for praise of that good friend of God, or even a canticle to joyfully honor his festive holy day." The languishing clerk heard about her challenge and quickly composed a composition honoring St. Nicholas, for he had reasons for winning. Unwisely, the widow had promised "any gift" to the clerk who could create an acceptable St. Nicholas *historia*.

The clerk then wrote a splendid *historia* which awed all who studied it, including the delighted widow, who asked him to name his reward. He demanded her love. Nothing could dissuade him in his determination to have her at all costs—not money, not power, not anything. He gave her but one day before delivering herself to him.

The broken-hearted and shamed widow wept most of that 24 hours, all that night she prayed that Nicholas would somehow save her from the clerk's demands. Meanwhile, the young clerk lay awake cursing the time he had to wait before the widow became his mistress. Suddenly, St. Nicholas entered his room, seized him by the hair, and began lashing him with his whip. Though the saint's face radiated compassion, there was no compassion in his whip. Nor in his words of condemnation. Finally, the thoroughly cowed young man exclaimed, "Lord, have mercy on me a sinner." At this, St. Nicholas identified himself and told him that the floggings would not stop until he promised to release the widow from her promise and to cease demanding that she give in to his lustful demands. Quickly, the chastened young man got up, went to St. Nicholas's tomb, found the weeping widow, and begged for her forgiveness. The widow granted that forgiveness and both lived out their lives in devotion to the saint, the widow founding a convent (Jones, 240–245).

The Cross Legend

This is the second St. Nicholas story to refer to the Reginold Eichenstätt *historia* that was then sweeping across Europe. The original account was penned by John the Deacon. In the story it appears that though the Nicholas *historia* was being sung, whistled, and performed everywhere, that was not the case in a certain Saint Mary of Charity cloister named after the Cross. Their prior, Dom Ytherius was finally approached by the senior monks and asked if he would permit them to "psalm the responses of the blessed Nicholas." The prior not only rejected their request, he

The great Nikolaaskerk in Amsterdam, Holland

Opposite right: The vaulted ceiling of St. Nicolas de Port Basilica in Lorraine, France; Far right: the golden altar of St. Nicholas Roman Catholic Church in Prague, Czech Republic

ONE FAITH

did it angrily. Surprisingly, the monks pressed him on the issue, with words such as these: "Why, father, do you disdain to listen to your sons? Why, when the *historia* of Saint Nicholas, full of sweet spiritual honey, is already honored through nearly the whole globe, cannot we chant it? Why cannot we, like others, be refreshed at such a feast? . . . Why, with all the churches committed to jubilation through this new leaven, must this cell alone now remain in mute silence?" They said more.

Finally, the prior exploded with blasphemies and ordered them out.

But that night, St. Nicholas appeared to the prior and castigated him in no uncertain terms. Not contenting himself with that, the good saint dragged him off his cot by his hair, and shoved him down on the dormitory floor. Then he began singing the Nicholas anthem, *O pastor aeterne*, and with each modulation he lashed the neck of the unfortunate prior

Stone relief of San Nicola di Bari, in Italy

with the whip which the saint had thoughtfully remembered to bring along. Eventually, the thoroughly beaten prior got the message and learned the words to St. Nicholas's satisfaction. By now near hysterical from all he had gone through, the prior began to sob loudly. Hearing this, the brothers ran into the room and were amazed to find the prior prone on the floor. But he appeared unable to provide them with a satisfactory explanation. So they carried him into the infirmary, where he remained for some days.

At last, restored to health by the intervention of the good saint, he summoned all the brothers and announced some unexpected news: "Observe, my dearest sons, that after I refused to obey you I underwent severe punishment for my hardness of heart. Now do I not only freely accord with your request, but as long as I live I will be the first and most accomplished chanter of the *historia* of that great father" (Jones, 116–118).

This has to be one of the funniest of the St. Nicholas legends. Just the thought of St. Nicholas whipping the good prior into liking the long anthem tickles the funny bone.

The Significance of these Stories

One can't help but notice in these stories that St. Nicholas is portrayed as a rather mercurial saint, oscillating between kindness and cruelty, giving and taking, blessing and punishing. Ancelet-Hustache explains the paradox in this way: "On one hand the beneficent saint, the light-bringing apparition; on the other, the enemy of mankind, the dark dweller in dark places. Nothing could be more in tune with the spirit of the Middle Ages than this violent contrast. The art and literature of the period, the legends, 'miracles' and other dramatic 'games'—all included the devil. The people of medieval days loved depicting the devil as hideously as they could, as we can see from the sculptures in the cathedrals, stressing the horns and claws, so that his final defeat might be all the more glorious. They saw the saints as their powerful assistants in their unceasing struggle against the Evil One, and above all they expected help from St. Nicholas, whom they placed so high in the hierarchy of heaven. Emperor Leo the Wise, who was writing in the tenth and eleventh centuries, summed up the thought of his time and the centuries to come when he wrote that the Enemy suffered a defeat whenever any saint's feast was celebrated, but that the feast of St. Nicholas caused him the greatest trouble, for it was celebrated all over the world (Ancelet-Hustache, 82).

Grotesque Krampus with a gentle Nikolo in this Austrian card

Normally, St. Nicholas, being a chaste ascetic, has very little to do with the fair sex. And certainly there is not even a hint that he would intervene in a case where lust was a factor. *The Bari Widow* is the one of only two exceptions to that rule, building a case for his being a protector of woman's virtue (the other is the much earlier story of *The Three Dowerless Daughters*).

And *The Cross Legend* tells of an overprotective saint who is so invested in the success of music dedicated to him that he is willing to whip anyone who fails to sing his praises. In fact, the whipping aspect of these last two stories reveals St. Nicholas in a most unflattering light. But, perhaps they do bridge to the later punishing dimension represented by assistants such as *Belsnickel, Pere Fouettard, Krampus, and Black Pete.*

The statue in St. Nicholas Anglican Church, Chiswick, London

CHAPTER 5

Nicholas Everyman

Now comes the Golden Age of the arts and of St. Nicholas as well. All things came together in the Renaissance, and nothing would ever be the same. With the rediscovery of the artifacts and literature of ancient Greece and Rome came the ancients' celebration of self, the will to challenge *everything*—even supposed absolutes.

But it was not so with the unlettered masses: for all practical purposes, humanism would by-pass them. Day after day, as they labored from dawn to dusk in the fields, manor houses, and cities, they had precious little energy left to think deep thoughts. It was enough that the church remained the rock it had always been. Since it was dangerous to question the aristocracy, they operated on the assumption that it was equally dangerous to question the clergy. Wasn't God clearly in control of every act of their lives? Wasn't God in constant communication with the earth (especially through the more approachable saints)?

So how did the Renaissance come about? And where did it come first? As fate would have it, the Renaissance would be born in that beautiful city of Florence, nestled in the hills of Tuscany, and sustained by the life-giving water of the undulating Arno River. Florence was ruled by Italy's most famous family, the Medici. The Medici served as the bankers of Europe. They were so powerful that they could stop wars in their tracks by calling in the loans of all citizens in a given state. The coat of arms of the Medici featured six (later only three) red balls on a field of gold. The three balls have symbolized mutual trust ever since. Many scholars feel that the three balls were predicated on the three bags of gold (each reduced to a sphere) given by St. Nicholas to the three dowerless maidens. Thus it was no accident that when a knight made a solemn vow, more often than not he would swear by St. Nicholas.

But the Medici were interested in far more than governing or banking. Their main interests centered in learning and the arts. No other family in the history of this planet has equaled the Medici in their patronage of learning and art.

Opposite: A statue in SS Peter and Paul Roman Catholic Church in Küssnacht am Rigi, Switzerland, home of one the great St. Nicholas traditions

Around that time, scholars and artists from the trembling Byzantine dominions began to flee what they feared was a sinking ship (Constantinople fell to the Turks on May 29, 1453). The art and literature of ancient Greece and Rome came with these refugees. Simultaneously, more and more Greco-Roman artifacts were being unearthed. Suddenly, it was as though the past seamlessly blended into the present. Gone was a thousand years of barbarism and gloom, born was this newly rediscovered *joie de vivre*: the headiest of wines. Well hidden in the luxuriant foliage of humanism was a poisoned apple. No one saw it until it was too late.

The oratory chapel in St. Nicolas Roman Catholic Church in Brussels, Belgium

In the previous millennium, Byzantine and Romanesque cathedrals had helped to freeze thought and limit challenges to authority. Now soaring Gothic walls and windows let in all the colors and ideas in the world. With them was born some of the most magnificent, inspirational, and enduring religious art this world has ever known.

Though it was not yet acceptable to produce secular art, the Greco-Roman fever permitted mythological scenes to be created. Renaissance artists climbed into that Trojan Horse and had it hauled into the City of God. Some of these depictions are among the greatest masterpieces ever painted. Since Greek and Roman mythology was so dissolute, the art (much of it nudes) tended to reflect that. The poisoned apple? Ah! It was revealed when the sensuality unleashed in pagan art began to appear in ostensibly Christian buildings, in the palaces of bishops, cardinals, and popes. As a result, hedonism began to edge out spirituality. The old gods began to return. Artemis was back. But not outside the church. Inside. Opening the door for Machiavelli. And *The Prince* was at least partially modeled on a Borgia pope and his son, art imitating life in that it was more important to be *perceived* as moral than to *be* moral. Somewhere the line of distinction between spirituality and hedonistic amorality began to blur.

> I n the Golden Age of St. Nicholas, he was the world's most popular non-biblical saint.

Statue over the entrance of the basilica at St. Nicolas de Port, France

St. Nicholas at the Zenith

It would be the Golden Age of St. Nicholas as well. He was now the most popular non-biblical saint in the world. He had already achieved preeminence in the East; now, no small thanks to the Bari Abduction, he achieved equal stature in the West. During these centuries, the shrine at Bari became almost as popular a pilgrim destination as Rome and St. James of Compostela. Especially attractive to pilgrims was the opportunity to acquire at the shrine bottles of the sacred manna (or myrrh) that emanated from the tomb. Miraculous healings continued to be reported as well.

Bari had a serious rival. To the north, in Lorraine, France, was a sleepy little town named Port. But that all changed with the decision to construct a church of St. Nicholas there. Result: the town became one of the largest and richest in Lorraine. In 1495, the decision was made to construct an even larger cathedral there. Much of the work was completed by 1518. Then the Emperor Charles V, ruler of half of Europe and all of the Americas, lent a hand, collecting money from all over the empire for the cathedral. In 1616, Pope Urban VIII announced a jubilee for the city, and more than 200,000 pilgrims answered his call. Then came war and fire and plundering in 1635, when French, Swedes, and Germans set fire to the cathedral roof, chopped down the doors, burned the city, and tortured the inhabitants. Shortly after this, Pope Innocent X confirmed Nicholas's position as patron saint of Lorraine. The church has since been rebuilt.

The list of famous pilgrims who came here to worship includes the Emperor Charles IV in 1335. Joan of Arc came here in 1429 to implore St. Nicholas to help her in her quest to secure an audience with Duke Charles II of Lorraine at Nancy. Margaret of Anjou celebrated at Saint Nicolas de Port her betrothal to King Henry VI of England. Poor Margaret would spend her last days a prisoner in the Tower of London, praying that St. Nicholas would intercede on her behalf. Francis Xavier came here on foot in 1536. Queen May of Hungary came in 1549. Charles IX of France and his mother, Catherine de Medici, came here in 1564. She returned later with another of her sons, the future King Henri III, whose wife, daughter of Nicholas of Lorraine, made weekly pilgrimages on foot to the cathedral from Nancy. King Henri IV, with his wife,

God, in you have I trusted,
St. Nicholas, to you I entrust my prayers,
Upon you both I cast my care,
even on you I throw my soul.
This is what you exact from me
You by your commands, you by your counsels.
Receive him who throws himself upon you both,
Have him who is prostrate before you.
Keep me when I sleep, help me in whatever I do,
Inspire me in whatever I think,
You, Lord, by your grace,
You, Nicholas, by your intercession
You for the merits of your so loved confessor,
You according to the name of your and my Creator,
who is blessed forevermore. Amen.

—St. Anselm, Archbishop of Canterbury, 1093–1114

From *Saint Nicholas: A Saint for Today: A Christmas Special*, a special supplement to *Anglican World*, 1999 Used by permission

The procession for Whitmonday celebration at St. Nicolas de Port, France

Marie de Medici, came in 1603. Also worshiping here was Henri VI, Charles VII, and Rene I of Sicily.

Perhaps the best way of measuring the universality of St. Nicholas's position in history is to point out the groups who chose him as their patron saint. For starters, there were Constantinople and the Byzantine Empire, Moscow and the Russian Empire, Holland, Norway, eastern Italy, Lorraine, and New Amsterdam (Manhattan, New York). Dr. Adriaan De Groot notes that he was not only the protector of helpless infants and children but also the patron saint of parenthood, of barren wives who sought to have children; and yearning virgins or spinsters who sought husbands (Jones, 370; Ebon, 53, 60). He was the patron saint of bankers, money-lenders, and pawnbrokers; of students, scholars, pilgrims, and travelers; of butchers, mercers, and coopers; of thieves, murderers, pirates, prisoners, and Vandals; of sailors, merchants, and

Illustrations of the legends of Nicholas's saving the soldiers from death and the three girls from poverty

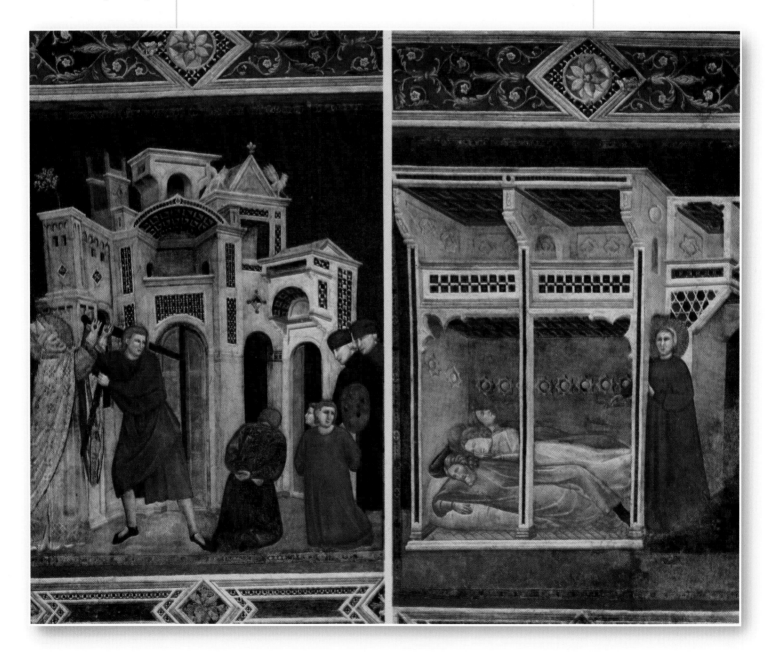

fishermen; of sawyers, dyers, turners, haberdashers, and cartmakers; of seedmen, packers, chandlers, winers, drapers, and brewers; of iron-mongers, coalmen, perfumers, and cobblers; of chemists, firemen, and Crusaders; of clerks, clerics, orphans, and royalty. He was always the protector of the weak against the strong, the poor against the rich, and, not coincidentally, the patron saint of giving and Christmas.

The Artists Who Celebrated St. Nicholas

St. Nicholas has been depicted by artists more often than any saint except Mary.

The earliest depictions of St. Nicholas are early Christian. Few of them survive today, mainly because of the wholesale destruction of this art during the periodic iconoclastic upheavals. The same was true

Banner at the Anglican Collegiate Church of St. Nicholas, Galway, Ireland

of early Byzantine depictions of St. Nicholas. Many of the later portrayals of St. Nicholas by Byzantine artists managed to survive. The oldest Nicholas artifact from the West to survive is a frescoed figure in the ninth-century Santa Maria Antiqua in Rome. Some of the oldest eastern icons and mosaics can be seen in places like Mt. Athos in Greece, the Kremlin, Assisi, and St. Mark's Basilica in Venice.

St. Nicholas has always been all things to all people, and each artist has found a perspective of him uniquely his own. In this respect, Jones notes that "Fra Angelico caught N in a studious moment (as always, in his iconographic bishop's robes)—the humane master, the patron of scholars, whose ghost today gives out diplomas at Cologne and Aberdeen. Veronese saw him as spokesman for the most powerful party of his day. He ranged N as front man before the Carmelite Madonna in all her glory. Ghirlandaio caught him as a pillar of the state, the way Borglum caught Washington, Jefferson, Lincoln, and Roosevelt the First. Along with Peter, John the Baptist, and Martin, he is Power. Titian followed N with his brush as Stuart followed Washington, producing a variety of results. In one, N dominates his committee, made up of Catherine of Alexander, as well as Peter, Anthony of Padua, Francis, and Sebastian. But in a lovely drawing he catches N alone and solitary, as the wisdom of the ages. Bellini sees N as overshadowing Augustine—the kind of invidious comparison that news photographers nowadays are trained to snap.

"Above all is Raphael's Ansidei Madonna, with N and John the Baptist located in London's National Gallery. Here is a Christian trinity just short of godhead—the Virgin as apex of a triangle which lowly man can comprehend, supported and supporting in a mysterious triangulation the dichotomized states of being that Western culture loved above all others: John and N, ascetic and secular, contemplative and active, claustral and worldly, individual and collective, monastic and episcopal, soul and body. Rafael brings out many traits in N: worldliness without pomposity, judiciousness softened by charity. Like a true head of the establishment, this N carries a book but never reads. Note how lightly the book is held, as he listens for the phone to ring (Jones, 3–4).

Other well-known artists who depicted him include the sculptor Bernini, Jan Steen, Cranach the Elder, Albrecht Altdorfer, Andrea del Sarto, Lorenzo Lotto, Morretto da Brescia, Vittore Carpaccio, Piero di Cosimo, Benedetto Bonfigli, Simone Martini, Giovan Battista Tiepolo, Jacques Callot, Pierre Claudin, Hans Baldung-Grien, Otto Van Veen, Cornelius Schut, Jean Girardet, Taddeo Gaddi, Jacobo di Robusti, Paul Troger, Hans Fries, Nicole Gauthier, Pietro Orioli, Margarito of Arezzo, Benvenuto di Giovanni, Lorenzo di Niccolo, Luca Signorelli, Giottino, L. Di Bicci, A. Lorenzetti, Francesco Pesselino, L. Monaco, Jean Fouquet, Jean Rexacht, Bartolomew Zeitblom, Fabio Christopheri—and he's even depicted in the world's most famous illustrated book, the Duke of Berry *Book of Hours* by Jean, Herman de Limbourg.

St. Nicholas was also depicted by many sculptors, on banners (such as those in the church in St. Niklaas, Belgium and the St. Nicholas Anglican Church in Galway, Ireland); icons, murals, mosaics (such as those in Venice's St. Mark's); statues (such as "Our Lady and St. Nicholas" in Liverpool, Salisbury Cathedral, St. Nicolas-de-Port, St. Nicolo in Venice, St. Nicholas Church in Amsterdam, St. Nicholas at Wade, U.K., and so many more); reliefs (found in churches all across Europe); images (appearing on reliquaries, croziers, ex-votos, and procession markers); and painted manna bottles such as those from Bari.

Nicholas and the Boy Bishops

Since Nicholas was so young when elected bishop of Myra, he became the prototype for the annual election of boy bishops in various parts of Europe. Though the custom was in vogue in Roman Catholic countries from earliest times, it was in England where this institution became the most popular. The boy would be

> **St. Nicholas was the prototype for European Boy Bishop festivities.**

"Sint Niklaas Bischop en Belijder," Door Pater Andreas Bosteels, OFM

elected bishop of St. Nicholas Day, would be dressed in pontifical vestments, and other boys would be given priestly robes to put on. Together, they would move in procession throughout the parish, the young bishop blessing the people who assembled along the way. Then the young bishop and his associates would take possession of the cathedral and its services; his reign would last until Holy Innocents Day, Dec. 28.

The earliest known reference to a boy bishop has to do with a visit by King Conrad II to St. Gall near Constance. The King found it "all very amusing and especially the procession of children, so grave and sedate that even when Conrad bade his courtiers roll apples along the aisle, they did not budge." In France, the tradition continued until 1721, in Germany until 1779, in Belgium until the nineteenth century. In England, it only lasted until the Reformation (McKnight, 66–78). However, an adapted ceremony still takes place today in Hereford Cathedral and English parishes such as North Walsum, Norfolk.

Patron Saint of Christmas

It is intriguing to note that as we describe the societal roles of St. Nicholas during the Renaissance, when he was literally, and figuratively, EVERYMAN, virtually omnipresent throughout Europe and the near East, his Christmas persona was comparatively a minor one.

Santa Claus, no, St. Nicholas. This image with a flowing beard, teddy bear, and bishop's miter blends the two characters.

This would be a good place to point out that the early Christians did not observe Christmas at all. In fact, Origen, one of the most eminent of the early church fathers, proclaimed that it was a sin to single out one day of the year as our Lord's birthday—as though He were a king or pharaoh instead of God!

That attitude began to change when Pope Julius I chose December 25 in 336 as the official date of Christ's birth. Arnest points out that this "was a deliberate attempt to co-opt the Roman festival of Saturnalia, a bawdy solstice celebration that lasted a week. It was easier to Christianize the festival than to abolish it" (Arnest, 1, 8). Today, for the same reasons, we celebrate Easter with bunny rabbits and colored Easter eggs. Saint Valentine has been all but forgotten on his birthday as we give out sentimental cards, candy, and flowers to those we love. St. Patrick isn't remembered as a real person either (at least in America), but rather his birthday is merely a reason to wear green, pretend you're Irish, and drink more than you should. And All Hallow's Eve has lost all spiritual significance in America, for we have made it instead the most occult of our holidays, complete with ghouls, goblins, witches, horror, jack-o-lanterns, and trick-or-treating. Intriguing, isn't it, that such Christianized pagan holidays end up being re-secularized by supposedly Christian nations.

As for Christmas, the biblical precedent for giving during this season was set by the Magi, who were the true first-givers of gifts: the three kings who brought precious offerings of gold, frankincense, and myrrh.

The young Nicholas, when he made selfless giving (in secret and without desire for recognition) habitual in his life, an integral part of his character, inseparable from who he was, had no way of knowing that he was establishing himself as the post-apostolic link between the Magi and posterity, the torch-bearer who would keep selfless giving alive down through the ages. In fact, it is said that giving a "Baker's Dozen" (13 for the price of 12) can also be traced to St. Nicholas.

Ebb Tide for St. Nicholas

Though St. Nicholas appeared more popular than ever at the close of the Renaissance, those appearances were misleading. For the poisoned apple had resulted in doubt where there had once been faith, skepticism where there had once been belief, mockery where there had once been praise. In this respect, St. Nicholas was anything but alone, but rather a symptom of a widespread malaise. The St. Nicholas stories appear relatively unchanged from those that came before. But it wasn't the stories that were different; it was the reception of those stories. With doubt and skepticism came ridicule and humor. When belief went out the window, we

The tomb of a Boy Bishop who died while serving in that role in Salisbury Cathedral, England. The cathedral continues the Boy Bishop ceremony each year at Nicholastide.

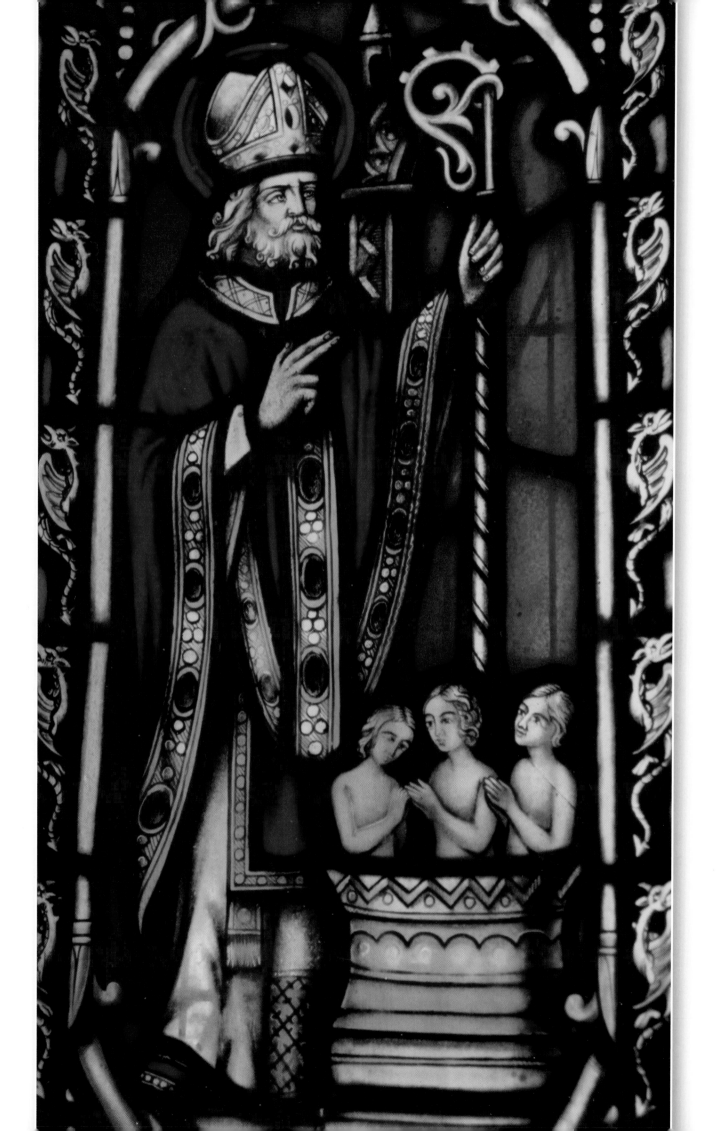

were left with quaint and simplistic stories that degenerated into archaic art forms. With that loss of belief, the stories lost their power to effect change.

The Stories Continue

The Three Children in the Salt Tub or Young Theology Students or Three Clerks 44

This particular story is one of the most famous, and oft-painted, stories about St. Nicholas. It also has many variations, both in subject matter and in geographical area.

Now for one of the better variants: Three theology students are traveling through France. As they see night approaching, they start looking for a place to spend the night. Finally they reach an inn, and gratefully enter it and ask for a room. The sharp-eyed innkeeper observes that their purses are heavy. Late that night, after they are all asleep, he softly enters their room. So soundly are they sleeping that they don't notice when he steals their purses. Not content with theft, however, the innkeeper kills them, perhaps by smothering with a pillow. Then he surreptitiously carries each one downstairs to the meat room. Here he strips them, cuts them up into slices, and puts those slices into casks used for salting meat. Variant accounts portray the innkeeper's wife as an accomplice.

Next morning, St. Nicholas arrives. Some versions have him ordering breakfast and catching the innkeeper and his wife in the act of preparing the slices of students for cooking. In others, he demands that the innkeeper take him to the room where the dismembered students are. Then St. Nicholas accuses him of murder. When he denies it, he restores the students to life in front of his very eyes.

Several centuries later, the same story has as its protagonists three small children (in most cases, three small boys) who late one night ask a butcher and his wife for lodging. During the night, the butcher and his wife sneak into the children's room, slit their throats, take them to the meat room, cut them up, then put the flesh into a tub of salt in order to preserve it in those pre-refrigeration days. Of course, first of all they thoughtfully salvaged all the children's valuables. Next morning, St. Nicholas appears, and the rest of the story continues according to the original pattern.

Image in the Iglesia de El Salvador y San Nicolas in Madrid, Spain. The statue is over six feet tall.

131

The Burtscheid Icon 37

Not long before the year 1000, the Emperor Otto III built a monastery at Burtscheid not far from Charlemagne's capital of Aachan. Otto appointed a monk named Gregory as abbot. Gregory built two chapels, one dedicated to Saint Apollinaris, the other to St. Nicholas. The Abbott also acquired a St. Nicholas icon that had been painted in Constantinople. Supposedly it was carried west by the son of the king of Greece.

On one occasion, it was carried to the house of a noblewoman who was about to be delivered of a child, and hung on the wall opposite her bed. During her delivery, in the sight of all who were present, the picture turned its face to the wall, as though to avoid seeing the woman in her labor.

This story is the earliest evidence we have to St. Nicholas's connection with childbirth.

Window in the Anglican Church of St. Nicholas in Floreat Park, Australia

Orthodox icon

How the Good Gifts Were Used by Two

Few people are aware that famed nineteenth-century artist Howard Pyle was also extremely interested in preserving (and illustrating) folk tales from around the world. This story is very much in the Grimm Brothers tradition. It is a fascinating rarity in St. Nicholas stories: it gives equal billing to another saint—St. Christopher:

"Once upon a time there was a rich brother and a poor brother, and the one lived across the street from the other. The rich brother had all of the world's gear that was good for him, and more besides; the poor brother had hardly enough to keep soul and body together, yet he was contented with his lot. One day who should come traveling to the town where the rich brother and the poor brother lived but St. Nicholas himself.

As chance would have it, St. Nicholas knocked at the rich brother's house first. St. Nicholas had walked a long way that day so was dusty and rather disreputable-looking. The rich brother gaped like toad in a rain-storm and directed him to seek lodging across the street.

This St. Nicholas did, and was right royally welcomed in. The good wife spread before him all that they had in the house: a loaf of brown bread and a crock of cold water from the town fountain. So the saint asked them to bring him an empty bowl and crock. Then he blessed them

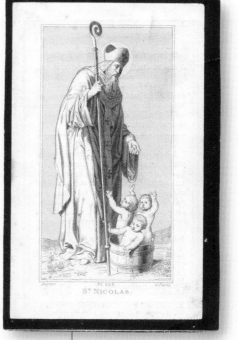

French prayer card

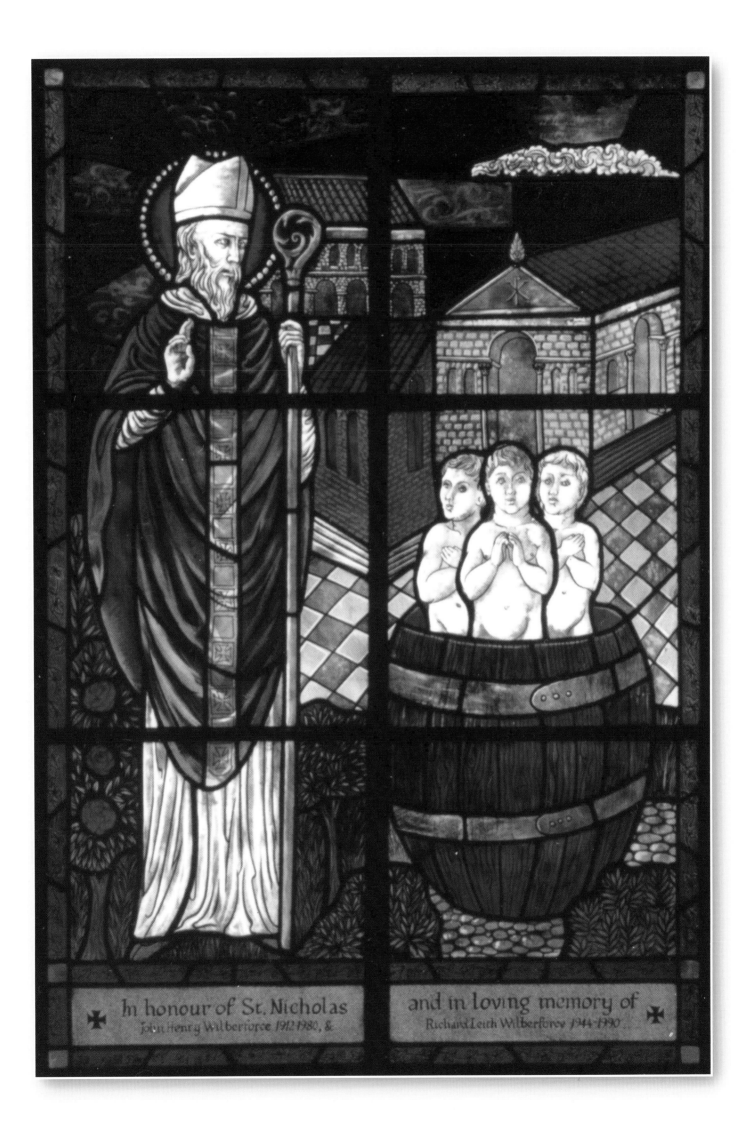

In honour of St. Nicholas
John Henry Wilberforce 1912-1980, &

and in loving memory of
Richard Leith Wilberforce 1944-1990

and said, "Bowl, be filled!" and immediately the bowl began to boil up with a good rich meat pottage. When it was full to the brim, he said, "Bowl, be stilled," and it stopped making broth. Then he turned to the crock and said, "Crock, be filled!" and it bubbled up with the purest of crystal water, only stopping with the command, "Crock, be stilled!" Then everyone ate and drank till there was no room for more. The next morning, St. Nicholas left them, but there was now no danger of hunger or thirst ever returning to that house.

One day, the rich brother got his brother to tell him the whole story while he watched the bowl and crock at work. He decided that he *had* to have them for himself! After repeated "No's" from his brother, he finally purchased them for a large sum of money.

The next day, the rich brother told his wife *he* would take care of dinner that day rather than she. At dinner-time, he gave the command, and sure enough, the bowl and crock were soon filled. Unfortunately, he didn't remember how to stop the process, so soon the broth and water filled the entire room, then the entire house—so the rich brother ran across the street and demanded to be told how to stop the process before the entire town was engulfed. But the poor brother was not to be rushed. Only after being paid another large sum of money would the poor brother agree to take back the bowl and crock.

Some time later, St. Christopher was thinking about taking a little journey to earth. St. Nicholas suggested that if he wanted real hospitality, he should drop by the poor brother's house. But when he arrived in town, the rich brother's house looked so much larger and finer that he knocked there first. The door was opened, then slammed in his face. So he went across the street and knocked there. He was warmly welcomed in, fed from the bowl and crock, and given a comfortable bed.

Window in the Garrison Church, Portsmouth, England. These images are from the school of Gioto/il Gotico.

The good wife had noticed how tattered St. Christopher's shirt was, so she spent much of the night making a new shirt for him. It was there by his bedside when he woke up.

Before he left, the poor brother emptied his stocking full of silver on the table, and told him to take all he needed of it. In gratitude, St. Christopher left him with a blessing, saying, "Whatever it be that you begin doing this morning, you shall continue doing until sunset." After he left, the wife decided to fold what new linen she had left after making the shirt, and her husband decided to put what was left of the silver away. So they did, but they couldn't quit: by the time evening came, the house was full of fine linen and every tub and bucket was brimming over with silver money!

When the rich brother came over, how his eyes bugged out with greed! He demanded that if either of the saints ever returned, he should be given first chance to offer them hospitality. Well, a year and a day passed, and both saints came to the poor man's door, who asked if they'd mind staying with the rich brother across the street. Rather grudgingly, they knocked on the other door. My! What a difference this time! They were given a great feast, new clothes were laid out for them, and next morning they were offered as much gold as they could stuff into their pockets. In return, they were left the same blessing as that left for the poor brother, and then their celestial visitors left.

The rich brother's wife decided that before she began to fold fine linen all day, she'd better feed the pigs and fill their water troughs. The rich man was so envious of his brother that he wanted to get even more silver than he had, but couldn't figure out how to do it. So he just sat there and smoked. Some time later he sought out his wife, and lo, there she was pouring out water for the pigs. That made him so furious he picked up a switch and struck his wife with it. And both of them continued doing so until evening. In the meantime, all the neighbors came out to see what the hubub was all about and laughed until they cried. In the evening they had nothing to show for the visit of St. Nicholas and St. Christopher but a wet pig sty and a badly bruised back!

For "even the blessed saints cannot give wisdom to those who shut their eyes to it" (Pyle, *Harper's Young People*, vol. vii, 415–417).

Interestingly, there was another saint who was often paired with St. Nicholas, Catherine of Alexandria, a post-apostolic fourth-century martyr. Catherine and Nicholas together are the leading tutelary saints of scholars and schools (Jones, 144). They are also the most popular names given to girl/boy twins.

> Catherine and Nicholas are the most popular names given to girl/boy twins.

The Accident of Birth

This is the only story that features St. Nicholas's relationship with the storks. It begins with these words:

"Saint Nicholas used to send, so I am told,
All new-born babes by storks, in days of old."

In the story, King Friedrich Max of Stultzenmannekim prayed for many years that St. Nicholas would send a baby

S. NICOLAUS.

audite filij··· donum bonum tribuam vobis prov: 4: v 2.

boy to him and his queen. Finally, St. Nicholas called Wilhelm Stork (a very sober bird) and told him to deliver a baby boy to the Queen. But Wilhelm Stork was old and hard of hearing, so ended up delivering the young prince to a cobbler who already had a half dozen children of his own! (Pyle, *Harper's Young People*, vol. vii, 205).

Impact of these Stories

The Three Children in Salt Tub/Young Theology Students story does a number of things: it strengthens the case for St. Nicholas's Trinitarian credentials, and it reinforces his position as a protector of children, students, and clerics. Since the story appeared late (in the twelfth century), and only in the West, the assumption is that it was intended to fill a felt need, a gap, in the St. Nicholas story canon. The story was also incorporated into several miracle plays. Besides those, artists all across Europe depicted the story in hundreds of paintings, sculptures, stained-glass windows, and in bas-reliefs.

Ebon feels that the student variant was most likely first. Perhaps because "Northern France was then the center of new spiritual, cultural, and artistic European initiatives, a period of early Renaissance. Young men in search of knowledge and stimulation were traveling to the region in large numbers. The educational institutions of northern France included a number of cathedral and bishopric schools. Travel was risky, and the young students could well have been in special need of the protection offered by a patron saint of the type other professions enjoyed and worshiped. Meisen notes that during the closing years of the eleventh century and the beginning of the twelfth, 'The cult of Nicholas made enormous inroads all over France. . . . Inasmuch as the boys and young men attending the convent schools were for the most part aiming at an ecclesiastical career, they would be the logical group to show an interest in worshiping the saint. Thus it would be easy to develop a new patronate by bringing the students into a special relationship of trust toward the saint."

As for the macabre, Ebon maintains that there was a definite crossover between miracle stories and folklore stories such as those retold by the Brothers Grimm: "The cannibalistic element in the student legend is just as crude as that in the story of Hansel and Gretel who are lost in the woods: the wicked witch tries to fatten up Hansel so that he will be good to eat. The Middle Ages, with

Gruesome stories helped St. Nicholas become the patron saint of children.

their child-like cruelties, their executions as public spectacles, crusades that mixed ecstatic Christian idealism with greed and bigotry, glorious cathedrals and ravaging epidemics—put their stamp on the Saint Nicholas cult, and they transformed the restrained, benevolent bishop of Myra into a folk hero of the marketplace."

Ebon also points out that there was a definite pattern in the story's evolution: the first version features older students whose hair is shorn in monk-fashion; but later on, during the thirteenth and fourteenth centuries, the threesome grow successively younger, until eventually they are portrayed as three little boys: "The resurrected victims became younger as the St. Nicholas patronate began to extend to younger pupils and preschool children. Who, after all, stood more in need of protection in an uncertain and hostile world than the small and helpless child?"

About this time, more and more often, artists began depicting St. Nicholas joining forces with the Virgin Mary in such a protective role. Secular schools followed church-based institutions in making St. Nicholas the patron saint of children, the falling dominoes cascading out of France to England, then Holland, Germany, and Denmark. And December 6 became a major children's holiday. Even today, Ireland's Montessori training center is named after St. Nicholas.

Greeten van Sint-Nicolaas

Dutch holiday card

There are obvious connections with the story of the three young men in Daniel who emerge unscathed from a fiery furnace (Shadrack, Meshack, and Abed-Nego). Jones points out that there is also the antecedent of the terrible famines that decimated Europe early in the eleventh century. During that period, "cannibalism was an attested fact" (Ebon, 54–9, this section).

The Burtscheid Icon is especially intriguing as it reflects the time's attitude toward partial nudity and childbirth. Even the St. Nicholas icon is so prudish that it turns itself over on the hook to avoid seeing the scene! In the companion childbirth story, *The Accident of Birth*, St. Nicholas is clearly singled out as the patron saint of childbirth, regardless of station in life. Reflective of modern times is its satirical tone, totally unlike the more reverential treatment in early St. Nicholas stories, and quite unlike the laudatory tone of the Brothers Grimm *How the Good Gifts Were Used by Two*, with its message that both St. Nicholas and St. Christopher seek out kindness and generosity in the world, and reward those who live by these character traits. Those who are unkind and greedy reap commensurate rewards—life coming full-circle according to how each one treats his/her fellow man.

CHAPTER 6

The Banished Bishop

The Second Transition

As we have seen, the first transition of St. Nicholas had to do with the impact of the abduction of his bones from Myra to Bari, which resulted in St. Nicholas becoming universal rather than merely eastern. Now came a second, equally significant transition: the unexpected secularization of a Christian saint. Let's look at the reasons why this occurred.

The Age of Faith was over, and the so-called "Age of Reason" had begun. A more apt term might very well be the "Age of Skepticism"—a very long age, seemingly without end, for it continues to this very day. We come back to our problems with labels, for faith, though uneven and diluted, continued, and men continued to slay one another in the name of religion. Though many may have given only lip service to a particular religion or sect, when it came to the bottom line, hundreds of thousands continued to kill any who espoused a different interpretation of the Bible than their own. Before, it had been Christian against Jew or Christian against Muslim. Now, with the advent of the Protestant Reformation, Christians were pitted against Christians.

There were no easy answers. For centuries, leaders within Roman Catholicism had tried to reform the system from within but had been stymied by political or financial realities. Without the wealth that came from selling cardinalships, archbishoprics, and bishoprics to the highest bidder, the church would have been hard-put to meet its fiscal responsibilities—supporting its religious power and the administration and protection of a third of Italy's land mass. The selling of indulgences generated a very large sum of money as well.

But there was another reason for the conflagration that was soon to engulf Europe. Over the centuries, so much property had been deeded to the church that it was by far the largest landowner on the continent, and rarely could it be taxed. It is conservatively estimated that it owned or controlled a minimum of 25 percent

Gruss vom Nikolo

Once a strong Austrian tradition, hundreds of "red" cards are found in antique collections in Europe.

of all land, and in some nations as high as a third. With the rise of nationalism came a dramatic increase in avarice on the part of secular authorities. Why should the church have permanent title to all that land? It was as though there was a state within the state, and both claimed sovereignty.

Protestantism was multilayered. On the surface were differences of Scriptural interpretation, some relatively minor and previously accepted as permissible within the church. But beneath were strong commercial tides—the church's negative attitude toward interest on loans, the church's insistence on celebrating a hundred-plus holidays each year (regardless of the effect on business productivity), and the lust for the church's land. Stir in the abject failure of the Crusades and France's virtual ownership of the papacy for most of a century, and you have reasons why the Reformation was almost a foreordained event.

Austrian card

Martin Luther had no idea that his attempts to reform the church from within would result in such a seismic upheaval. He certainly didn't intend to leave the Roman Catholic Church and sire a new form of religion. But things evolved, and forces over which he had little control made him almost a prisoner to events. For instance, Luther started out as the apostle of the common people, and urged them to assert their God-given rights to be free. When they took him at his word and savagely attacked the nobility and ransacked or destroyed churches, castles, and palaces that had taken centuries to build, he was appalled at the forces he had set in motion. Neither could he deny that it was the princes who had saved his hide again and again. Belatedly, he reversed his earlier counsel to the common people and urged them to accept the political status quo. Time and again it appeared that Luther and Protestantism were doomed, and time and again, *something* would happen to give both a reprieve. By the time the Emperor Charles V finally found breathing room and didn't need the military and political support of northern Europe anymore, it was too late. The political and religious map of Europe had changed forever. Luther had inadvertently helped to accelerate nationalism (the modern state) and modern commercialism (more powerful even than most states). The two together—with plenty of greed for church wealth—added up to Henry VIII's far-reaching decision to separate the Church of England from the Church of Rome.

Elegant German postcard showing Saint Nicholas with Angels; Th. Gäammerler Jr., Bavaria, Germany, 1933

As ideological differences were hammered into creeds, and Europe was subjected to centuries of bloody conflict in the name of those creeds, the proverbial baby tended to be thrown out with the bathwater—in this case, the saints—saints such as St. Nicholas. Apparently, it mattered little that the process of canonization had not really gained momentum until after A.D. 1000, or that saints such as Nicholas dated clear back to post-apostolic times. Most of the figures that had been revered for so long by the church were now discarded by Protestants who sought to eradicate all things associated with the Roman Catholic Church, and they fired their big guns at sainthood. Jones notes that, "They attacked no instinct or perception so hardily as that of *mediation:* they asserted that the God-Man alone could mediate, not one of His creatures like the Church, and certainly not the saints. The Augsburg Confession (A.D. 1530), . . . 'But scripture teaches us not to invoke the saints, or ask help of them.' Luther was silent about the saints in his Ninety-five Theses, but the Thirty-nine Articles were unambiguous: 'The Romish doctrine concerning Purgatory, Pardon, Worshiping and Adoration as well of images as of Reliques, and also Invocation of Saints, is a fond [meaning "foolish" or "silly"] thing, vainly invented.'" Within Roman Catholicism, "The Council of Trent, desperately attempting to hold a severed world together, mildly recommended the assistance of the saints while stating, 'No divinity or power is thought to be in them for the sake of which they may be worshiped, or anything asked of them, or any trust put in images.'" Many, even within Catholicism, believed the "Church would have done well to leave canonization or any other judgment of sanctity to the direct action of the Holy Spirit" (Jones, 285–286).

Patron saint of those in love, another example of the many Austrian-designed cards

Saints such as St. Nicholas now began to lose some of their universality. True, St. Nicholas was still revered within Roman Catholic and Orthodox Christianity, but he began his long decline in lands controlled by Protestants. Luther himself, where St. Nicholas was concerned, was ambivalent, for initially he continued to give presents to his children and other members of his household on St. Nicholas's feast day. As time passed, however, he began to have second thoughts on the matter. Eventually, he and other Protestant thought-leaders decided that a substitute for St. Nicholas would have to be found. And who more appropriate than the Christchild as a bringer of gifts?

For Protestantism, this attempt to turn away from St. Nicholas resulted in the opening of a Pandora's Box, which unleashed a host of semi-pagan pseudo-St. Nicholases. Instead of making the observance of Christmas more sacred, the reverse occurred. In essence, they were inadvertently responsible for replacing a sacred icon with a secular one. For out of the woodwork of European and near eastern mythology arose long-slumbering pagan deities that now, by default, were given new life. As for the St. Nicholas persona, Protestant leaders grossly underestimated his resilience and the hold he had on the minds, hearts, and souls of Christians everywhere—or his protean ability to reshape his persona without completely losing the magic that had kept him alive for over a thousand years. Luther himself, finding it impossible to defeat St. Nicholas, ended up compromising by declaring that St. Nicholas was the messenger who relays to the Christchild all requests for presents. Anglicans retained the date December 6 in the calendar of their 1662 *Book of Common Prayer.*

When the *Christkindel* failed to fill St. Nicholas's considerable shoes, who were these pagan or semi-pagan deities that were reborn? Well, first of all there was *Befana*, who predated Christianity, dating clear back to early Roman times. *Befana* was a genial hag who supposedly traveled the world searching out children; the good ones she would reward with candy and sweets, the bad with stones and charcoal. Christians in southern Europe retrofitted her for her Christian role by creating a new legend for her, a legend that had no truth in it at all. She was now presented to children as a fourth member of the Magi, who was summoned by God to join the other three and seek out the newly-born King and present Him and His parents with a valuable gift. But *Befana* had the Martha-ish tendency to prioritize housework above answering the divine call; hence she missed her appointment with the other Magi. In consequence, *Befana* was now doomed for all time to search for the baby Jesus every Epiphany Eve.

Berchta, a hook-nosed Germanic counterpart, was also trotted out during the Christmas season; her main role was to check up on the behavior of German children, and give appropriate rewards. This indefatigable woman also checked up on the adults. Woe be to the man who had a dirty barn or the woman who was sloppy or careless in her spinning!

Protestant opposition to the veneration of saints unleashed a host of semi-pagan pseudo-St. Nicholases.

Then we have that male hag Germans know as *Knecht* [servant] *Ruprecht*. He is very ancient and originated in pre-Christian pagan times, a fertility relic of winter solstice celebrations. *Knecht Ruprecht* was about as scruffy as they come and was usually attired either in straw or in skins. He also differentiated between the naughty and the nice in his gift-giving. Protestants now donated him to poor St. Nicholas, whether the saint wanted him around or not.

St. Nicholas left such a vacuum when he was edged aside that it took many figures to replace him. The first of these is *Black Pete*, who in his earliest manifestations was horrible to behold—dark grungy face, horns, extra-long lolling bright red tongue, fiery eyes, and chains that clanked whenever he moved—a veritable Beelzebub! Children were terrified of him and would flee to St. Nicholas for protection from his clutches. *Ruprecht's* counterpart in Denmark is known as *Nissen*, a ghoulish fellow with a long red tongue and a big tail.

Closely related to both is the demonic *Krampus* (or *Grampus*), native to Austria's mountain towns. The *Krampus* is a goatman who wears an immense wooden mask, has glaring eyes and jagged teeth, and his goatskins descend clear to his ankles. Around his waist he wears loose rattling chains, and on his back are hollow iron balls that give out a drumming sound whenever he moves.

Austrian postcard

Close kinsmen to the *Krampus* include *Hans Trapp* (Alsaace-Lorraine); *Ru Klaus* (Rough Nicholas); *Hans Muff* (Rhineland); *Bartel* (Silesia); *Gumphinkel* (Hesse); *Pelznickel* (Furry Nicholas); *Aschen Klaus* (Nicholas carrying a bag of ashes and switches); *Sami Klaus* (a frightful-looking Swiss bogeyman), whose Bavarian counterpart is called *Buttermand*; *Hoêsecker* (Luxembourg children dread him as he carries switches, which he uses to whip lazy or disobedient children); *Tompte Gubbe* (Sweden); and *Pere Fouettard* (Father Whipper, an ugly mean-spirited figure who wears a dark-colored robe, sports a gray rather mangy-looking beard, and has been known to break into houses and drag French children out of bed for a spanking). Although some, in local instances, were stand-alones, almost invariably these repulsive figures insisted on attaching themselves to St. Nicholas. Christina Hole

Folktale characters associated with St. Nicholas were often terrifying.

points out that ". . . these terrifying creatures seem strange companions for a saint who is otherwise remembered chiefly for his kindness. In reality, they are far older than he, relics of pagan conceptions, probably were once fertility spirits associated with winter solstice. But now they are his, drawn into his orbit when he became the gift-bringer, and for thousands of European children (Catholic as well as Protestant), they are as essential a part of Nicholastide or Christmas Eve as is the gentle saint himself" (Hole, 10).

Although the devil was mentioned in Catholic and Anglican liturgy and worship, Protestants greatly intensified awareness of the devil as an ever-present force to be reckoned with. He was no mere abstraction to them but a malevolent physical presence. The many burnings of those accused of being witches during this time period testifies to their fixation with all things demonic. Thus we should not be surprised that these demonic Christmas-related figures were now introduced as being subject to God's power as manifested in the life and ministry of St. Nicholas.

Now we turn to some stand-ins of St. Nicholas (figures trotted out to impersonate him, to assume his roles after he had been ungraciously shoved off regional stages). In France, he is called *Pere Noel* (Father Christmas); in Germany, *Weihnachtsmann* (Christmas Man); in Finland, Old Man Winter (who drives reindeer down from the mountains and brings snow with him). But in Holland and lowland countries, St. Nicholas dug in his heels and adamantly refused to be displaced: *Sinterklaus* he was, and has remained through the centuries. As for *Christkindel*, in Spain, he was called *Niño Jesús*; in France, *Petit Noel*; and in Italy, *Gesu Bambino*. Though sometimes portrayed as the Child Jesus, he mutated into a cherubic little girl, and later into an angelic teenage girl, and yet later into a devout young woman. In America, *Christkindel* mutated through those three feminine stages into a male St. Nicholas counterpart: Kris Kringle. In Czechoslovakia, he is known as *Svaty Mikulas*, and was lowered from heaven on a golden cord by an angel.

Eastern European greeting, a whimsical image of St. Nicholas

Unquestionably, Steen's famous painting "The Eve of St. Nicholas" is the most significant of all St. Nicholas-related art. Significant because in it Steen was breaking new ground. The Dutch were among the very first in art to dare to leave religious, mythological, landscape, portrait, and historical subject matter behind them and turn to the common family. It is safe to say that we learn more about the average seventeenth-century Dutch family in this one painting than in volumes of history books.

Olive Beaupré Miller, in 1926, wrote a wonderful beautifully illustrated book for children titled *Tales Told in Holland*. In it she approaches Steen's painting from the fresh vantage point of a child's perspective:

> But for all his roistering and recklessness, Jan was a lovable fellow. He painted the comedy of human life with genial tolerance—tavern scenes of jollity, card parties, marriage feasts, festivals of St. Nicholas, and children. Ah! what children!
>
> Once on St. Nicholas Day, Jan Steen's whole family gathered together to enjoy the gifts St. Nicholas had left the night before in the shoes of the children. One little girl went toddling about with a pail full of toys and a doll clasped tight in her arms. Tenderly the mother held out her arms toward the happy child. Behind these two, a big boy with a baby perched on his arm, pointed skyward to show the baby and a little fellow beside him how St. Nicholas came riding over the roofs on his great white horse and listened at the chimneys to find out if they had been good. Beside this group, a little boy, his eyes dancing with mischief, pointed laughingly to his big brother, who was howling in dire distress and digging one fist in his eyes. Alack, he had set out his shoe the night before, but what had he received? Nothing, nothing at all, nothing, that is, but a switch. He had been a naughty boy. St. Nicholas had brought him nothing, nothing but a switch. His older sister joined the little fellow in laughing at the offender, while Grandfather Steen sat smiling in the center of the group. But, in the background stood Grandma, and what was Grandma doing? If

French card with St. Nicholas and his donkey on a rooftop

no one else felt sorry for the lad who had been naughty, there was still Grandma. She was going out of the room, but as she went, she turned around and smiled and beckoned. Ah, Grand-mothers' hearts are very soft! She could not let her grandson take his punishment unrelieved. She meant to beckon him out of the room and give him something in secret to make up for the switch in his shoe.

It was thus that Jan Steen set the family down to live through the ages on canvas. All across the front of the picture he painted a litter of things—a child's shoe, two bright colored balls, a basket full of little cakes, each painted in such detail that one can see the squares in the waffles, and could almost pick off the nuts and the tiny black caraway seeds that adorn the crisp, brown cookies. Against a table leans a great square loaf of bread with chickens and animals traced on the crust, and how that crust shines with butter!

No picture could better express the sense of innocent fam-ily festivity. The room, indeed, is a muddle. The mother has hard work before her, if she would restore it to a Dutch pitch of order and cleanliness, but how jolly every one is. To this very day, when the dignified quiet of Dutch family life has been disturbed by feasting or upset by the play of children, with toys strewn all about, they say in Holland:

Rare Eastern European card from the Rosenthal Canterbury Collection, Hungary, 1933

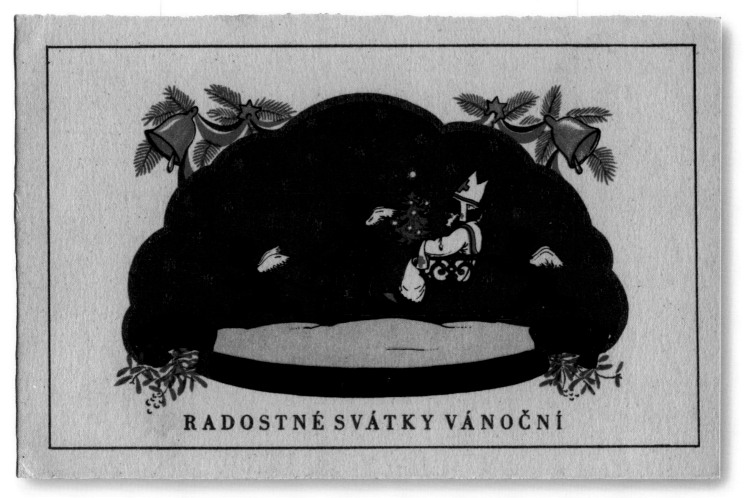

RADOSTNÉ SVÁTKY VÁNOČNÍ

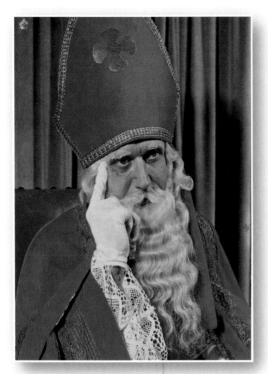

A thinking Sinterklaas. Dutch card from the 1950s

"This looks like a household by Jan Steen" (Miller, 160–162).

As was true in other European countries, St. Nicholas's persona continued to evolve in Holland, Belgium, and lowland countries. The most significant factor in that evolution was the addition of the rat pack to the saint's retinue. Holland's contribution is known as *Zwarte Piet* (Black Pete). His coloring should not be taken as a racial statement, but rather that he originated as a representation of the devil and was originally portrayed as evil and sinister. Ancelet-Hustache, discussing demonic figures such as Black Pete, notes "Thus St. Nicholas had triumphed over the devil and made him his servant. With this second figure so constantly depicted, it followed naturally that, as time went on, they should divide the saint's roles between them: it was for the bishop in heaven to reward the good, while the emissary from hell was given the job of punishing the wicked at his master's command. He occasionally carried a bag on his back from which the legs of a punished child protruded as a salutary example" (Ancelet-Hustache, 83).

Black Pete was originally portrayed as a Turkish orphan who traveled with St. Nicholas, and since his swarthy complexion seemed so dark to the Dutch, eventually they considered him to be black. In medieval and Renaissance paintings, Black Pete was depicted in garish Turkish garb with bright red lips and a golden earring.

Gradually, the tradition developed that St. Nicholas and Black Pete spent most of the year in Spain and would arrive in Holland by ship from a Spanish port. Doubtless that tradition has its roots in the long occupation of Holland by Spanish imperial forces.

Over time, another tradition developed, one that would bear fruit later on in America. On St. Nicholas Eve, the saint and Black Pete ride the Dutch skies, landing

German postcard of the Christkindel

"The Feast of St. Nicholas," c. 1660-65. Oil on canvas by Jan Steen. Rijksmuseum-Amsterdam, The Netherlands.

on housetop after housetop, and listen in at chimneys. St. Nicholas always rides his great white horse. His magical robe gives him the power to travel in the twinkling of an eye wherever he and Black Pete wish to go.

In America, when the Dutch landed in what soon became known as New Amsterdam in 1624 (and later yet, New York), they brought St. Nicholas with them. In fact, the ship that brought them had St. Nicholas on its figurehead, the first church within the walls of New Amsterdam was named after him, and he remains to this day the patron saint of Manhattan, the island the Dutch settled first. For some unknown reason, the Dutch settlers left Black Pete behind.

Spain brought St. Nicholas with them to the New World as well; in fact, Jacksonville (in what is today Florida) was originally named after the saint.

German migration to America really began when William Penn invited his continental neighbors to immigrate to his British colony in 1682—Penn's Woods, or Pennsylvania. By 1689, several thousand Germans had moved to the new colony; by 1742, 100,000 had arrived—and by 1783, almost 300,000. Eventually, more than one-third of Americans would have German in their ancestry.

Both Roman Catholic and Lutheran Germans brought *Christkindel* and *Pelsnickel* [keep in mind that anything with "nickel" in it translates "Nicholas" (a shortened version of the name)] with them.

St. Nicholas is the patron saint of Manhattan.

Only in America, the P was dropped over time and B was substituted, hence *Belsnickel*. The use of *"nickel"* enabled Germans to give a double

Image from a Dutch cigar band

KAREL I   1963

meaning to the word, as the ancient meaning of the word encompassed "fur demon," "fur imp," and a devil-like aspect. In portions of Germany, he was called *Pelsmartel* (in honor of Martin Luther), and his visit was tied to Luther's birthday on November 11. *Pelsnickel*, on the other hand, would come on December 5, the Eve of St. Nicholas.

The *Christkindel*, later on Christmas Eve, supposedly would return when all were asleep and enter the house through such openings as an open window, a keyhole, the fireplace (rarely), or through the walls, and would place the gifts on the table—*not* under a tree!—in the Christmas room. Although it was known that she came on a donkey or a mule with great light around her, no one ever was privileged actually to see her during those later deliveries of presents and coins.

Some farm households each Christmas Eve would leave hay outside for the animal that had the honor of carrying the Christ-child. On Christmas morning the hay that remained—blessed also by the dew of that holy night—would be fed to the animals on the assumption that it now held special powers and would fortify the animals for the coming year.

Inside the house children would place empty plates on tables or windowsills, with the expectation that if they had been considered good, the *Christkindel* would leave them something special. If they had not, then they would get whatever the *Belsnickel* felt they deserved—most likely a chunk of coal.

On the stairs—as is done on Day of the Wise Men, January 6, in many parts of the world—children would place their shoes (cleaned and polished) on Christmas Eve, hoping the *Christkindel* would fill them with nuts, candy, and that rarest of delicacies for nineteenth-century children—an orange.

So angelic was the *Christkindel* that it is easy to see why her visits were perceived as spiritual ones. The time varied, but usually it would be Christmas Eve, after the lamps were lit, that one of the

St. Nicholas and company in mime outside St. Stephen's Cathedral in Vienna

Christkindel's companions would ring a bell in front of the window. Then after establishing contact with those inside, the question would be asked: "May the *Christkindel* come in?" Answered in the affirmative by the lady of the house, the entourage would enter and almost immediately the *Christkindel* would begin questioning the children as to their behavior during the year.

Children would often be frightened by all this commotion. They would be asked standard questions such as "Have you obeyed your parents all this year?" "Have you said your prayers every night?" If they had been good, they were rewarded with gifts. If they had been bad, they'd receive blows or be switched. Some *Christkindels* would affect great doubt about the regularity of their prayer life, causing all the children to fall on their knees and recite their prayers as proof of their assertions, just as St. Nicholas would have done.

If there were children who had misbehaved—usually recalcitrant boys—a signal would be given that would summon the *Belsnickel.* In the early days the two traveled together. The *Belsnickel* would usually be a strong male with a deep booming bass voice. He would be covered by a shaggy fur coat (often with the fur worn on the inside). Generally, he would either wear a grotesque mask or his face would be blackened with burnt cork.

Iffelen are the lighted headdresses worn by the men of Küssnacht am Rigi, Switzerland, each December. These were created by Ernst Sidler.

The *Christkindel* filled shoes with nuts, candy, and fruit.

On his back would be a long chain that rattled terribly when he wished to frighten, and in one hand a bundle of switches. Oftentimes, he'd wear patchwork clothes—everything he wore or carried was of antique vintage—and carry a large bow and a quiver of arrows. Attached to his long coattails would be bells. His stockings would be of green buckram, on his feet would be Indian moccasins, around his ample waist a wide belt, and on his head would be an ancient hat worn low over his forehead. His old clothes would be ill-fitting, so pillows often would exaggerate the already well-nourished figure. If he was beardless, he would most likely don an artificial one; above it would be his trademark: a sinister upward-curving horned moustache.

He or an associate would carry a large feedsack in which to stuff bad boys and carry them away—usually no farther than a snowbank in the vicinity. Another sack or basket would hold gifts for those who had been good.

Unlike his gentler counterpart, he rarely deigned to ask if he could come in but stormed into the house like an avenging demon, rattling his chain, shaking his bells, and making fierce noises no one could understand. Bad boys would cringe in terror, but there was no refuge for them. Custom dictated that even brothers or sisters would propel the erring ones forward to be punished with voice, switch, or lash.

English postcard. Cards with "Father Christmas" are rare.

Every child knew he'd be coming and awaited his arrival with a curious mixture of eagerness, dread, and outright terror. On Christmas Eve they knew his onslaught was imminent by the sound of his bells, the rattling of twigs across the window, a rude knock, and the thumping of his booted feet on the stairs.

In remote villages the *Belsnickel* would sometimes attract children by slamming open the front door. He would throw handfuls of nuts and candy on the floor, and then after children would scramble after his bait, pounce upon them, wielding whip and sticks right and left indiscriminately, on the basic premise that the unrighteous deserved it and the righteous weren't as righteous as people thought they were.

The secret of his [sometimes the *Belsnickel* was a woman] apparent omniscience was known to the adults, because he was

A postcard showing the tradition of leaving gifts in shoes

in reality usually a neighbor, friend of the family, or close relative such as an uncle or grandparent. Such a relationship guaranteed inside knowledge of behavior, secrets known only to family members, personal idiosyncrasies, frailties, etc., which made his (or her) pronouncements and questions so terribly dreaded. Even good children shook to their core, wondering which of their hidden sins would be found out.

When he had stomped up the stairs into the parlor, the family would be waiting—the older children huddled in corners, the baby on father's lap, and the next smallest either hiding behind mother's skirt or cowering under her apron.

Without any preliminaries, immediately the inquisition would commence:

"Have you said your bedtime prayers every night?"

"Have you memorized all your Sunday school verses?"

"Can you repeat the catechism?"

"Have you been naughty?"

"Did you play hide-and-seek near the furnace—as you were warned not to?"

"Did you faithfully do your chores every day?"

"Did you snitch any charcoal from the charcoal house?"

"Did you mistreat your little sister?"

These were not merely general questions he asked. They got very specific and personal. And some of the *Belsnickels* would carry big black books with them, and inside would be written specific misdeeds that would be incorporated into the interrogation:

"Did you or did you not, last October, deliberately let out of the corral widow Schmidt's favorite milk cow, Old Bossy?"

"Weren't you the one who pushed over the outhouse two weeks ago, knowing full well the schoolmaster was in it?"

Or for a child who professed good behavior:

"That won't do! Last year you promised not to sleep in church. And just last Sunday night, you embarrassed your entire family by snoring. *By snoring!*"

He would often make them recite poetry or Bible verses they had learned for the Christmas program in the church. And many children were so petrified with fear that they could not remember a word. Again, all these are questions St. Nicholas would have asked had his persona been there instead of the *Belsnickel's*.

> # The *Belsnickel* kept a book of good and bad deeds.

When there was erring to be punished, *the Belsnickel* would flail out with his long lash—often making more noise than inflicting pain—or rap on the head, back, hand, etc., with the switches. After the grilling was over, he would toss down on the floor pieces of candy, nuts, etc., and roar with laughter as the children fought each other for pieces.

Through it all, he laughed . . . a lot. And it was funny—to the adults. Well, not always. Not when he severely reprimanded father for failing to keep the harness well greased, the horses properly shod for winter's icy roads, or the snow shovel in its proper place. Neither was Mother exempt. Woe to her if she had failed to keep the dishes clean or the furniture dust free!

Once the serious part was over, the *Belsnickel* distributed the goodies he had brought with him: toys, oranges, apples, and transparent candy in the shape of toys. At that time, his job done at that house for the year, he would often reveal who he was and take refreshments. But just as was true with the *Christkindel*, the *Belsnickel* had another job to do that night, returning when all were asleep to punish the bad and reward the good. It was he who supposedly filled stockings, hats, caps, and the Christmas boxes that were set apart just for him.

In later years, as America became more secular and the old traditions lost their force, *Belsnickeling* became merely a form of Christmas roistering. More masks were sold at Christmas than at Halloween as gangs would flood the urban areas with hilarity. Many would perform music, with and without instruments, "mumming" at each door for treats. On Christmas Eve the streets would be filled with revelers out for fun and mischief, costumed as bandit chiefs, Indians, clowns, harlequins, devils, demons, ragamuffins, minstrels, and performers. Many, having had far too much to drink, made the night hideous with

Classic image of St. Nicholas on cookie paper, France

162

Gelukkig Kerstfeest

Classic Santa from Holland

kettle drums, trumpets, penny whistles, cornets, violins, bones, and tambourines.

The institution of the *Belsnickel*/the *Christkindel* survived for about 150 years in America before it was replaced by that kinsman of the Dutch *Sinterklaas*, Santa Claus (this section: Wheeler, *Christmas in My Heart 4*, 15–19).

Frohe Weihnachten!

CHAPTER 8

Santa Claus Comes to Town

St. Nicholas Comes to America

This book would not be complete without sharing one of the most fascinating stories in American history: how St. Nicholas came to America and what his relationship is to Santa Claus. It's all Dutch, from beginning to end, and it all started with a ship, only two years after Captain John Smith had founded England's first American colony in Jamestown.

Blame it all on the explorer, Henry Hudson. Though English, when his ship, "The Half Moon," entered what we know as New York Harbor in 1609, he was in the service of the Dutch East India Company. As was Columbus before him, Hudson was seeking a short-cut to the East Indies. When he sailed into the great river that would later bear his name, he hoped it would be that long-sought water passage to the East.

The five nations of the Iroquois ruled this region at the time, and they were eager to trade their rich furs for European goods. Having regained its independence from Spain, Holland was eager to become a major player in world exploration and colonization. Within a year trade began with the Indians. The New Netherland Company began the trade, and the West India Company continued it. In 1615, a stockaded trading post they named Fort Nassau was erected on Castle Island (within today's city limits of Albany). In June of 1623, the Dutch formally decreed that the entire region (land between latitudes 40 degrees and 45 degrees) be organized into the province of New Netherland.

In March of 1624, thirty families (mostly Walloon) set sail for the New World in a ship appropriately named *Nieu Nederland*. They were led by Cornelius Jacobson Mey, the first governor of the colony. It was May before the ship reached Manhattan, where some of them decided to put down roots. More than half of the families stayed on the ship and disembarked up-river at Fort Orange (which grew into Albany). Within a year, three more shiploads of colonists arrived. Governor Peter Minuit arrived in

Opposite: Fatherly Saint Nikolaus in Germany cradling the Christkindel

1626 with more colonists and bought Manhattan Island from the Iroquois for a reputed $24 worth of beads. Fort Amsterdam was erected on its lower end. The first church was dedicated to St. Nicholas.

Then more colonists flooded in, settling up the river into what is now Connecticut, New Jersey, and New York. Trouble with Indians followed, and with it came the realization that a strong leader and some sort of centralized authority was needed. Peg-legged Peter Stuyvesant arrived in May of 1647. Under his autocratic leadership, the colony's population increased from 2,000 to 10,000.

Additional trouble was not long in coming. On the basis of Cabot's discoveries in 1498 and the patents to the London and Plymouth companies in 1606, the British contended that the Dutch were intruders. The Dutch, quickly realizing that a showdown was imminent, built a wall (whence Wall Street gets its name) across Manhattan Island. In March of 1664, King Charles II of England deeded the entire land mass to his brother James, Duke of York and Albany. The duke sent four ships with five hundred fighting men and 125 guns demanding the surrender of New Amsterdam. The Dutch were armed with less than two hundred fighting men, and little gunpowder for the few cannons they had. Finally, the doughty governor, recognizing that he had no alternative if he wished to save his people, sadly hoisted the white flag.

The English may have defeated them militarily, but the land—its very heart and soul–remain Dutch. The presence of St. Nicholas has been in the Hudson River country of America ever since the beginning. The New Amsterdam Dutch shortened *"Sinterklaas"* [or *Sinta Claes*] to "Santa Claus." They mean the same thing: "Holy" or "Saint" Nicholas.

Saint Nicholas Wishing Well in Santa Claus Park, Santa Claus, Indiana

SAINT NICHOLAS WISHING WELL

Named after the Patron Saint of Santa Claus Park—a well more than a hundred years old . . . which attracts children and parents from near and far . . . to look into its depths while facing the east and earnestly wish that desires come true.

This photograph from the Rosenthal Canterbury Collection shows a vintage New York bus heading for the famous St. Nicholas Avenue, one of the longest streets in the Big Apple.

Wishing You a MERRY CHRISTMAS

SWEETS · TOYS

FAT... Chris... laden wi... never... GOOD GI...

Father Christmas is unique to Great Britain.

As for the Dutch, they still permeate every pore of that land.

Forging a New Myth

Because of their peaceable surrender the Dutch were permitted to hold on to their possessions. They were astute businessmen in the Old World, for a time dominating European finance. And they were equally astute financiers in the New World. After all, it is their street, and their city, that today is the financial nerve center of the entire world.

The Revolution came, and America went into a kind of holding pattern, during which time a baby was born in old New Amsterdam/now York. Like so many boys born during this period, he was named after that long-enduring general—*Washington* Irving. In 1789, George Washington would disembark in New York and be

sworn in as America's first president, and New York would be its first capital.

Originally, Irving had intended to become a lawyer, but a debilitating illness forced him to end his studies. Since his family was a wealthy one, he was sent to Europe during his recuperation period. Upon his return, he faint-heartedly attempted to take up law again. Then, with a sigh of relief, he turned to writing. Given that his family ran the New York *Morning Chronicle*, and the fact that he had a real gift for humor, getting published was easy. America owes a great debt to a gentleman by the name of Samuel Latham Mitchell, for when his pontifical, erudite, and stodgy tome, *The Picture of New York*, was published in 1807, Irving and his brother Peter laughed so hard at its pretentiousness that they decided to write a mock epic spoof of it. Not long after, Peter went off on a long trip to Europe, so it was up to the younger brother to write it. Washington Irving invented a Dutch scholar by the name of Dietrich Knickerbocker, and, under that name wrote *A History of New York from the Beginning of the World to the End of the Dutch Dynasty*. It was first published in 1809. In the seven books of this magnum opus, Irving tells the epic story (tongue always in cheek) of the forty-year-long Dutch "dynasty." What added humor was that Irving filled the books with literary imitations and parodies of the likes of Homer, Cervantes, Malory, Fielding, Stern, and Swift.

The following excerpt provides an example of its "high tone":

"Enraged to see his military stores laid waste, the stout Risingh, collecting all his forces, aimed a mighty blow at the hero's crest. In vain did his fierce little cocked hat oppose its course. The biting steel clove through the stubborn ram beaver, and would have cracked the crown of any one not endowed with supernatural hardness of head; but the brittle weapon shivered in pieces on the skull of Hardkopping Piet [Peter Stuyvesant], shedding a thousand sparks, like beams of glory, round his grizzled visage.

The good Peter reeled with the blow, and turning up his eyes beheld a thousand suns, besides moons and stars, dancing about the firmament—at length, missing his footing, by reason of his wooden leg, down he came on the seat of honor with a crash that shook the surrounding hills, and might have wrecked his frame, had he not been received into a cushion

Greetings for Nikolaus Day in Austria

169

softer than velvet, which Providence, or Minerva, or St. Nicholas, or some cow, had so benevolently prepared for his reception" (Blair, Hornberger, Stewart, 238–46).

Irving's genius was such that readers of the mock epic found
it almost impossible to separate the truth from the fiction. It
was read, and chuckled over, across the nation as well as
in England and its empire, where Irving first attained
real fame (the first American author to be counted
as an equal by England's literati).

Irving's brother-in-law, John Pintard (merchant and founder of the New York Historical
Society), was instrumental in making George
Washington's birthday and July 4 national holidays. Pintard was a remarkable visionary,
desirous of not merely reflecting or recording events but also effecting change. As he
studied the history of his state, he became
convicted that many of the Dutch contributions
were in danger of being forgotten. He decided to help
bring them back to life. And who better than St. Nicholas
to serve as the catalyst? As early as 1793, Pintard had included St.
Nicholas in his personal almanac. Now he determined to reintro-
duce New York's under-appreciated patron saint.

The momentum began when, at the Society's annual
banquet on January 10, 1809, Dr. David Hosack
said, in delivering a toast, "To the memory
of St. Nicholas. May the virtuous habits
and simple manners of our Dutch ancestors be not lost in the luxuries and refine-
ments of the present time." At that same
dinner, Irving was nominated for member-
ship (Ebon, 91). Pintard had long objected
to the roughness and rowdiness with which
Christmas was then celebrated. Even was-
sailers, as they tramped through the New York
streets singing Christmas carols, would quickly
turn hostile and even violent if they didn't get
offered what they were after (usually liquor).
Pintard advocated the return of St. Nicholas
into the life of New Yorkers so that Christmas celebrations would be private and fam-
ily-oriented like they were in Holland,
and earlier in New Amsterdam, rather than
public and brawling (Arnest, 1, 18). Clearly,

> **W**ashington Irving was instrumental in creating the modern Santa Claus.

ges. gesch.

Printed in W.-Germany

Traditional scrap from Europe; Kris Kringle is rarely found on a greeting card.

Art.-Nr.: 7194

Card featuring lines from "A Visit from St. Nicholas," commonly known as "Twas the Night before Christmas"

Pintard infected Irving with the same virus, for St. Nicholas/Santa Claus makes twenty-five different appearances in the *Knicker-bocker* history. This passage is particularly noteworthy:

> "And the sage Oloffe dreamed a dream—and lo, the good St. Nicholas came riding over the tops of the trees, in that self same wagon wherein he brings his yearly presents to children, and he descended hard by where the heroes of Communipaw had made their late repast. And he lit his pipe by the fire, and sat himself down and smoked; and as he smoked the smoke from his pipe ascended into the air and spread like a cloud overhead. And Oloffe bethought him, and he hastened and climbed up to the top of one of the tallest trees, and saw that the smoke spread over a great extent of country—and as he considered it more attentively, he fancied that the great volume of smoke assumed a variety of marvelous forms, where in dim obscurity he saw shadowed out palaces and domes and lofty spires, all of which lasted but a moment, and then faded away, until the whole rolled off, and nothing but the green woods were left. And when St. Nicholas had smoked his pipe, he twisted it in his hat-band, and laying his finger beside his nose, gave the astonished Van Kortlandt a very significant look, then mounting his wagon, he returned over the tree-tops and disappeared" (Ebon, 94).

Jones notes that "Without Irving there would be no Santa Claus. The *History* contains two dozen allusions to him, many of them among the most delightful flights of imagination in the

Gathering at the tomb of W. Clement Moore in the cemetery at the Episcopal Church of the Intercession, New York City (Photo courtesy Trinity Church, Wall Street)

In 1963, a traditional Christmas Eve Pilgrimage Service where children gather with lanterns at the grave of author Clement Clarke Moore in Trinity's 155th Street cemetery to hear Twas the Night Before Christmas.

21062 Printed in Belgium

A Belgian card showing St. Nicholas checking off his shopping list

volumes. *Here* is the source of all the legends of N in New Amsterdam—of the emigrant ship *Goede Virow*, like a Dutch matron as broad as she was long, with a figurehead of Saint Nicholas at the prow; here are the descriptions of festivities on St. Nicholas Day in the colony, and of the church dedicated to him; here is the description of St. Nicholas bringing gifts, parking his horse and wagon on the roof while he slides down the chimney. . . ." (Jones, 344–345). The *Knickerbocker* books resulted in the overnight popularity of St. Nicholas in America.

But Irving wasn't through with Christmas yet. In *The Sketch Book*, probably his most popular book, he portrayed an idealized Christmas as celebrated in England. It was also the work that included Hudson River tales of the likes of Rip Van Winkle, Ichabod Crane, and the Headless Horseman.

However, St. Nicholas was not yet firmly imbedded in American psyche.

Enter the distinguished Episcopal clergyman, Dr. Clement Clark Moore (1779–1863), Hebraic scholar at New York's General Theological Seminary. The story that has been told so often it has become part of the American myth is this:

> As Christmas 1822 approached, Dr. Moore, an accomplished poet, decided to write a present for his children. Suddenly, the concept came to him: Bring to life via poetry Irving's unique depiction of St. Nicholas. So it was that Moore put all Irving's ingredients together, added some of his own, and on the evening of December 23, 1822, read "A Visit from St. Nicholas" to his children [significantly, "St. Nicholas," not "Santa Claus"]. That might have been the end of it had not a lady visitor been there that night; she begged a copy, and had it published anonymously in the *Sentinel* of Troy, New York at Christmas time 1823. And the rest is history.

"A Visit From St. Nicholas"

'Twas the night before Christmas when all through the house
Not a creature was stirring, not even a mouse;
The stockings were hung by the chimney with care,
In hopes that St. Nicholas soon would be there;
The children were nestled all snug in their beds,
While visions of sugar-plums danced through their heads;
And Mamma in her kerchief, and I in my cap,
Had just settled our brains for a long winter's nap—
When out on the lawn there rose such a clatter,
I sprang from my bed to see what was the matter.
Away to the window I flew like a flash.
Tore open the shutters and threw up the sash.

175

The moon, on the breast of the new-fallen snow,

Gave a luster of mid-day to objects below,

When, what to my wondering eyes should appear

But a miniature sleigh, and eight tiny reindeer,

With a little old driver, so lively and quick,

I knew in a moment it must be St. Nick.

More rapid than eagles his coursers they came,

And he whistled, and shouted, and called them by name;

"Now, Dasher! now, Dancer, now, Prancer and Vixen!

On, Comet! on, Cupid! on, Donder and Blitzen—

To the top of the porch, to the top of the wall!

Now, dash away, dash away, dash away all!"

As leaves before the wild hurricane fly,

When they meet with an obstacle, mount to the sky,

So, up to the house top the coursers they flew,

With a sleigh full of toys—and St. Nicholas, too.

And then in a twinkling I heard on the roof,

The prancing and pawing of each little hoof.

As I drew in my head, and was turning around,

Down the chimney St. Nicholas came with a bound.

He was dressed all in fur from his head to his foot,

And his clothes were all tarnished with ashes and soot;

A bundle of toys he had flung on his back.

And he looked like a peddler just opening his pack.

His eyes how they twinkled! his dimples how merry!

His cheeks were like roses, his nose like a cherry;

His droll little mouth was drawn up like a bow,

And the beard on his chin was as white as the snow.

The stump of a pipe he held tight in his teeth,

And the smoke, it encircled his head like a wreath.

He had a broad face, and a little round belly,

That shook when he laughed, like a bowl full of jelly.

He was chubby and plump—a right jolly old elf;

And I laughed when I saw him, in spite of myself.

A wink of his eye, and a twist of his head,

Soon gave me to know I had nothing to dread.

He spoke not a word, but went straight to his work,

And filled all the stockings; then turned with a jerk,

And laying his finger aside of his nose,

And giving a nod, up the chimney he rose.

He sprang to his sleigh, to his team gave a whistle,

And away they all flew like the down of a thistle;

But I heard him exclaim, ere he drove out of sight,

"HAPPY CHRISTMAS TO ALL AND TO ALL A GOOD NIGHT!"

Ho Ho Ho, European die-cut images

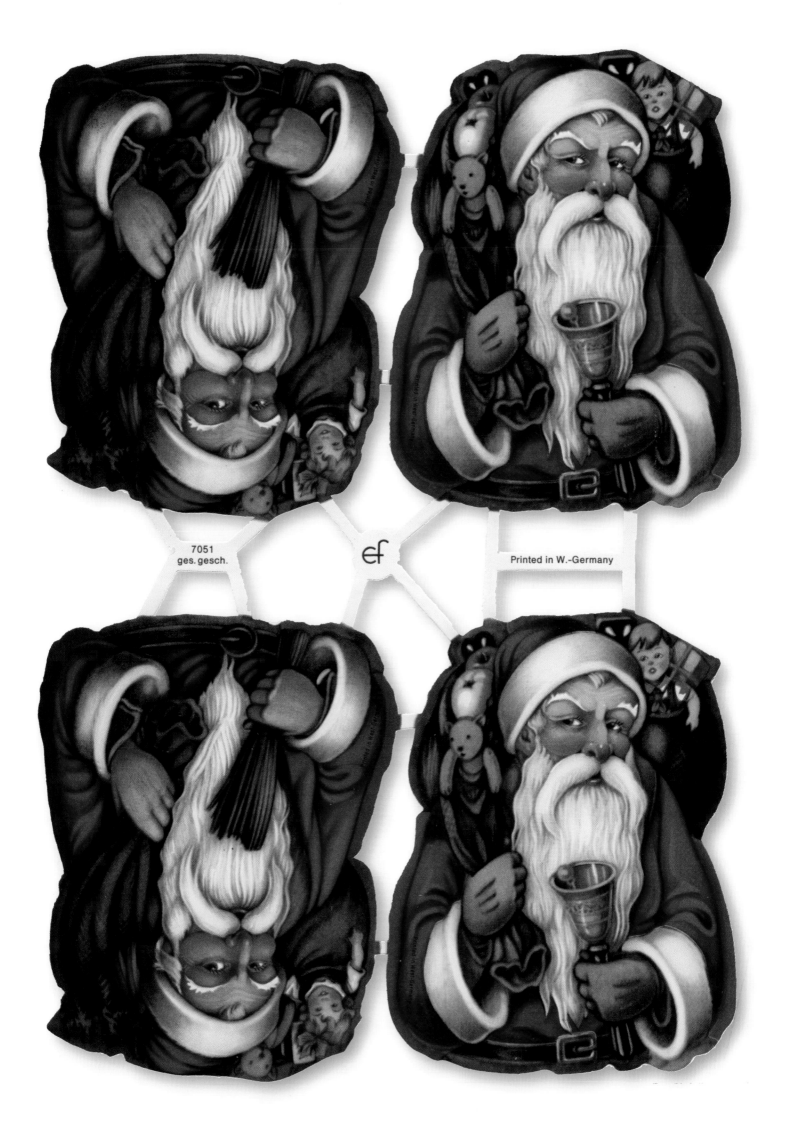

7051
ges. gesch.

Printed in W.-Germany

7151

PRINTED IN GERMANY

"Santa" or "Father Christmas"— costumes and names change, but Nicholas is the true name of the beloved saint.

From here, in reprints and anthologies, its words entered the language: "'Twas the night before Christmas," "visions of sugar-plums," "Now, Dasher! now, Dancer! now, Prancer and Vixen!" and "a sleigh full of toys," "a bundle of toys he had flung on his back," "a right jolly old elf" who "filled all the stockings" and "up the chimney he rose" to enter "his sleigh."

It would be twenty-two years later before Dr. Moore would admit publicly that he had written the poem—after all, what would people say? "A divinity professor writing such things! What is this country coming to?" Finally, in 1844, Moore included the poem in a collection of his poetry that he published (Ebon, 96–98).

It has been said that this poem may have been reprinted more than any other poem ever written. Clearly, it is based on Irving's *Knickerbocker* imagery, even to "laying his finger aside of his nose." What *is* different is miniaturizing St. Nicholas, making him the size of an elf; and his reindeer are to scale. And there is no mention of reindeer in Irving; St. Nicholas drove a horse.

Nordic image of Father Frost

Rare French pen and ink drawing of St. Nicholas holding his miter

Propagation des Images religieuses.

S. NICOLAS. | S. NICOLAS.

Mark Arnest maintains that "More than anything else, 'The Night Before Christmas' changed the public perception of Christmas—and its mention of St. Nicholas leaving gifts for children was particularly influential." And Arnest maintains that it helped to accomplish other things as well: "giving gifts to children instead of social inferiors removed it from class consciousness. Second, it turned the traditional public celebration inward toward the family. A child-centered celebration was new in the United States." Third, it loosened purse strings (Arnest, 8).

But there remains a controversy. A number of scholars, including Don Foster and Tristram Potter Coffin, maintain that the poem was written by a major in the Revolutionary War: Henry Livingston, Jr. (1748–1828), later on, a land surveyor and Renaissance Man. There certainly is the possibility—since Livingston never claimed authorship [Livingston had six years to admit he had written the poem after it was published, but never did]—that Livingston *did* write the initial version, and Moore adapted it. Since copyright protection was virtually non-existent in those days, a lot of writers took credit for whatever their hands touched. Jones doubts Coffin's contention: The poem "is thoroughly Moore's, whatever legends to the contrary. Even *belly-jelly* was good classical rhyme in Moore's eighteenth century models." Since Moore even published a hand-written facsimile edition, declaring it to be the original, it seems almost inconceivable that a professor of divinity, and scholar of his stature, would stoop to outright plagiarism.

Others disagree: Vassar professor of literature Don Foster first made academic headlines by his contention that an unknown 1612 funeral elegy by one W. S. had actually been written by William Shakespeare. But he really became a celebrity when he helped to identify the Unabomber (Theodore Kaczynski) and successfully identified the anonymous author of *Primary Colors* (a novel based on Bill Clinton's 1992 presidential campaign).

David Roberts' article on Foster, "The Word Sleuth," was reprinted in the April 2002 *Reader's Digest*. In it, Roberts notes that "Foster became convinced that any writer's style was so full of quirks and idiosyncrasies it could render one's identity almost as accurately as fingerprints. His technique depended mostly on an acute analysis of word choice, punctuation, spelling, habitual phrasing and poetic devices" (Roberts, 85–89).

In an October 26, 2000 article in *The New York Times*, David D. Kirkpatrick researches this debate in depth. He notes that in his book, *Author Unknown*, Foster, maintains that Dr. Moore was too much of a grouch to write such a playful poem: "He took a stern approach to being

Victorian representations of Santa Claus

Prize-winning drawing of St. Nicholas by Helen Read of All Saints School, Harwich, England.

a parent, and his poems and writings often focused on the annoying noise of 'clamorish girls' and 'boisterous boys.'" Foster also points out that before Moore finally stepped forward to claim credit for the poem, he first wrote the owner of *The Troy Sentinel* (first publisher of the poem) to ask if anyone knew where it came from. Even more conclusively, "Whoever wrote it," Mr. Foster says, "followed closely in the tradition of the 18th century poets William King and Christopher Antsey. Both wrote popular, bawdy poems in an anapestic meter, with the accent on every third syllable. . . . But Moore wrote only one undisputed anapestic poem, 'The Pig and the Rooster,' moralizing about laziness and arrogance. . . . Henry Livingston, however, lifted frequently from such bawdy anapests. Livingston wrote anapestic verses to his family every Christmas. Many of them borrow language and form from King and Antsey, and so resemble *A Visit*." Also, unlike Moore, Livingston's writing is "peppered with the unusual use of 'all' as an adverb, as is true in this poem: 'All snug in their beds,' 'all through the house,' 'dressed all in fur.' . . . *A Visit* is a hodgepodge of Livingston's favorite images," Mr. Foster writes. "Livingston's light poems are crowded with flying children, animals, ferries, boats and other vehicles, like Santa's flying sleigh and reindeer."

Even so, declares Kirkpatrick, "Mr. Foster faces an uphill battle in convincing historians that Moore did not compose the famous poem, at least until other scholars test his assessment." Some experts cite the evidence that Moore wrote out four copies of the poem by hand late in life. They have become among the most valuable documents

Charles Dickens remembered in this antique postcard

in American history. Seth Kaller, a New York antiquarian dealer, bought the fourth in 1997 for $210,000 in an auction at Christie's. "It's like someone coming forward and saying that he wrote 'The Star-Spangled Banner,' not Francis Scott Key,' Mr. Kaller said, 'or that he wrote the Gettysburg Address, not Lincoln'" (Kirkpatrick, E1, E9).

What about the reindeer, though? Did Moore invent them? Not so, responds Jones: One year before Moore wrote his poem, in a juvenile book titled *The Children's Friend,* (published in New York) appeared a poem about "Santeclaus," written by an anonymous author. The first stanza reads:

> Old Santeclaus with much delight
> His reindeer drives this frosty night
> O'er chimney-tops, and tracks of snow,
> To bring his yearly gifts to you.

Jones feels that the reindeer connection was in all likelihood even older than this particular poem. Actually, at least in New York during the early nineteenth century, Christmas was overshadowed by New Year's: "New York's New Year was a big affair, with much firing of guns as well as visitations; 'an ancient but foolish custom

French card

of ushering in the New Year with merriment and noise,' reported the *Packet* in 1785. "We may with safety say that there were more than a thousand guns and pistols fired on Friday night in this city, attended with excessive vociferation and uproar." Moore's poem was soon serving a dual purpose, as one version now began, "Twas the night before New Year.' Jones feels that this may very well be where the "compromise greeting, 'Merry Christmas and Happy New Year," gained stature. In fact, many quipped that poor "Santeclaus" had to work *two* nights each year (Jones, 349–350).

By the process of evolution, St. Nicholas's reindeer grew from one to two to eight, and by 1841, short breeches were being called *Knicker-bockers*. But across the nation there was still no consensus as to what Christmas was or wasn't, or what St. Nicholas wore or did not wear.

Prince Albert, Scrooge, and Tiny Tim

By the mid-1800s, England was the strongest power on earth, and fashion leader as well. It was London that ruled the world of finance. In 1840, when Queen Victoria surprised her beloved German-born husband by having a Christmas tree set up in Windsor Castle, Prince Albert was (in the Queen's words) "quite affected . . . , turned pale, and had tears in his eyes." Only eight years later, Victoria and Albert were depicted next to the Christmas tree in the pages of the *Illustrated London News*. The Christmas tree proceeded to sweep across the British Empire and the parts of America where the German immigrants hadn't already introduced it (Highfield, 4).

The year 1843 was pivotal in the life of Charles Dickens. His American Tour had not been a success, and the sales of *Chuzzlewit* had not lived up to expectations. For the first time, he had to face the possibility that he might have peaked and that the rest of his life would be all downhill. His wife was pregnant with their fifth child, and his bills were mounting.

Dickens' life and career had one constant: he never ceased caring. Especially did he care about the poor, the downtrodden, the disadvantaged, and the children. On October 5, 1843, he shared the Athenaeum stage with the man who would go on to become one of the British Empire's greatest prime ministers, Benjamin Disraeli. The subject of the day was the poor and the need for education. The audience's applause was so enthusiastic and supportive that Dickens couldn't get the subject out of his head. Wasn't there some way he could do more?

> **T**he message of love and selfless giving in *A Christmas Carol* is the message of St. Nicholas.

185

A hand-painted envelope with the 2001 St. Nick holiday stamps. This letter was cancelled on the first day of issue of the stamps in Santa Claus, Indiana, U.S.A.

During a three-day visit to Manchester, Dickens' mind kept returning to want and ignorance. One evening, en route to an appointment, the story concept of *A Christmas Carol* was born. On his return home, he was so overcome by the concept that he wept and laughed and wept again, and excited himself so much that he walked the back streets of London, fifteen to twenty miles a night, feeling his characters gradually becoming flesh.

For the root of his story, Dickens started with Christmas-related sections in his *Pickwick Papers, Sketches by Boz*, and "The Goblin Who Stole a Sexton" —but from these he launched into uncharted waters. The theme he began to articulate was one he never let his readers forget: that Christmas "is a time of all others when want is keenly felt and abundance rejoices."

Having chosen the theme, Dickens created Scrooge next; in his boyhood state—even to the books he loves—Scrooge is Dickens himself. The pathos of Tiny Tim Dickens drew from those in his own family who had died as children or teenagers. The Ghost of Christmas Present clearly articulated the plight of children in mines and schools like the ones in Yorkshire that Dickens had studied firsthand.

As momentum increased, Dickens dropped everything else in his obsession to stay with his characters—for his characters were every bit as real to him as any friends or loved ones in actual life. For a month and a half, he lived, slept, and dreamed the story, delivering it to his publishers, Chapman and Hall, in mid-November.

He didn't have to wait long for the public's verdict: the sales were tremendous. On Christmas Day alone, 6,000 copies were sold. But the impact upon himself was even more significant. As he had feverishly scribbled his way through the story, he learned some jolting things about himself. He gradually became aware that he had almost destroyed himself and his craft by egocentricity; that somewhere along the way he had himself become a Scrooge. He had felt so secure in his gifts that he assumed his preeminence would last forever. Before he completed the book, Dickens was able to pull himself back from the brink and realize his need for others. He began to wonder if he had ever really known who he was. (It would take writing the autobiographical *David Copperfield* to complete his inner quest to find that out.) Without question, writing *A Christmas Carol* dramatically changed the rest of his life.

St. Nicholas *magazine* *was the most* *successful* *children's* *magazine in* *the history of* *publishing,* *running from* *1873 to 1939.*

So it happened that in the last quarter of Dickens' life, in his 450 public readings (an average of one performance every twelve days for fifteen years), the story of Scrooge became as indispensable as singing the national anthem at a sports event. And as Dickens' life drew to a close, an even higher percentage of each evening's performance was devoted to *A Christmas Carol* and its lessons of agape love. On March 15, 1870, an exhausted Dickens made his final appearance on the stage. After reading the trial sequence from *Pickwick Papers*, he launched into *A Christmas Carol*, draining his last

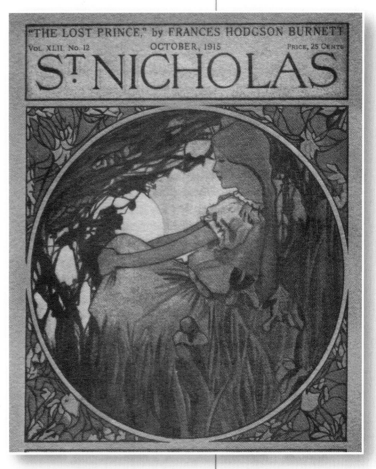

reserves in order to read with verve and brilliance. The applause was overwhelming and seemed to go on and on. When silence had finally been restored, Dickens informed his listeners that they had just listened to his last public performance, and concluded with these words: "From these garish lights I now vanish evermore, with a heartfelt, respectful, and grateful farewell," and walked off the platform. By June 7, he was dead (Wheeler, Intro. to Dickens' *A Christmas Carol*, xiv–lxxv).

He had accomplished more than he knew. He had written the greatest Christmas book ever written, the prototype by which all other Christmas literature would be measured against. A book that would but gather strength, stature, and momentum with the passing of the years. A book that would, quite simply, sweep the world. A book that would do more than any other outside Holy Writ to create a Christmas season around the world. Thomas J. Burns labels it, "The Second Greatest Christmas Story Ever Told" (Burns, Wheeler, 165).

Externally, the Three Christmas Spirits can well be likened to the rather paganish Father Christmas persona, but internally, in the spirit of the book, it is all St. Nicholas. It is his message of love and selfless giving that permeates every page of the book. Without that power, the book would long since have ceased to matter.

Nast, Virginia, and Sundblom

No small thanks to Irving, the Christmas tree, *A Christmas Carol*, and the sentimentality of the times, Christmas as a season now rushed into being. But it needed a catalyst. That was provided by a German immigrant. Thomas Nast was born in Landau, Bavaria, in 1840. When he was only six years old, his mother and sister decided to join the hordes of their countrymen who were emigrating to the New World. The trio settled on New York's Greenwich Street. Thomas grew up in a veritable Babel of voices and languages. Whereas there had been only 90,077 immigrants in the decade of the 1820s, during the 1850s, Ireland alone sent over a million, and Germany almost a million. With great difficulty, the nation's cities struggled with the herculean task of trying to assimilate the never-slowing torrent of people. The heaviest burden by far was borne by the city of New York itself, the port of entry. By 1850, Manhattan struggled to accommodate half a million people, Brooklyn a hundred thousand, and Williamsburg and Jersey another hundred thousand. And that was before the real rush began!

New York's schools were flooded with children who knew little or no English. Thomas was one of them. The overburdened

Angel bears the banner ST NICHOLAS in the parish church of St. John Baptist in Newcastle upon Tyne, England.

Classic elegant French photo card

Vive St Nicolas

1440

teachers did their best to make Americans out of each of these confused but eager children. At Christmas time, whatever gifts the children received tended to come in the name of Santa Claus, for by now, the Americanization of the Saint had reached the point where the European term for his name, St. Nicholas, was used less and less.

In those days, the North Pole was on everyone's lips, reaching it the equivalent of landing on the moon to that generation. Sir John Franklin (1786–1847), English rear admiral and explorer, early on was caught up in the excitement of finding the fabled Northwest Passage. In 1818, he commanded one of the ships in Captain Buchan's Arctic expedition. In 1819, he commanded his own expedition, which suffered greatly before returning to England in 1822. In 1826, his and Richardson's expeditions added 1,200 miles to the maps of the American continent. Franklin returned the next year, then moved to Tasmania. Returning to England in 1843, he was again caught up in Arctic fever.

On May 19, 1845, Franklin's ships, the "Erebus" and the "Terror," sailed from Greenhithe with 129 officers and men, supplied with food for three years. The ships were last seen at the entrance to Lancaster Sound on July 26. When three years had passed without any word from them, an expedition was formed to seek them out and see if they needed assistance. They were not successful. From that time on, expedition after expedition sailed north, for the fate of Franklin's men was being discussed everywhere. But it wasn't until 1859, fourteen long years afterward, that the skeletons of the last survivors of the expedition were found.

New Yorkers, who had sent out several search and rescue expeditions themselves (one in 1850, another in 1853, resulting in the founding of the American Geographical Society), by the mid-1850s felt almost a proprietary interest in the North Pole (Jones, 353–6; *Encyclopedia Britannica*, vol. 9, 695–6, this section).

A child's prayer and a listening saint. Dutch postcard

Veselé Vánoce!

A Santa-looking Nikolaus with a sack and a tree and Christkindel

And no small thanks to *The Children's Friend*, and its emphasis on a sleigh and reindeer, by the 1860s it was assumed in New York that Santa's home was at the North Pole rather than Spain. The boy Thomas assimilated all this.

The second half of the nineteenth century was to spawn the greatest explosion of magazine publication in the world's history, thousands emanating from those two great publishing meccas, New York and London. One of the greatest of these, *Harper's Weekly*, began publication in 1857. The House of Harper was at that time the preeminent publishing house in the world. Harper also published a monthly magazine and *Harper's Young People* that extended the reach of its weekly. Five years later, the twenty-two-year-old Thomas joined *Harper's Weekly* as a staff illustrator. Nast had been sketching ever since he could hold a pencil in his hand; by the age of fifteen, he had already become a professional artist.

America's Civil War was raging, and the fortunes of President Lincoln and the North appeared bleak that winter of '62. Since their fighting men were weighing heavily on everyone's hearts, Nast capitalized on that and for the Christmas issue drew a double-page "Christmas Eve." On the left was a lonely fatherless group at home; and on the right, an even lonelier soldier-father stared into the campfire, seeing only his loved ones at home through

Groeten van St. Niecolaas.

Dutch postcard

the flames. That two-page spread touched the hearts of Americans everywhere, and launched Nast on his road toward immortality. Letters poured into *Harper's* from all across the nation thanking the editors and Nast for that inspiring picture. That was it: the editor told Nast that Christmas two-pager was his from that time on. Although that first two-page spread didn't feature Santa Claus, the frontispiece, "Christmas in Camp," did. In it, Santa (robed in the stars and stripes) was depicted as distributing presents from his reindeer-pulled sleigh to the cheering soldiers. Above was a triumphal arch reading "Welcome, Santa Claus." In 1863, Nast's double-pager was titled "A Christmas Furlough," and was structured as a triptych: the center panel featured a furloughed soldier coming home to his eager family waiting beside a heavily laden Christmas tree. On the left ("Eve") was an illustration showing Santa, toysack on back, bending over two sleeping children; on the right ("Morning"), the children finding the bulging stockings hanging on the fireplace. That same Christmas, Nast featured Santa Claus with reindeer and sleigh on a snowy rooftop (Jones, 354–5, this section).

Nast's intricate woodblocks took a great deal of time and effort to produce; nevertheless, he was able to complete two a week for *Harper's* during the quarter century (1862 to 1886). During that time, Nast became the most famous cartoonist in America, creating both the Republican elephant and the Democrat donkey, as well as almost single-handedly destroying New York's infamous Tammany Hall with his devastating caricatures. In spite of all these other involvements, Nast's Christmas Santa Claus spreads continued faithfully year after year. According to Coffin, "In them Santa Claus's year-round activities are described: his work in making toys and filling stockings, his use of a spyglass to check up on young behavior, his decoration of Christmas trees, his trips about the sky in the magic sleigh. Santa Claus is even made to distribute gifts to good (that is, Union) soldiers in the Civil War" (Coffin, 93). It has been reported that President Lincoln personally requested Nast to create Christmas illustrations depicting Santa with Union troops. After the war, many ex-Con-

Sint and Piet arrive from Spain on a steamboat.

federate troops reportedly admitted that those were some of the most demoralizing moments in the entire conflict: seeing Santa side with the North in the Nast portrayals. Lincoln maintained that Nast was his best recruiting agent.

It is intriguing to see how Nast's depictions of Santa changed as time went by. His earliest Santas were small and gnomelike. Gradually, Santa changed and blurred in to the Germanic *Belznickel* appearance-wise, life-size, and complete with fur, only Nast transformed the rather scroungy-looking fur worn by the European rat pack into a handsome-looking fur coat an Astor wouldn't have refused to wear. By the 1880s, Nast's Santa had grown undeniably

St. Nicholas magazine with St. Nicholas and children on the cover

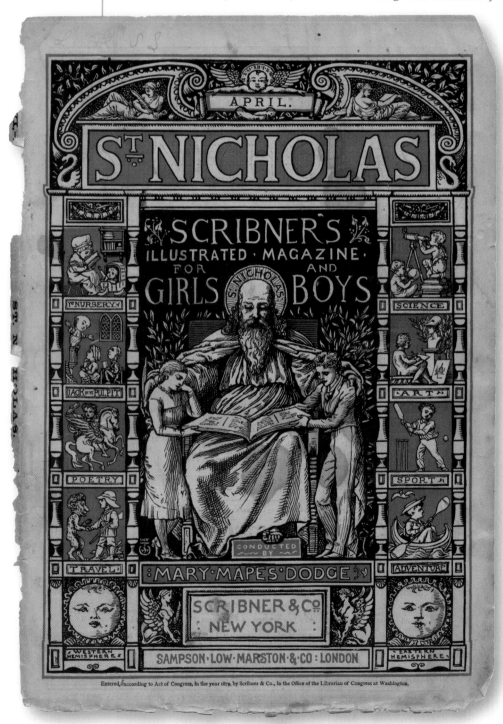

The miter marks the man in these German Oblaten scraps

Printed in
Germany

7208/1
ges. gesch.

St. Nicholas Center Exhibition in Holland, Michigan, U.S.A.

ers who used his paintings extensively include Procter and Gamble, Palmolive, and Maxwell House Coffee. However, the world remembers him most fondly for the memorable paintings he did of Santa Claus for Coca-Cola. For over twenty years these riveting illustrations (usually positioned on back covers of the nation's leading magazines) went *everywhere*. Sundblom took Thomas Nast's woodcuts as a starting point, polished the rough edges off, then colorized and contemporized Santa for the twentieth century. By the time Sundblom was through, only one thing was lacking to complete the persona of Santa Claus (Reed, 202–203).

And that contribution was written by Robert L. May for the advertising department of Montgomery Ward in 1939. His story of "Rudolph, the Red-Nosed Reindeer" was used as a give-away that Christmas. Before they finished the season, Montgomery Ward had given away over two and a half million copies. In 1946, Wards used it again, this time giving away three and a half million copies. Then, the story's immortality was assured when Gene Autry and Bing Crosby made the Phi Bete/Johnny Marks song by the same name a best-seller around the world, quickly selling over 50,000,000 copies. In it, Rudolph, the ugly duckling of a reindeer, stuck with a red bulb of a nose, is despondent because he feels rejected and miserable. Santa, confronted with the foggiest of nights, decides to enlist him and have him guide the other eight reindeer through the night. So it was that this ninth reindeer com-

Santa Claus gets caught raiding the refrigerator in this painting by Haddon Sundblom. Image courtesy of the Archives, The Coca-Cola Company.

Coca-Cola
REG U S PAT. OFF

pleted the persona (at least our conception of him) of the American St. Nicholas, Santa Claus.

"Santa remains one of the few excursions we can allow ourselves into the world of make-believe where right is right and wrong is wrong—period. As Gamaliel Bradford wrote, 'the fairies are gone . . . the witches are gone . . . the ghosts are gone. Santa Claus alone still lingers with us. For God's sake, for Heaven's sake, let us keep him as long as we can. If God's in His Heaven, He must agree that Santa Claus is 'all right for the world'" (Tristram Potter Coffin, 95–96).

They Are Still Being Written

The Miracle of St. Nicholas

St. Nicholas stories have continued to be written—in fact, are still being written today. Because of space constraints we are selecting only one as a prototype. This masterfully written 1920 story is significant in a number of ways: First, because it graphically depicts the end of faith and hope in Russia; second, because it captures what it must have been like to see Bolshevism substitute communist ideology for God; and third, because it prophesies the endurance of St. Nicholas in spite of all the Soviet attempts to kill his spirit, and his reemergence after the fall of the Berlin Wall.

The story begins in muted tones. On a bank, along a river of palest gold, a boy sits with a girl's dark head on his shoulder. Only a week ago they had married. Now they have but one night left together, for tomorrow he must leave to fight the Germans.

There are no words possible, so they watch in silence their last shared sunset. The imperial decree has already gone out so all Praskovia, the child-wife, can do is wait, pray for Kolia every day, and once a week burn a candle for him before the icon of St. Nicholas.

Summer turns to autumn, and autumn to winter. At first the letters come regularly: the armies are advancing into Prussia, the Germans are flying before them, and the war will soon be over.

The icon of St. Nicholas in the Russian Orthodox Cathedral of the Resurrection in Berlin, Germany

Statue in St. Nicholas of Bari Roman Catholic Church in Toronto, Canada

In the spring, a son is born. How the bells of the little wooden church ring the day he is christened! Proud, happy letters from Kolia reveal his joy at being a father. But then, there is silence, no more letters. Word comes that, unbelievably, the entire Russian Army (almost out of supplies and ammunition) is in retreat. Wide-eyed and terrified, Praskovia listens to the news reports from neighbors. Surely, St. Nicholas will protect them!

Then they hear the sound of guns, and horsemen ride in, telling everyone in the village to leave immediately, for the army is burning every village as it retreats. Now the long heartbroken journey to no one knows where begins and seems to have no end. Hunger, exhaustion, and disease travel with them each step of the way. Big Kolia's mother dies of fever and exhaustion—then her grandson, Little Kolia, dies as well. For a long while, Praskovia babbles in a delirium, caring little whether she lives or dies.

Later on, she is heaved into a cattle car, and far ahead an engine jerks the train into motion. She is told it will eventually stop at Petrograd. There she asks everywhere about the whereabouts of her husband, but with the central government collapsing, and 20,000,000 Russians either dead or dying, who is there to know—or care— about someone's husband? At last a kind woman gives her a job, food, and a place to lay her head.

But Kolia is not dead, though he's close to it . . . in a filthy German prison camp. After a long time, he and a big-hearted Cossack escape. Along the way, after unbelievable hardships, the Cossack dies. But Kolia gets through to the French line . . . then is shipped to England. Later on he reaches Sweden, Norway, and other countries he has never heard of. Eventually, he and his fellow scarecrows cross through Finland into Russia. But no one can tell him what may have happened to his family. His village has been in German hands for over a year. His search proving fruitless, he apathetically watches as the Revolution sweeps away everything of substance he has ever known. Then a

dirty-looking man with greasy black hair and narrow shifting eyes comes to camp and speaks to the regiment about "freedom, and promises, and food, and peace, and glory." What cares Kolia for any of these without Praskovia and Little Kolia? And there is no longer any God to comfort him.

Kolia has been hardened by years of bloodshed. Eventually, however, one day his eyes are opened, and he is blinded by the glare of intolerable anguish, vain regret, and shame. On he walks, past the vast battered Winter Palace, until he comes at last to a little white church standing among green trees. Kolia, obeying some instinct that craves shelter and relief from the desolate dirty streets, opens the door and walks in.

Before the altar, Kolia pauses, then kneels down. He wishes he had a candle to light. Almost unconsciously he finds himself praying again, praying for the impossible to happen: he whispers, "Have mercy on me—forgive me—have mercy upon me and bring Praskovia back to me . . ." Over and over till awareness of where he is ebbs away.

The door of the little church opens softly, and someone creeps in. Very slowly and very wearily. There is fumbling, rustling, and suddenly a faint light as a trembling hand places a small yellow candle before the image of St. Nicholas. Kolia wonders who in this dead city of despair still prays; who still retains any hope or courage? Nevertheless, he continues kneeling there alongside this unknown woman. At last the candle sputters and goes out.

The largest parish church in England is St. Nicholas Great Yarmouth, Norfolk. Nicholas greets those coming to church.

With a sigh that is weary beyond belief, the woman rises. Without knowing why, Kolia rises and follows her. Her hand on the heavy door, she feels him close behind her, and she is filled with fear. "What is it you want?" she whispers, staring up at him with wide, dark eyes. "It—" she begins, and then her voice breaks. "Kolia—it can't be you—is it *you?*"

He is on his knees before her now, his trembling arms flung round her, his tear-wet, ravaged face pressed into the folds of her skirt, and, incapable of speech, she lays her hands on his rough, tumbled hair. All the questions and answers . . . they will come later. For the present they only know that they have found each other, that the miracle they had prayed for has come to pass. And perhaps in the shadows, St. Nicholas smiles with an infinity of compassion and understanding. (Meriel Buchanan, "The Miracle of St. Nicholas," *Scribner's Magazine*, July 1920, 137–45, abridged).

CHAPTER 9

St. Nicholas Around the World

Now we finally arrive at our own time, especially the last three quarters of a century. What has happened since Sundblom's Coca-Cola ads and "Rudolph the Red-nosed Reindeer"? Has anything really changed? Has Santa Claus replaced St. Nicholas around the world? Let's find out.

The Orthodox World

A good place to start would be *Beit Jala*, in Palestine or in Demre, Turkey, and experience the East that gave birth to St. Nicholas. In the Muslim world, St. Nicholas is known and revered, but he is not a central figure to them. The Turks call him *Noel Baba* and are proud of him. Increasingly, they are realizing that he represents a potential gold mine in twenty-first century tourism as an icon, as a bridge between East and West, and as a magnet for world peace.

The St. Nicholas Church of Myra (Demre, now) has been partially restored. An orthodox liturgy is offered in the church, which is attended by an ecumenical and interfaith gathering there early each December. The sarcophagus that once contained St. Nicholas's body can still be seen in one of the side chapels, as can icon-like murals. A great statue of Santa Claus has been erected in the garden, indicating a call for peace to the children of the world.

Without question, St. Nicholas's greatest bastion remains what it has always been—the far-flung world of Orthodox Christianity. Even though Turkey is today predominantly Muslim, the nominal head of Orthodox Christianity remains the patriarch of Constantinople (Istanbul). For most of the twentieth century, it appeared the largest number of Orthodox believers in the world had been disenfranchised, but when Communism fell, once again it became apparent that Orthodox Christianity remained alive and well in Russia, and St. Nicholas was still the most popular saint in

Santa Claus goes around the world in this painting by Haddon Sundblom. Courtesy of the Archives, The Coca-Cola Company.

all Russia. In fact, it appears that almost every church in Russia has at least one St. Nicholas icon.

Should you wish to get a feel for what St. Nicholas means to Eastern Orthodoxy, all you have to do is check to see if your nearest Eastern (or Greek or Russian) Orthodox church has services on December 5, St. Nicholas Eve. Chances are they will. You will note that the faithful will leave their shoes outside the church door; upon leaving the services each will find gold coins (actually chocolates wrapped in gold foil) in them, symbolizing the gold dowries for the three dowerless sisters. During the services you will see St. Nicholas appear in his traditional bishop's garb.

One of the great hidden St. Nicholas treasures is that of his cave at the Greek Orthodox Church in *Beit Jala*. This war-torn and somewhat neglected church resounds with the echoes of praise from the thousands of pilgrims who gather here for the annual St. Nicholas festival. Beneath the main cave is the cave where St. Nicholas is said to have lived during his time in the Holy Land.

Image of St. Nicholas at the Russian Orthodox church in Bari, Italy

But what will surprise you most will be St. Nicholas's place in the daily spiritual life of Orthodox Christians (he is honored twice: both on December 6 and on May 9, celebrating both the ancient Rosalia festival and the removal of his bones to Bari). Interestingly enough, in both Orthodox and Anglican/Episcopal churches, St. Nicholas is revered most, not for his gift-bringing, but for his being the ultimate pastor, the ultimate shepherd, second in that respect only to Christ Himself. This aspect has never been articulated more beautifully than in Michael Ramsey's (he was then archbishop of Canterbury) sermon on Ascension Eve, 1956. In that sermon, he noted

"These [St. Nicholas] stories, blending memory and legend . . . tell the impact upon Christendom made by a real personality who could not be forgotten or ignored. The crop of legends has fact behind it. Just as when a stone is dropped into a pool, the ripples of water circle far beyond the central point so the impact upon humanity of a man of power and saintliness creates ripples of story and legend across the Christian world.

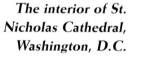
The interior of St. Nicholas Cathedral, Washington, D.C.

Right: The St. Nicholas Shrine Church, Flushing, New York, U.S.A., where relics from Bari have been sent in an extraordinary ecumenical gesture by the Dominican Fathers in Bari, Italy

In the shadow of the World Trade Center there once stood St. Nicholas Greek Orthodox Church, crushed and destroyed on 9/11, 2001. Plans to restore a St. Nicholas Church are underway.

"[St. Nicholas] is an illustration and proof of one of the great gifts of God to the world: the pastoral ministry of the Christian church.

. . . [Today, after the example of St. Nicholas], we "will teach the Christian faith with conviction, not trimming it after the prejudices of this age. . . ." That we will have, like him, "a love for children . . . to do far more that children may grow up in the knowledge and love of our Lord . . . ." That "the church is their home where they are loved and cared for. . . . Like St. Nicholas, the parish priest is the stiller of stormy seas, bringing peace to hearts failing them for fear. . . . Many are frightened about the world we live in, about the insecurities of life, about guilty fears which they do not always face or admit; and lives are battered like vessels without a course."

The rare Bari medallion of Nicolaus

Perhaps it is because of this pastoral dimension that Orthodox Christianity, in its weekly liturgical cycle, singles out only three persons by name: Mary, the mother of Christ; John the Forerunner; and St. Nicholas.

Bari

Bari remains one of the great St. Nicholas centers. Because of St. Nicholas's presence here, Bari has become one of Europe's greatest ecumenical centers. Case in point: an Orthodox chapel can be found inside the Roman Catholic Basilica. Here Christians from many different denominations come each May for symposiums, worship, and, of course, the annual celebration commemorating the Translation of the Relics of St. Nicholas of Myra to Bari in 1087. During this period an image of St. Nicholas is taken from the Orthodox church and carried in procession down to the port. There it is placed in a boat and carried out into deeper water. It is returned during an unforgettable night procession. Several days of celebration follow. In the Basilica, after a solemn mass, the prior (in the presence of the archbishop of Bari) withdraws the "Holy Manna" that has accumulated

St. Nicholas has made Bari one of Europe's greatest ecumenical centers.

in the crypt during the year. This manna is then poured into hand-painted bottles and made available to pilgrims (for a hefty price). Also an integral part of the annual celebration is the sailing of the Ship *Caravella* (a replica) that brought the St. Nicholas Relics here nine centuries ago.

Offered for sale everywhere in Europe are four types of St. Nicholas icons. First is the type found in Bari. In these, St. Nicholas is portrayed in Western church vestments that have an Orthodox flair to them; there is no headdress, but instead a nimbus surrounding his head. The color of this nimbus is universally a bright yellowish gold, and the dark skin color seems consistent with the fact that Nicholas was born in what is today Turkey. Second, there is the classic Russian Orthodox icon of a rather stern and powerful saint in vestments, with Jesus and Mary on either side. Third, there is the Byzantine Greek Orthodox icon that usually depicts the bishop in finery encrusted with gold, with a face that often is cheery, and almost invariably an enormous forehead. Fourth, and most familiar to aficionados, is that of the Western bishops. Roman Catholics, Armenian Orthodox, and Episcopal Anglicans are familiar with the miter as the headdress of a bishop, and the pastoral staff (or crosier) that their bishops carry, and they feature these in their icons.

The great statue in Siggiewi, Malta

It is this fourth type that so many collect today because of its many fascinating variations: (some of the folk art, especially Polish, include the figures of the three children saved by St. Nicholas). Some of them depict the three bags of gold thrown through the window. Especially in religious art from Spain, Portugal, and Mexico, the saint is usually portrayed with a beard.

The Dutch World

We turn to the Netherlands next, for they have celebrated St. Nicholas for close to a thousand years (there were over twenty St. Nicholas churches as early as the twelfth and thirteenth centuries). What is called *Oude Kerk* on *Oude Kerkplein* (Old Church on Old Church Square) in Amsterdam was consecrated to St. Nicholas back in 1325. So total was their devotion to the saint that people in those days often called the citizens of Amsterdam *Sinter Klassmannen.*

Early in November (even earlier for many Dutch shopkeepers), St. Nicholas begins to make his presence felt. Shop windows begin to fill up with St. Nicholas goodies and memorabilia—giftwrapped cardboard boxes, replicas of St. Nicholas and Black Pete, chocolate letters, *pepernoten,* and a host of related things. Each day that passes, the anticipation of children continues to build.

Toward the latter part of November, there comes an event that even today brings virtually the entire nation to a halt: the arrival of St. Nicholas and his Black Pete contingent from Spain.

A stern looking St. Nick from France, used as a cookie sheet or scrap

Amsterdam has long held the honor of welcoming them first, and the ship invariably bears the name, *Spanje* [Spain]. At the same time, there are similar arrivals all over the nation: some by boat, some by jet, some by helicopter, some by conveyances such as trolleys, carriages, trains, bicycles—even taxis.

In Amsterdam, the steamer docks amid the sounds of church bells, cheering crowds, and booming guns. Hundreds of thousands of Amsterdamers crowd the streets. Creeds mean little on this day, for St. Nicholas has become a universally beloved ecumenical figure. Now the stately saint descends from the ship and mounts his great white horse. Invariably, his beard will be long and white, and he wears gloves, a white robe, crimson mantle, and tall red mitre headdress. In his hand he carries a golden crosier, a staff shaped like a shepherd's crook.

Along the way, it is clear that the saint enjoys being in the company of the children, each of them craning their necks for a glimpse of him. "Most fortunate are those perched on the shoulders of an adult, thus gaining a better view. *Sinterklaas* is profoundly obliging. He never hesitates to stop and tweak a miniature nose or grasp a small outstretched hand along the way . . . . *Sinterklaas* may possibly stop to remind some children about their conduct records, which he has been keeping in his Big Red Book. He often reads from this carefully recorded log when out among his

Classic visit to Sinterklaas, shown in an old photographic souvenir card from Holland

SINTER CLAES

Royal location in Dam Square, Amsterdam, for the symbol of the city's friend and saint. Sint and Piet greet thousands the third weekend of November.

juvenile followers. It reveals his intimate knowledge of their year's activities, good and bad" (*Christmas in the Netherlands*, 13).

Some of the children rush toward him (especially when he later on descends from his horse and is walking among them); others, however, shyly hold back, clearly awed by the immortal bishop. As he speaks with them he is likely to drop hints about what kind of tidbits his horse likes best. The children know exactly what he's talking about, for each of them will leave such a snack in a shoe near the hearth at home, in hopes that St. Nicholas will come during the night and leave a treat behind—if they have been good, of course.

Black Pete, on the other hand, couldn't be more of a contrast. He, and his fellows, are usually dressed like medieval Spanish pages, complete with "long stockings, short, puffed britches, tight-fitting jacket, pleated collar, and plumed beret tipped over one ear. All are in bright contrasting colors" (*Christmas in the Netherlands*, 8).

The children are everywhere and have been waiting for what seems an eternity to them. Many of them don paper bishop's miters bought in costume shops as they prepare to greet their saint. As the procession moves away from the ancient St. Nicholas Church, little else can move on the snarled streets. While St. Nicholas waves, the brigade of Black Petes ham it up: they dance, they ride funny little motor scooters, they tell jokes, and pass out cookies, marzipan, and other sweets to each of the children within reach.

Pete carries with him certain standard props. The most important—and dreaded—is the famous Big Red Book in which *Sinterklaas* keeps those all-important records of child behavior. Pete lets them know that keeping those records is a full-time job for him and the saint back in sunny Spain. Pete is also likely to carry a handful of birch rods or switches. The switches are enough to keep the children on their best behavior. Bad children may receive no treats at all, only the rod or a switch. But the third prop is everyone's favorite: the big sack filled with goodies. Continually, he tosses cookies, fruits (the children love oranges), chocolates, and other sweets. Especially *pepernoten* (small round hard cookies made with seasonal spices).

"Pete enjoys engaging with foolery with the children. Often he will not only join them in singing and dancing but will lead them in a chorus. He is always available to introduce a willing youngster to the famed *Sinterklaas* or to tousle a nearby head of

People in the Netherlands have celebrated St. Nicholas for nearly one thousand years.

hair. Tots and teens alike delight in his tricks and silly actions. Consequently, wherever Pete is found, there will inevitably be a group of young people surrounding him" (*Christmas in the Netherlands*, 14).

Everyone tries to get in on the act: civic officials, brass bands, acrobats, entertainers, children's organizations, floats, and police motorcades throng the street in the wake of St. Nicholas. In Amsterdam, the parade often winds its way clear to the Royal Palace, where, in all likelihood, the queen will be waiting. The lack of support of Dutch Protestant leaders for all this has had a predictable result: every year the crowds are larger than those of the previous year.

The days and nights that follow are busy ones for all the St. Nicholases and Black Petes, for the genius of the Dutch St. Nicholas season is that the two principals are tightly woven into the very fabric of their Christmas season. Much more so than is true with Santa Claus in America. At nighttime it is assumed that they are riding across Holland's rooftops, listening in at chimneys to verify their suppositions as to children's behavior. Pete supposedly slides down each chimney (or otherwise gains admittance to the house) in order to exchange small gifts for the hay or carrots left in the children's shoes for the horse. During daylight hours they are even busier: visiting classrooms, hospitals, department stores, restaurants, offices, and innumerable private homes. There are parades to ride in, additional gifts to distribute, enthusiastic but sometimes off-key singing to listen to, confessions to hear, admonitions to give. Hardly a minute can they count their own ("Santa Claus: The Dutch Way," n.p.).

It is at schools, however, that they spend the most time. As they draw near a given school, the children will be waiting for them in the schoolyard, their exuberance poorly contained. Almost invariably they will now welcome the saint by singing a *Sinterklaas* song such as this one:

Sunday school attendance stamp showing St. Nicholas and the children

II. St. Nicholas and the Children.

Good St. Nicholas is in Holland once again
With his horse and Peter from sunny Spain.
And even if he can't stay long,
We hope he'll stop to hear our song.
Dear St. Nicholas the door is open wide,
For you and Pete to step inside.
And we're singing, voices ringing, and our hearts rejoice
'Cause the saint loves all good girls and boys.

After listening to their entertainment, the group will usually proceed to the school gymnasium or a large classroom. For weeks the children will have been planning for this moment; now their paper-chains adorn walls, doors, entrance-ways, and light fixtures. Attached to the walls or suspended from strings are colorized drawings, sketches, or montages depicting the saint's earlier disembarkation and parade. Nor is Pete neglected: portraits and masks of him are everywhere as well. The children even imitate their guests by wearing mitres made of red construction paper or brightly colored berets complete with paper plumes.

Pete's sack of goodies is full, so now he heaves *pepernoten* in great handfuls everywhere in the room, laughing at the confusion and bedlam he creates, his voice as loud as theirs as they scramble around on the floor. Meanwhile, *Sinterklaas* may look reprovingly at Pete, shake his head, and even order him off. After all, he's supposed to be behaving, too. But Pete's high spirits cannot be squelched that easily, for he hops on and off chairs, tables, and shelves—even surreptitiously pokes wadded paper inside *Sinterklaas's* mitre. Occasionally, he stuffs an unruly child into his sack and threatens to haul the naughty child back to Spain with him.

Finally, the big moment arrives: there is sudden and total silence as *Sinterklaas* opens his Big Red Book. Pete stands close by, birch rods at the ready. The children all press close so as not to miss a word. Does he know about their misdeeds? What a ques-

GROETEN VAN St. NICOLAAS

SPANJE

Wie komt er alle jaren
Daar heel uit Spanje varen

This card shows the moment of arrival of Sint and Piet from Spain. Children sing the traditional "Steamboat Song" to mark the occasion each mid-November.

The Liverpool Anglican Parish Church of Our Lady and St. Nicholas, on the Mersey River, England

tion! Of *course* he knows: he knows *everything*! They are astonished as they listen to their names and acts. Could the teachers have blabbed on them? Preposterous idea! *Sinterklaas* obviously needs no help from anyone else.

Next, the saint is likely to invite children to the front to perform, sing, or answer questions dealing with their behavior. "They may be brave, confident, apprehensive, shy, or even fearful of the overwhelming *Sinterklaas*. On some cheeks, an occasional tear of fright might glitter. This, however, quickly disappears at the comforting touch of an adult or through the twinkling smile of the loving bishop himself."

Before leaving, *Sinterklaas* almost always has additional surprises to hand out. Then, he turns back to promise to visit each of them personally in their homes if they in turn promise to be good. Who could reject such a deal? (*Christmas in the Netherlands*, 28–30).

But everything else pales beside the great night itself, for this time not just the children, but the entire family is involved: "The exchange of gifts among family and friends on December 5 is an incomparable event. The presents are never highly expensive or extravagant, nor are they beautifully wrapped. The tradition is, rather, to disguise or camouflage each present in an imaginative way. Its creative wrapping is a most important feature. Everyone calls the gifts 'surprises.'

T he tradition in the Netherlands is to disguise gifts as creatively as possible.

"A rhyme or poem always accompanies each surprise. Sometimes it expresses gratitude. More often, it humorously points out one of the recipient's quirks, foibles, or habits. Gentle teasing is the rhyme's goal. It is never meant to cause pain. The time is a special one, when good-natured kidding is not only expected but applauded. The camouflage and the verse, for example, might commemorate an incident or mishap of the past year. Although embarrassing at the time, it is now a source of joking. None other than *Sinterklaas* himself signs the surprises and verses, so that the giver remains anonymous. In some areas, Pete signs his name, too.

"The clandestine activities of St. Nicholas Eve have given rise to the Dutch saying that best describes the Netherlands at this time of year. The entire nation 'goes mysterious.' For weeks, all have been shopping alone, secretly preparing surprises, and frantically writing verses in the isolation of dim corners of the house. Sometimes family members confine themselves to their rooms for long stretches. They even slam doors in faces, then stuff cotton in their ears while trying to compose choice rhymes. At work, no one is astonished to see an otherwise dignified physician hunched over a custard pudding on a desk. It will conceal a special gift. The nurse may be struggling to secure a package in the hollow of a loaf of bread. Everyone knows home is no place for this delicate task.

The great duo, Sinterklaas and Zwarte Piet

"For those who don't feel up to writing their own poems, local department stores generally employ a professional rhymester called a *sneldichter*. Sometimes with the aid of a rhyming dictionary, these speed poets can dash off a jingle in no time, all typed and ready for presentation. Half the fun of the holiday for many, however, lies in drafting these jolly rhymes on their own, regardless of the poetic quality. The more imperfect the verse, the more to laugh about" (*Christmas in the Netherlands*, 31).

December 5 finally arrives. At school, teachers rarely try to get much accomplished during that morning, and instead permit the students to sing, play games, or open surprises. Often names have been drawn ahead of time so that each student may now open a package, read the verses out loud, and be prepared for the resulting hilarity. Then, at noon, the best surprise of all, when they are sent home early.

That evening's Vigil of St. Nicholas is traditionally a time for the family to gather together, and all generations share the fun. It is said that Dutch who are abroad suffer more homesickness on St. Nicholas Eve than at any other time of the year.

After supper, the children become very quiet as they listen intently for the sound of hooves on the roof. Someone, more often than not Papa, belatedly remembers that he left something at the office and rushes off, promising to return quickly.

Suddenly, there is a loud knock at the door—or sharp taps on the window. Mama opens the door just enough for Pete's hand to come through; then he scatters handfuls of candies and *pepernoten* on the floor, and the children all race for it at once. Pete then disappears, but not before leaving a big sack or basket of gifts on the doorstep.

Now *Sinterklaas* makes a personal appearance, is ushered into the house, and is awarded Papa's chair (Papa still being gone on his "errand"). *Sinterklaas* now opens his big book and lectures each child: "Hans, you waste everybody's time by dawdling at your food." "Katrina, it's never right to be cruel to animals—look what you did to poor Grimalkin last April!" "Hilda, a game is just a game; remember that next time you play chess with Matt." The children can't help wondering just how it is that *Sinterklaas* knows so much about their private lives. Just before leaving, the saint is likely to leave a gift for each child. But he is not yet through: hidden in secret places in the house are other gifts; sometimes directions are left behind so that they can embark on a treasure hunt following up each clue. Before retiring, the children place their shoes by the chimney and sing St. Nicholas songs.

But for the older children and the grownups, the evening has only just begun. There in a big heap on the floor are many packages of all sizes and shapes, each with a name attached, hence a term used for this evening, *Pakjesevond* (parcel evening).

The Dutch are unexcelled in the art of surprise-giving. And not least of the fun is the fact that the guessing never stops. *Who could have planned this one? Who could have written such inspired verses? How did I get found out?* That's what is *thought*. What is *said*

Candy shop in Flanders, Belgium

will be quite different, for *Sinterklaas* has signed every package.

No one hurries, for they've been waiting all year for this. As each person begins to unwrap a given package, all listen intently and watch every movement of the hands. Teenagers especially relish the subtleties in the poetry, the hidden jokes. And often nothing is as it may seem: "A surprise, for example, may lie in a sausage, in a glove filled with wet sand, or in a gelatin loaded with fruit. A bracelet may come in a raw potato dressed up like a doll" . . . but the potato might instead be wrapped in tape, put into a milk carton, and placed in a bucket of ice. "Thank you, *Sinterklaas!*" Mother may respond to such a gift. Sometimes very

223

Gift wrap, cards and decorations all feature Bishop Nicholas

small items like pocket knives may be buried deep in an extra-large beef roast (which turns out not to be beef at all but merely cotton basted with burnt sugar). A plaster-filled cast may be given to someone who recently broke a leg; if the plaster is broken into there may be a pair of miniature skates buried therein. The person who absolutely detests porridge is likely to be given an extremely large bowl of it. And custom dictates that the recipient must eat the whole bowlfull in order to reach the surprise at the very bottom. In some cases, the parcels will contain merely treasure maps, leading everyone on a wild chase through the house and yard in order to find the surprises. Who knows, it might be hidden deep in a coal cellar or potato bin, high up in the eaves, in a closet or flower pot, stove, or drain-pipe.

Or sometimes the package will contain only a blank piece of paper—or at least it appears that way. Finally, the recipient sniffs the paper and notes a strange lemony fragrance. Holding the paper next to an open flame reveals the written clue as to where the surprise might be found. The fun is in the chase: the longer it takes, the better job "that clever *Sinterklaas*" has done! So . . . sometimes *Sinterklaas* confuses everyone by putting the wrong name on a given package: "Mother opens it, only to find a small box with Father's name on it. Father opens the box to find a note sending his oldest son out the front door. There, on the step, is a molded chocolate figure. Ten minutes later, when the son breaks off a piece of the candy to eat, what should appear but a note for his little sister. She follows directions, looks in the kitchen sink, and there is a storybook signed by the saint."

And sometimes the surprises turn out to be hoaxes. "Candies filled with mustard, crackers made of soap, cookies with toothpaste icing," etc., but all laugh heartily at how innovative *Sinterklaas* was with each one.

By this time, the place is in such disarray it appears to be a painting by Jan Steen. Strewn about are reams of torn paper, poems long and short, boxes, bags, crumbs, and clutter of all kinds.

If no one is sleepy yet, they may place surprises on other people's doorsteps, ring the doorbell, and run. Finally, exhausted, everyone partakes of pastries and hot chocolate, to bring another year's celebration to its close. That night the children are likely to dream of *Sinterklaas*, on his way back to a much needed rest in sun-baked Spain (*Christmas in the Netherlands*, 32–39, this section).

Some of *Sinterklaas's* innovative gifts are pranks.

Thus concludes the St. Nicholas period of the Dutch Christmas season. The excitement has been so intense that everyone is more than ready for a change of pace. The serenity of the Advent season enables the Dutch to prepare to welcome the Christchild. Family-togetherness is everywhere the societal norm.

Most towns sport a majestic Christmas tree in their main square, brilliantly lit each evening. Stores are seasonally decorated with greenery and colorful decorations. More and more, Santa Claus decorations and memorabilia appear as well. Bright flower exhibitions bring additional color into Dutch homes as people carry their decorations home. Since the Dutch love to sing and listen to music, chimes and carillons play every day, and people throng to churches and concert halls for musical performances.

Trimming the Christmas tree is an activity the entire family participates in. Many, especially those who live in apartment complexes, place three-dimensional Advent stars in their windows. The Dutch love to make their own ornaments and decorations; they also hang apples, oranges, and tangerines on their Christmas

Die-cut images from Germany, O Tannenbaum, the Christmas tree

trees. Last to go on are small candles (which needless to say, require continual vigilance lest the tree catch fire).

At the center of each Roman Catholic home there will be a *kerstal* [or creche] near the Christmas tree, and creches will appear in their churches and chapels.

At night, the Dutch love to share Christmas stories, reading aloud by the soft light emanating from the Christmas tree candles.

Then comes Christmas Eve. In the evening many families attend church services. December 25 the Dutch call "First Christmas Day," and it is considered a very holy day. Many Dutch attend church with their families on Christmas morning . . . and each person they meet they wish *Vrolijk Kerstfeest* [merry or joyful Christmas]. An early breakfast before church will be followed by a post-church breakfast-lunch.

Flemish card showing the mystery and magic of St. Nicholas

It is becoming more common for some presents to be given on Christmas morning, but they are simple, such things as carefully chosen books. In the afternoon, most homes open their doors to family and close friends. It is a quiet time, graced with puzzles, board games, and the singing of favorite Christmas carols.

And how everyone hopes a hard frost will have set in by now so that the entire family can enjoy the most popular Dutch pastime of all—ice skating on nearby lakes and canals. *Everyone* skates, from grandparents to small children. Even baby carriages on runners are pushed along on the ice. Families stay together by each hooking an arm over a long pole as they skate.

Seven o'clock in the evening means it's time for the traditional Christmas feast. Many Dutch families read from the Bible at this time, and all generations share favorite biblical passages. Flowers, such as red and white poinsettias, irises, and tulips, make the tables almost a fairyland.

December 26, the Dutch call "Second Christmas Day," and it is as subdued as December 25. The difference being that families call on their friends, attend performances, dramas, and concerts,

**Station at
Sint Niklaas,
Belgium**

and dine out. Children participate in Nativity plays, and no child is left out.

But Christmas is not even yet over for the Dutch, for the Twelve Days of Christmas continue. In the country, during this period, there are the final judging of midwinter-*hoornblazen* (great alpine-like horns that can be heard three miles away on icy nights). These contests date all the way back to 2500 B.C. And in the cemeteries of Friesland the practice of continuous bell-ringing takes place.

New Year's Eve, the Dutch call "Old Year's Evening," and it generates great excitement. Unlike many other parts of the world, in the Netherlands they choose not to party with others but rather with their families. By late afternoon, the streets are crowded as everyone rushes home from work, greeting all those they meet with *Zalig Uiteinde!* ["Blessed End!"] The entire nation shuts down to celebrate. Many families attend church services early in the evening, or have Bible readings at home. All generations of a given family are likely to meet in one location and spend the evening playing games, charades, and eating. After listening to the year's wrap-up on television, the entire family rushes outside to prepare the fireworks, which are permitted only on New Year's. "The clock strikes 12 and boom! The noise begins. All factories in the towns and all the ships in the many harbors blast their whistles. Church bells peal and carillons play. Firecrackers explode on the ground and fireworks light up the sky."

Then back inside, there is a moment in which to give thanks, to embrace one another and wish each other Happy New Year. After the toasts, the adults go back outside and start visiting their neighbors. They sleep late that morning.

Finally the Twelfth Day of Christmas, the feast of the Epiphany or Three Kings Day, arrives. This day the Dutch generally dedicate to their children. An Epiphany cake with a bean cooked inside is the center of all attention, for whichever child finds the bean in his/her cake automatically becomes monarch for the day and dons a gold paper crown. In Catholic parts of the Netherlands, children dress as the Three Kings, shepherds, and angels and parade through their streets carrying candles, homemade stars, and Chinese lanterns. They sing Epiphany songs as they march.

On that day, January 6, families take down their Christmas trees and thereby bring to an end their long and joyful Christmas season. (*Christmas in the Netherlands*, 40–63, this section).

The foregoing is a picture of the traditional Dutch Christmas season, but in recent years a wave of secularism has resulted in Santa Claus boomeranging his way back to the Dutch people from America, complete with songs such as "Jingle Bells." And politically correct animal lovers have condemned *Sinterklaas* for sometimes wearing a furry mantle, feminists have condemned the bishop for not having more female pages in his train, anti-discrimination groups have condemned the Moorish *Zwarte Piet* because he stains his face black, and others maintain that *Sinterklaas* is just out of touch with modern values.

The bridge to St. Nicolas de Port, France

"Humbug!" retort untold thousands of Dutch of all ages, who post signs with X-ed out Santa Clauses that prohibit Santa from showing his whiskers and red-nosed reindeer until *Sinterklaas* is safely back in Spain—and who could even imagine a Christmas devoid of the tall bishop and his coterie of Black Petes! (Chao, n.p.; Marlise Simons, n.p.).

Alsace-Lorraine, France

St. Nicholas is as beloved in Lorraine as he is in Holland, and his appearances there are similar to those in the Netherlands. When the children see him coming down the street in his crimson bishop's robe and pointed miter, they cheer and clap. But they tend to recoil in fear when they see St. Nicholas's inseparable companion, *Pere Fouetard*. Like *Zwarte Piet*, he carries a bundle of switches with him. And he appears to have an uncomfortably accurate memory, remembering which boys and girls misbehaved during the past twelve months. Now and then he will playfully whack certain children's toes as they pass.

In some places in Lorraine, a standard feature of the procession will be a cart carrying a salt barrel. Sticking out at the top are three naked boys (Spicer, n.p.).

Just as is true in the Netherlands, the gifts children receive are given in the name of St. Nicholas. Shoes, stockings, or baskets left by the fireplace on the Eve of St. Nicholas are found filled the morning of December 6 with sweets, gingerbread figures, and fruit. Carrots and hay are left for St. Nicholas's horse (or donkey), a glass of wine for the saint. In Lorraine, on December 4, children intently watch the sky: if it is red, it means that St. Nicholas is busy cooking the cakes he'll be delivering the next night. St. Nicholas is also extremely popular in Alsace (Strich, n.p.).

Today, the Church of Nicolas de Port in Lorraine is one of the grandest such churches in the world. Its history goes back to St. Nicholas Day, 1244.

St. Nicholas arrives at Canterbury Cathedral accompanied by the Dean and the Archbishop. Photo: David Manners

In much of France today, *Pere Noel*, a St. Nicholas surrogate, rules over the Christmas season. Like St. Nicholas, *Pere Noel* is tall, thin, has a white beard, and wears a long red robe. On his back, he often carries a sack of treats and toys for the children. Sometimes a donkey carries that sack for him. Antique dealers, however, offer dozens of Bishop Nicholas tinted postcards created in France. *Pere Noel* is a strange amalgamation of both St. Nicholas and Santa Claus in that he brings small gifts and candy treats to children both on December 6 and on Christmas Eve. Like Santa Claus, supposedly *Pere Noel* lives at the North Pole. *Pere Noel* has a helper, too, *Pere Fouetard* [Father Whipper], who informs his master which children have not behaved; however, *Pere Fouetard* is not nearly as visible in France as Black Pete is in the Netherlands. Many children put their shoes near the fireplace, creche, or Christmas tree on Christmas Eve, hoping that *Pere Noel* will leave presents in them. The children open their presents on Christmas Day, the adults on New Year's Day (Thoemnes, 17).

Flanders, Belgium

Since Flanders has, throughout history, been so closely associated with Holland, it should come as no surprise to discover that St. Nicholas is deeply revered here. The city of Sint Niklaas here has a St. Nicholas church, outside which has been erected an enormous image of St. Nicholas and the three children in a barrel. St. Nicholas is even part of the official city seal and street decor. The people of Sint Niklaas have their own

Shield of Sint Niklaas, Belgium

French photographic postcard

231

unique way of greeting the arrival of St. Nicholas and *Zwarte Piet*. A weekend family celebration in the style of a circus is held, and St. Nicholas presides from a throne with his helpers. Several times during weekend performances, he directly addresses the children.

The people of Flanders have an ongoing battle with the intrusion of the Americanized Santa Claus. Staged arrests of Santa Claus are sometimes held on their streets, and Santa Claus is forbidden to appear before December 7.

Luxembourg

On the Sunday preceding the December festival of St. Nicholas, the Grand Duchy of Luxembourg welcomes the saint in its cities, towns, and villages. In some places, such as in Echternacht, St. Nicholas and his companion, *Hoêsecker*, arrive by boat. Waiting for them on the shore will be the town mayor, resplendent in his robes, as well as the aldermen by his side. These officials escort their distinguished visitors to town in a horse-drawn carriage. A large procession follows, including a local band that makes a great deal of noise. In the town itself a throng of children "shout, hop, and jump excitedly as Nicholas and *Hoêsecker* make their triumphant approach to the old Town Hall in the market place. The band plays all the songs the boys and girls know. The children dread *Hoêsecker* as much as they love Nicholas. Like *Pere Fouetard*, *Hoêsecker* carries switches on his back, and he never hesitates to whip a lazy or disobedient child. At the ceremonies in the market place, each one receives a big paper bag bulging with apples, cakes, and bonbons. The little ones in their mothers' arms get their presents first, then the children up to twelve. . . . Meanwhile the band strikes up one lively Christmas tune after another" (Spicer, n.p.).

German card circa 1900

Gruß vom Nikolo!

European elegance expressed in this German card

Gruß vom Nikolo!

Austria and Germany

St. Nicholas is very popular still in both South Germany and Austria. In Austria, *Krampus* (one of the more frightening assistants of St. Nicholas) terrifies many of the children. Reports of near violent attacks by this assistant does little to enhance the public perception of the saint. St. Nicholas is found shaped into breads, candies, and almost every other imaginable food in Austria. Christmas markets in Salzburg and Vienna have vast arrays of St. Nicholas items to delight the shoppers.

United Kingdom

St. Nicholas has long been beloved in Britain. In fact, there are almost 500 churches dedicated to St. Nicholas here (over 400 in England alone!). The most famous of them is probably Kings College Chapel in Cambridge, this splendid chapel known the world over for its great medieval stained-glass depictions of St. Nicholas and its annual Festival of Nine Lessons and Carols on its Christmas Eve broadcast around the world. In Aberdeen, Scotland, there can be found the Kirk of St. Nicholas, which is both Congregational and Presbyterian Church of Scotland. Just about a mile from it in the St. Margaret of Scotland Episcopal Church can be found one of the most exquisite Comper chapels of St. Nicholas in the world. One of England's most famous churches is St. Nicholas Church of Durham, and another is St. Nicholas Cathedral in Newcastle upon Tyne.

Famed British composer Benjamin Britten composed a cantata for St. Nicholas that is performed every year in concerts and Advent services throughout Britain.

Today, Anglican leaders have begun a strong movement to bring back St. Nicholas and the spiritual dimension of Christmas in order to counter the secularizing effects of Father Christmas. All too often today, it is the pagan antecedents of Christianity, with their Winter Solstice connections that are popularized by the media.

> Anglican leaders are working to bring back St. Nicholas and the spiritual dimension of Christmas.

The United States

Without question, Santa Claus is the most pervasive Christmas presence in America today. He is the force that propels the nation's most lucrative selling season, and he appears in malls all across the country, and there long lines of children climb up on his knee and tell him what they want for Christmas. He has become a staple of secular Christmas music.

Santa has also been incorporated into the day-to-day life of church members, and one of each family is likely to dress up in a Santa suit come each Christmas. Santas ring Salvation Army bells as they encourage shoppers to help the needy and destitute. Many of those who wear Santa suits are involved in admirable philanthropic causes, seeking to make a real difference in their communities.

Having said this, beneath the surface of things, St. Nicholas has remained at the core of American life, as the latest Christmas stamps so graphically remind us. And it was not so long ago that the greatly beloved St. Nicholas Church (dubbed the Protestant Cathedral) ministered to members of the Reformed Church of America just a short distance from the famous St. Patrick's Roman Catholic Cathedral on New York's Fifth Avenue. In an almost unbelievable chain of circumstances, that St. Nicholas Church was destroyed during the 1940s to make possible an extension of the Shell/Rockefeller Center. Currently, there is an ongoing movement to reestablish a St. Nicholas Church elsewhere in the city. The same is true for the 169-year-old St. Nicholas Greek Orthodox Church that stood only 500 feet from the World Trade Center, and was a casualty of September 11, 2001. Many other St. Nicholas churches can be found across the nation, and St. Nicholas-related celebrations are becoming popular in Episcopal and Lutheran circles as well.

. . . and the World

St. Nicholas churches and cathedrals can be found not just in the cities we have mentioned but around the world—in places as far-flung as Seoul, Korea; Johannesburg, South Africa; Aberdeen, Scotland; Galway, Ireland; *Beit Jala*, Palestine; Lisbon, Portugal; Madrid, Spain; Paris, France; Zanesville, Ohio; Dallas, Texas; and Juneau, Alaska; Cardiff, Wales; Prague, Czech Republic; Moscow, Russia; Venice, Italy; and Sydney, Australia. He is indeed a universal symbol.

Jolly old Saint Nicholas,
Lean your ear this way!
Don't you tell a single soul
What I'm going to say;
Christmas Eve is coming soon;
Now, you dear old man,
Whisper what you'll bring to me;
Tell me if you can.
When the clock is striking
    twelve,
When I'm fast asleep,
Down the chimney broad and
    black,
With your pack you'll creep;
All the stockings you will find
Hanging in a row;
Mine will be the shortest one,
You'll be sure to know.
Johnny wants a pair of skates;
Susy wants a dolly;
Nellie wants a story book;
She thinks dolls are folly;
As for me, my little brain
Isn't very bright;
Choose for me, old Santa Claus,
What you think is right.

—Traditional Christmas Carol

CHAPTER 10

A New Way to Celebrate Christmas

The Missing Piece of the Puzzle

Now we have come to the end of our seventeen-century-old story. No—not end—for such a story is not likely to ever die. Now that we have vicariously experienced the entire incredible saga, *what do we do with it?*

It appears that we have two options: either we treat it as merely a "good read," consider it to have little relevance to the rest of our lives, and go on to other things that interest us more—or we treat it as a map book to our future. Might it even be that long-missing piece to the puzzle of our lives?

Knowledge. Never in human history has there been this much of it at our beck and call. Only clicks of a computer away. Yet, there are nagging questions: "What knowledge?" "What are we to do with it?" "How am I to differentiate between mere knowledge and wisdom?"

Brrrrrinnnnng! It's that wretched alarm clock! Groggily, you reach for it, turn it off, sit up, and scrape the cobwebs out of your eyes. Then it comes to you: *There's so much to do today!* and you leap into action. Wake up the three kids. Get them up (not the same thing as waking them). See that they wash up, dress, eat, put everything into their knapsacks they'll need for the day, and get them off. Then clean up the house so it won't look like a wreck when the plumber comes to fix the broken valve. The telephone rings. "Oh no! How could I have forgotten: I'm in charge of PTA [Parent Teacher Association] tonight! . . . It can't be my turn again this soon! . . . Bye!" The telephone rings. "Honey, I forgot that important Huntington contract. And the big meeting's in 45 minutes! Would you mind grabbing it for me? It's in the top drawer of the file cabinet. And buzz it down to me quickly, please. You will?

St. Nicholas has traded in his donkey for a Vespa. "Christmas is Coming" by Inkognito, Berlin, Germany.

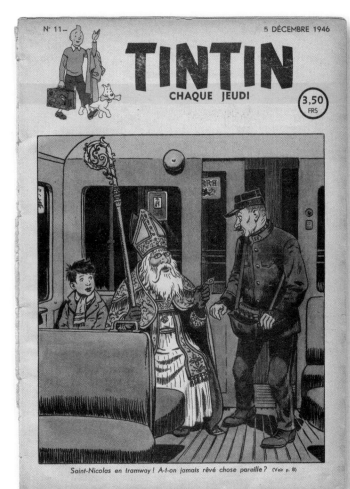

Saint-Nicolas en tramway! A-t-on jamais rêvé chose pareille? (Voir p. 8)

The popular French comic book Tintin features St. Nicolas in two issues from the 1950s

Bless you! Bye." The telephone rings. *Not again!* "Hello?" (ungraciously). "Oh, hi, Becky."

"Oh, Mom!" she wails.

"What's wrong, Dear?"

"Oh, Mom, I . . . I . . . slipped getting out of the school bus . . . fell into a big puddle . . . I-I'm a wreck! Oh, *Mom!*"

"Don't worry, Dear. I'll come down and pick you up in fifteen minutes—oh, make that thirty! Gotta get an important document to Dad quick! . . . I know, Dear, I know, you're a mess . . . I'll get there soon as I possibly can! Bye!"

And that's only the first two hours of the day.

Later on, there's housework, appointments, civic responsibilities, shuttling the kids to their music lessons and sports activities, seeing that they practice their music lessons at home, do their homework—each of them—and help those who need it, get supper ready, afterward see that the dishes are done, everything's put away, and—see that no child joins the others at the TV until caught up with all the assignments. Answer the telephone. "Oh no! I'm late for PTA! I'm, I'm, I'm . . ."

And so it goes. Day after day. Hardly ever a quiet moment. When once in a while it does get quiet, the TV set's turned on in order to find out what's happening in the world.

St. Nicholas fulfilling his tasks in this pastoral representation, complete with the expected toys

De nuage en nuage, Saint-Nico...

JOYEUX NOËL

French card showing St. Nicholas and the toys he left on the doorstep

The house is running over with electronic gadgetry, and none of the family are ever far from any of it. Every member of the family has a cell phone, and they're *always* talking to someone about something!

Oh yes. Christmas. Everybody—grandparents, uncles, aunts, nieces, nephews—they'll all be here this year. I think I'm going stark raving mad! . . . There on the coffee table is that new book on St. Nicholas that I finished last Sunday evening. What was it George and I decided to do to save our sanity? How the Christmas madhouse was going to be different this year.

For many years, I had a standard assignment I'd give all my college freshman students. It was called "The Nightingale Assignment," and it usually took up half the second semester of Freshman Composition. During those seven weeks, they were to ask themselves Life's Three Eternal Questions: *Who am I? Where have I come from? Where am I going?* They were to repeat over and over Rabbi Hillel's (first century A.D.) "Eight Magic Words": *If not now, when? If not me, who?* They were to memorize Kalidasa's (India's greatest writer, fifth century A.D.) "Salutation to the Dawn," so that they would realize that every day is a miniature lifetime, with a beginning, a middle, and an end. And that each evening, they were to face God and share with Him what had been accomplished during the day. How had they grown in wisdom? Who had they helped? And then, could they honestly say, "Lord, if you were to judge my entire life by today, I would be confident that I'd done my best."

Crucial to the assignment's success was finding out who or what their inner nightingale was (as articulated in Zane Grey's "Monty Price's Nightingale"). Who or what was the driving force that propelled them from day-to-day? And so that they could *know* the answer—a mandated one hour of absolute silence every day.

What amazed me most? That most of them could not remember the last time they had experienced silence. They literally did not know what to do with it. Some would tell me, "The TV is on in our house from the moment the first person gets up until the last person goes to bed."

By the time they were through with the assignment, not one of them was the same person they'd been six weeks earlier.

Life's Three Eternal Questions: Who am I? Where have I come from? Where am I going?

German Oblaten and scraps of Santa Claus, St. Nick, and Nikolaus

So what is that missing piece to the puzzle of our lives? I believe you know the answer by now. It is silence. It is serenity. It is quiet time in which to dream, to conceptualize, to become. Longfellow used the term, "The long thoughts of youth."

Look around at the people you meet. Notice how many race through their days with their inner tachometer needle perpetually in the red zone. How *driven* they appear to be.

Yet there's the nagging question: *Do they have any real idea where they're going?* What will happen to them after the inevitable crash?

The 52 Days of Christmas

The Squirrel Cage

Fifty-two days of Christmas! You have to be out of your tree! Perhaps. Perhaps not. That's the length of time it took to do the Nightingale Assignment. It would represent one-seventh of every calendar year.

Interesting thing about sevenths. They are built into our inner psyches. We were created to need rest, changes of pace, every seven days. One doesn't have to believe in a Higher Power here. Test yourself. If you go longer than six days at something your inner gears begin to slip, your brain loses its edge, your muscles tighten. You inevitably reach the point of diminishing returns. We were each programmed to need Sabbaths.

Some years ago, I was interviewed for a position by one of America's top consultants. Many of the nation's top CEOs, those that ran Fortune 500 companies, paid him $2,000 an hour for counsel. I asked him a candid question: "Tell me, Sir, what could you possibly tell them that would be worth $2,000 an hour?" He leaned back in his chair, looked at me long and searchingly, then sat up straight and said with a smile: "You kind of caught me flat-footed on that one—no one's ever asked me that before . . . but the truth of the matter is . . . and I can't believe I'm telling you this. In fact, I'm almost ashamed to admit it."

"I can't wait to hear it," I said, afraid he'd keep the secret to himself.

"Well, it's unbelievably simple. I tell them to take one more week vacation this year than they did last year."

"WHAT?" I sputtered, unbelievingly.

He proceeded to explain. He said that most CEOs are driven to succeed. Almost to the panic point. They work day and night. Weekends, too. So desperately afraid someone will catch up with them and take their job away from them.

He used a metaphor to explain: "They race and race and race inside the wheel of their squirrel cages. Faster and faster and faster. But they don't get anywhere."

I was beginning to understand. "So . . . they aren't learning anything new anymore."

"Precisely. I tell them that neither their minds nor their bodies can take a steady diet of squirrel cage racing. I tell them to get out of their squirrel cages. Often. Go somewhere. Explore the world. Do crazy things. See what other people are doing. But get *out*. And take one more week off than they did the year before—and their productivity will be greater next year than it was last. I guarantee it. I stake my fee on it."

I've never forgotten that admission. Sabbaths. Even though he apparently had little room for a High Power in his life, he knew one thing: To continue performing at peak output, we *must build in regular changes of pace*. Sabbaths.

So what we are proposing is that we get out of our squirrel cages for one seventh of the year.

Flemish card

LEVE St-NIKLAAS

Rare postcard expressing Eastern European splendor

MIKULÁŠSKÝ POZDRAV

How Would It Work?

This way. It can't be a matter of voting. Not at first. Parents must be in control, and stay in control of the entire process. And it cannot possibly work unless serenity is made possible.

"How can that happen?"

"Easy. Beginning mid-November, pull the plugs."

"Huh?"

"Yes, pull the plugs every evening: TV, videos, DVDs, radio, computer, telephone, even overhead lights. Metaphorically of course: I don't mean to literally yank the wires out of the wall. We almost have to present the season to our children in this manner: "We are going to travel to a different country for 52 days. The school and work routines will continue as usual, of course, but our evenings will be different."

Each evening, instead of the dominance of our lives by electronic gadgetry, the family will gather together as a unit, beginning with a candle-lit dinner. If the telephone rings, the answering machine will pick up the messages. They can be answered later. We will not hurry but rather talk about whatever comes to mind. Share what happened during the day. After the dishes are cleaned—we'll all help—we'll take the lanterns and candelabra into the front room (or family room), and the fireplace will be the focal center of our lives until January 7. First will be story hour. Afterward, there may be family music, followed by table games. Later on, some may prefer to read until bedtime.

"And that's it? Fifty-two days of that?"

"Guess we'd better explain."

Nicholastide (Mid-November till December 6)

Dennis Engleman has long advocated a return to the longer Christmas season, and anchoring it to the good bishop:

> "Why is St. Nicholas so closely associated with Christmas? Perhaps because he loved to give, as did the Magi who brought gifts to Baby Jesus, and because he had a special love for children. Or perhaps simply because he was so devoted to Jesus Christ. Most likely, it is because his feast day of December 6 falls within what the world knows as the 'Christmas Season.' (In the Orthodox Church, the time from November 15 to December 24 is a penitential, anticipatory season known as Advent or Christmas Lent. The true Christmas season, the time for rejoic-

Photograph card from France

ing in Christ's birth, runs for twelve days, *beginning* December 25)" (Engleman, 77–78).

The season of St. Nicholas will anchor the tripartite Christmas season, each with its own distinct personality and beauty. In family councils, it will be decided which St. Nicholas-related activities and events will be emphasized most. During the first and second weeks of November, the family will study the Dutch way of celebrating Nicholastide, in chapter 9. This way, if it is decided that there will be a reenactment of the arrival of St. Nicholas and Black Pete from Spain, plans must be made immediately. Perhaps extended family, neighbors, or fellow church members can be brought in. Maybe the entire block or neighborhood can be incorporated into the circle of fun, with St. Nicholas playing his role and Black Pete his (cutting up and clowning for all he's worth).

Rare die-cut images from Germany

Every evening, a St. Nicholas story, or a story incorporating selfless giving into its plot, will be read. Or it can be enacted in family or church dramatic performances. But these stories need to be put into action, or they will mean little. Involve the children, teenagers, groups, or church in seeking out needs in the community that need to be met. Then have the young people address those needs secretly so that the recipients remain unaware of where the help comes from.

A very special tradition (memorably articulated in story-form in Paula McDonald Palangi's "The Last Straw" (Wheeler, *Christmas in My Heart 2*, 44–48) has to do with acts of kindness. Ideally, the activity would begin on the first day of Nicholastide and stretch through Advent to Christmas Eve. On the first day, set up a small cradle-sized manger in the house, then have everyone draw names; continue doing so once a week. Each person then tries to perform as many acts of kindness for whoever's name is on that piece of paper. In the true spirit of St. Nicholas, every effort should be made to keep such acts secret. And for every secret act of kindness, that person ads another piece of straw to the cradle of the Baby Jesus. The object is to make

Emmanuele Luzazati, "San Nicola i bambini," Citta Di Bari poster

or present the story in drama, mime, or puppetry. Conclude the celebration with a visit by St. Nicholas, who, after encouraging children to live good lives, then takes out his Big Book and points out specific misdeeds in the lives of children present. He will then toss out treats for them to scramble after.

Or, we can follow the Dutch way. Just as is described in chapter 9, after dinner, the children will listen intently for the sound of hooves on the roof, a knock on the door, sharp taps on the window. Then in will come *Sinterklaas* and Black Pete, carrying the Big Red Book. The grilling of each person and the gift-giving by the saint follow, then the visitors leave. The children may have a treasure hunt of their own, followed by singing St. Nicholas songs prior to placing their shoes by the chimney and going to bed.

The Austrian manifestation of Nikolaus with the devilish Krampus in a rather playful disguise

Ah! But then the adults and teenagers reach *Pakjesevond* (Parcel Evening) that they've been planning for so long! What hilarity! And how clever *Sinterklaas* proves to be! Later on, it'll be time for pastries and hot chocolate.

We have already discussed the St. Nicholas-related institution of Boys' Festivals, during which choirboys elect a Boy Bishop, attendant dean, archdeacons, etc., on St. Nicholas Day. Today we find that, after a lapse of a number of centuries, Boy Bishop celebrations are coming back. It offers a special opportunity to make boys feel more invested in the activities and goals of the church. Those who bring back this institution thereby extend St. Nicholas's presence far into the Christmas season: to Childermas on December 28 (Hadfield, 135).

Now St. Nicholas and Black Pete return to Spain, their direct role in our season over for another year.

Gruß vom Nikolaus!

Window of St. Nicholas and the Virgin Mary in St. Nicholas Anglican Cathedral, Newcastle upon Tyne, England. Exhibitions are now held with the St. Nicholas Society in December and May each year.

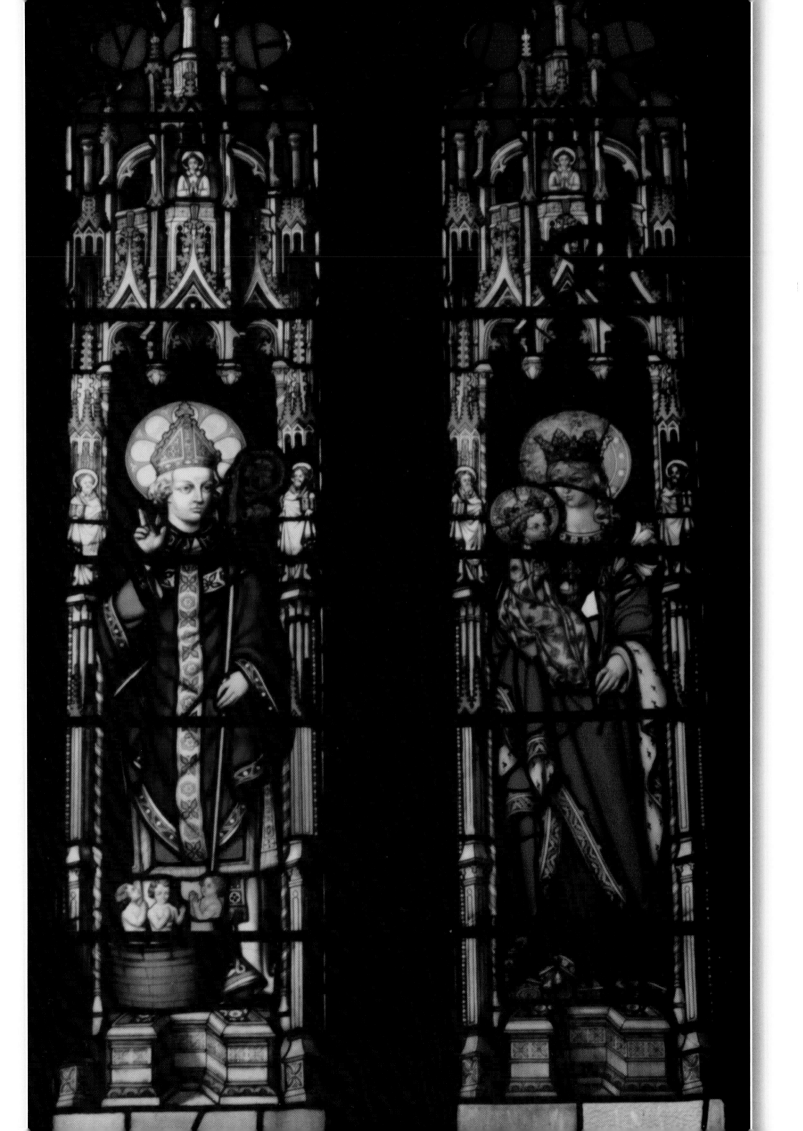

Enter Santa Claus

By December 7, Santa Claus (the secularized St. Nicholas) enters into our season. Those who prefer to remain with the real persona, St. Nicholas himself, will continue to incorporate him into the season, as will those who prefer not to confuse children by incorporating both. This will be especially true for all the thousands of parents who now tell the truth about St. Nicholas to their children from day one. What a relief to know that they'll no longer be presenting Santa Claus as a real person when they know that someday they'll have to do an about-face and admit they lied.

However, since children will see Santa Clauses in every mall and on every other street corner, he is a figure that must be dealt with and explained. Parents really cannot honestly maintain that they are the same person, for they no longer are. They were, four-hundred years ago, but their paths diverged afterward, as we discovered. Some may prefer to emphasize Santa Claus over St. Nicholas simply because they'd rather deemphasize the spiritual and concentrate on the secular. That is a privilege each of us has. And Santa Claus will not let those down who retain him as a central Christmas figure, for he remains a kind figure in an otherwise often unkind world.

Illustration of "St. Nicholas in his Study" by Scott Gustafson. For more information, please visit www. scottgustafson.com

Santa Clauses ring bells for the Salvation Army, do good for innumerable worthy causes, and bring joy to children of all ages. All this we ought to share with our children. And I cannot forget one of my oldest and fondest personal memories: my conservative minister father in his Santa Claus suit, playing "Jingle Bells" on his harmonica outside the door, on his way in, every Christmas.

255

The Advent Season

Advent traditionally includes four full weeks before Christmas, however, in America, some like to graft the last Thursday in November, Thanksgiving, to it. Thanksgiving Night, the family sets up the creche or Nativity set and reads the first non-St. Nicholas-related story of the season. Others may prefer to wait and begin the celebration of Advent on the traditional fourth Sunday before Christmas. Since Christmas falls on different days each year, Advent may vary in length from 22 to 28 days.

Unlike the more rollicking Nicholastide, Advent is a more serious season. The stories will continue; only these will emphasize the life of Christ while on earth. In truth, we cannot emphasize too much the role of stories during our 52-day Christmas season. When the years have flown by and the children grown old, chances are that it will be the reading of these stories that will have impacted their lives the most. For the values internalized, as these beloved stories are read and reread from year to year, become part of the very fiber of their beings. In truth, we do grow into, *become* our favorite stories. The greatest possible bond between two people is created when a mother or father hold a child on their lap, or sit with arm around a child, and read stories aloud. The sound

Antique card for Epiphany

THEY PRESENTED UNTO HIM GIFTS; GOLD, AND FRANKINCENSE, AND MYRRH.
MATT. II-11.

of those stories being read remains in the reader's conscious and subconscious thoughts as long as life shall last. It is the ultimate memory of home, and reason enough to cause grown-up children to travel thousands of miles just to be home with Mom and Dad, and experience those stories once again. No grown-up child ever travels thousands of miles just to sit in front of a television set!

As to what the season of Advent accomplishes, Advent specialist L'Tishia Suk submits that its most important function is that it restores Christ back to being the center of the Christmas celebration, because on each Advent day, the birth of Jesus is read, sung, and talked about. She suggests that parents either purchase or make an Advent wreath and five Advent candles (one white, one rose, and three purple), an Advent calendar, with 24 windows to open each day in December, and Christmas carol books. To make Advent especially meaningful, she recommends the following:

In medieval times the Irish began a custom of placing a candle in the window and lighting it each evening. The unspoken message—that any stranger was welcome to enter (in the name of Christ), and share the family's hospitality. This particular tradition can be incorporated into the entire 52 Days of Christmas. Parents today who incorporate this lighted candle in the window into their festivities may also wish to keep a plate of freshly baked cookies, and have a hot drink ready, for all who call on them (Cheney, 68–70).

L'Tishia Suk suggests that parents do the following:

> Light the first purple candle, known as the prophecy candle. The liturgical color purple is a sign of penance and longing as we wait for the birth of Jesus. With the lighting, talk about Jesus being the light of the world. Read the Advent Scripture of the day. Conclude by singing or praying. Have one child blow out the candle.

A classic St. Nicholas Day card

257

SENDING LETTERS TO SAINT NICHOLAS.

Letters and stockings, children and a fireplace—the making of a visit from St. Nick

Light the same candle each day of the week. Follow with the reading, Christmas carols or other meaningful activities.

On the second Sunday light two purple candles, both of which are relit each night. The second candle is known as the Bethlehem candle.

The third week light the two purple candles and then the rose candle, or shepherd candle. Rose is a sign of joy and hope that He is coming.

Conclude the Advent season by lighting all four candles and placing an additional white candle in the center in its own holder. Have a birthday party for Jesus complete with cake, the Happy Birthday song, candles and presents of nonmaterial gifts such as singing, reading, a nativity play, etc.

Additionally, Ms. Suk recommends that, as Christmas cards arrive, save them and pray for the senders during the Advent time each night. Do an Advent service for the needy. Incorporate the animals in your nativity set into the stories. Occasionally, add related crafts to the Advent time. Make cookies or candies to add a festive feeling.

Following are 28 Advent readings.

First week: Is. 40:1–5; Is. 52:7–10; Is. 40:9–11; Gen. 3:8–15; Gen. 15:1–6; Deut. 18:15–19; Ps. 89:1–4.

Second Week: Is. 11:1–10; Zech. 6:12–13; Mic. 5:2–4; Mal. 3:1–6; John 1:1–8; John 1:9–18; Mark 1:1–3.

Third Week: Luke 1:5–13; Luke 1:14–17; Luke 1:18–25; Luke 1:39–45; Luke 1:46–56; Luke 1:57–66; Luke 1:67–80.

Fourth Week: Is. 7:10–14; Luke 1:26–35; Is. 9:2–7; Matt. 1:18–25; Luke 2:1–20; Matt. 2:1–2; Luke 2:21–35.

Again, the entire Advent emphasis should be on giving rather than receiving. It is easy for parents and grandparents to forget that only by giving does a child develop a generous spirit. All too often in America today, Christmas is merely a time when children hand

Rare Nativity scene, with a stairway from heaven for the Holy Night itself

Mater Amabilis.

Gentle child and gentle mother

over a list of demands to their parents. Gone is the time when children were content with one or two long-desired gifts. This sad state of "gimme, gimme" needs to change in our new season. During Advent, the emphasis should be on each person (young or old) making or preparing gifts that are hand-made rather than store-bought.

Many families act out St. Luke's Gospel during Advent. The living room becomes their stage, Mother's stash of fabrics and draperies are raided, odds and ends are accumulated by Father, bathrobes are brought out. Toy and stuffed animals are brought in by the children. Dolls, too. Each evening one person reads (slowly) a selection from Luke, and the others spontaneously act out what is being read. No rigid rules. Some families may mime the Gospel story. Some may wish to create their own script or borrow someone else's.

These evening plays may be spread out over the entire Advent season if so desired. Same for Christmastide (Chaney, 67–68).

Since December 16 is also the start of that most beloved Hispanic tradition, *Las Posadas*, this would be an excellent addition to your group or church's Christmas season. In Mexico, for example, every home is expected to be decorated and ready to receive guests by that date. Lilies, Spanish moss, poinsettias, evergreens, colored paper lanterns, have been brought in; and in the very center of the home, a nativity scene or creche will have been set up. All this, in preparation for *Las Posadas*.

"Starting near the first of December, children's thoughts center increasingly on the coming nine nights. Who will get to be the Virgin Mary? Who will get to be Joseph? Who will get to be the hard-

Santa Papers, used by the kind permission of Hunter Inc., lithograph images used for wood ornaments or for cookies and biscuits, with unique representations of St. Nicholas

An Italian Happy Nativity postcard

Buon Natale

hearted innkeeper when Mary and Joseph seek *posada* (a place to rest for the night), and who will at last get to welcome them in? Every time children pass a creche, their thoughts turn to that dramatic reenactment only days away.

"Finally, on the night of December 16, nine families choreograph the festivities. The starring roles are assigned to children. At certain homes, as the guests and extended family arrive, they are arbitrarily separated into two groups: the cruel innkeepers and the holy pilgrims. Each pilgrim is handed a lighted candle, and a procession is formed, with an angel leading the way, followed by Mary, Joseph, and the pilgrims.

"No one who has ever seen *Las Posadas* can possibly forget how moving it is. Once it begins, all else in the life of the town seems to stop while the two-thousand-year-old drama is once again played out.

"The long journey from Nazareth to Bethlehem is represented by two children. Carrying his staff, Joseph leads a donkey. On the donkey's plump back is the most precious thing in the universe: little Mary, who we 'know,' carries within her the Savior of the

German die-cut images and scraps

world. Friends and relatives surround the pair as they make their way down the street. These friends are also attired in costumes of the time. The mood is set by candlelight and sacred music. Joseph and Mary and their attendants stop at nine houses. At each door, Joseph pleads for *posada;* at each door, he is unceremoniously turned away. Except at the ninth house—the door is opened wide, the procession comes in, and all sing their thanks.

"For nine consecutive nights, the pageant is repeated, for on each night, *posada* is offered in a different home.

". . . Also each evening [in the ninth house], blind-folded children take turns swinging at piñatas—then, when one eventually smashes it, there is a wild scramble for the shower of fruits, gifts, and candy. . . .

"The last night (*La Noche Buena* [Christmas Eve]), is the most lavish of all, and *posada* is usually at the home of someone affluent enough to entertain lots of guests. In this home, the altar is decorated with tinsel and flowers, and the infant Jesus is found in a moss-lined crib. The whole party sings many more songs . . . and that is followed with food, sweets, liquors, and dancing until it is time to go to the cathedral for midnight mass. . . ." (Wheeler, *Christmas in My Heart: A Second Treasury,* 4–9).

Another great tradition that deserves wider celebration comes to us from medieval Poland. Participants are called "The Star Boys," and every Advent season groups of boys carry the props for their impromptu play performances. The stable they called the *Szopka.* Children watch enthralled as puppets enact scenes set in long-ago Bethlehem. These Star Boys continue their performance through both the Advent and Christmastide. To gain a better feel for them, let's drop into the pages of Eric Philbrook Kelly's wondrous Christmas story, "The Christmas Nightingale":

> Two boys rose and brought the little puppet show forward. Stefan adjusted a chair and extinguished all the candles except for those which illuminated the little stage, so that nothing was perceptible save the space where the Christ Child in roughly carved wood lay sleeping, and the Madonna hovered above him. Behind the rude stall were seen the heads of cattle, and in the front shepherds were kneeling. . . .
>
> "I am Bartek, the shepherd," recited one of the boys. 'It is Christmas Eve and I am sleeping on the hills.'
>
> "And we are shepherds," shouted four others.

The performances of the Star Boys is an Advent tradition from medieval Poland that deserves wider celebration.

The play proceeded. The angel comes from the sky to rouse the shepherds to make the pilgrimage to Bethlehem. They meet a soldier at the Bethlehem gate who warns them that Herod dislikes shepherds. Herod in his robes shouts at the top of his terrible voice when he hears that a new king is born and orders the children of Bethlehem to be put to death.

At this point the first act ended, and the chorus came forward to sing. (Wheeler, *Christmas in My Heart* 3, p. 68).

The Holy Nativity on an Eastern European postcard

Finally, we come to the third high day of our season, December 24. On this evening, a beautiful way to begin the festivities is to read Bill Vaughan's "Tell Me a Story of Christmas." In it, a little girl keeps asking her father to tell her a story of Christmas, and he obliges, again and again—with every type of Christmas story he can think of—but she cuts him off, satisfied with none of them. Finally, almost in desperation, he leans back and says, "And it came to pass in those days, that there went out a decree from Caesar Augustus . . ." [and he "tells her a story of Christmas"]. Then finish reading Luke's Nativity story to the family (Wheeler, *Christmas in My Heart* 2, 119–120). Many families open their presents during this evening. Others wait until Christmas morning. More and more are incorporating "The Trading Game." For information on it, read "Hans and the Trading Game." So beloved has this game become that, for our family, Christmas would not be Christmas without it. (Wheeler, *Christmas in My Heart* 5, 115–128).

Many Christians conclude this memorable evening with Midnight Mass.

The Twelve Days of Christmas (or Christmastide)

Although the commercial world is taking down its trees and tinsel on December 26 to make way for the January white sales, the Church is only beginning a full twelve days of high feasting which will reach their climax and zenith on January 6. Then, in the regal splendor of Epiphany, we see another facet of the Incarnation, a facet which completes the Christmas mystery: the tiny Baby born on Christmas night is in reality the King of the whole world (Chaney, 7).

A unique French photograph card transformed into an embossed cartoon, one of the rarest images in the Rosenthal Canterbury Collection

Traditional face of Santa/ St. Nick

It was not so long ago that most everyone in Christian nations celebrated the twelve days following Christmas Day. Today, so many have ceased to observe these days that people lift their eyebrows in puzzlement when Shakespeare's *Twelfth Night* play is discussed or "The Twelve Days of Christmas" is sung. "Twelve days of Christmas? How quaint!" Or "Twelfth Night?" "Twelfth night of *what*?" But now, more and more, people everywhere are recognizing the desirability of recapturing the rest of the old-time Christmas season.

Christmastide has been one of the most cherished seasons of the church for a long time. The Festal Tide Council of Tours (A.D. 567) ordained Christmastide to run from December 25 to January 5. The shift to January 6 took place some centuries later. All during medieval history, it was a time for special religious services, biblical mystery plays (many having to do with the Nativity), games, dances, hunting jousts, and feasts. In Bavaria, it was called the "Twelve Quiet Days" because housewives abstained from spinning, baking, washing, or cleaning during this time. All across Europe, it was expected that Yule logs would burn in fireplaces from December 26 to January 6 (Gulevich, 194–196).

Drama has remained a constant in Christmastide ever since the earliest miracle plays. In court circles, the masque ruled supreme for centuries until displaced by pantomimes. In London, even today, the theater season and Christmastide remain almost inseparable (Hadfield, 130).

One question has to do with the First Day of Christmas: does it land on Christmas Day or the day after. Those who answer "Christmas Day" tend to consider "Twelfth Night" to be the evening of January 5; most people, however, consider it to be the evening of January 6.

Another question has to do with the Christmas tree: when should it be put up and decorated? Obviously, to those who have considered Christmas to reach its end on December 25, the Christmas tree ought to be put up earlier in the Advent period. But once we accept the longer Christmas season we have the luxury of a different option, one well articulated by Elsa Chaney: "Families living close to the spirit of the liturgical season do not, on any account,

Veselé vánoce

The visit of the Magi, the Three Kings, Epiphany, as portrayed in an antique card

A Holy Happy & Christmas & be Thine.

May Time smooth out
thy lines of care
And gently deal with thee,
my friend!
May shadowy places brighter grow,
And peace, God's peace on thee descend.

C-80
© ℳ

Antique English card

set up the tree and other decorations ahead of time. They do not want to spoil the last lovely days of Advent longing and expectation by starting Christmas too early" (Chaney, 40).

Elsa Chaney, a specialist on Christmastide, suggests that we remind our children that the Christmas tree is a symbol of "the great Tree of the Cross"—it is by a tree that the whole world has been redeemed. And the evergreen aspect of our tree reminds us that the everlasting life Christ promises us was won through His Incarnation, Death, and Resurrection (Chaney, 45).

Chaney also suggests that parents consider adopting a certain custom: on December 26, St. Stephen's Day, all the children are to be gathered together and retold the story of the Magi. They are reminded that each of the Wise Men has to come from a far away country—and the journey to Bethlehem will take twelve days (best not to be too literal with them, given the slow speed of travel in those days). Caspar with his camel will be taken to one of the most remote rooms of the house and there positioned. Melchior will be placed in another distant room, and Balthasar in yet another. Then, each day that passes, the family will watch as each Wise Man journeys over obstacles (over bookcases, mantelpieces, dressers, cornices, etc.) in the rooms that correspond with the real-life geography of his travel route. All will discuss climate, dangers, cities, peoples, etc., that fall within that segment. On Epiphany, they will all arrive at the stable, in their splendor, to pay homage (Chaney, 67–68).

Away in a Manger: Shepherds visit the Virgin and Child.

268

A Happy Christmas

Chaney also suggests that families secure a large white candle (a symbol of Christ the Light) and light it each time they have a Christmastide function. When mealtime arrives, the candle is moved to the center of the table and lighted as a reminder that Christ is present. Some place the candle by the creche, crib, or Nativity scene, and light it for the singing and prayers (Chaney, 68).

Cheney points out that since St. Stephen was stoned to death while praying for his enemies, children celebrating this day should be encouraged to likewise pray for those they dislike. Also to pray for all those around the world who are being persecuted for their faith. Since Deacon Stephen was one of the first recorded social workers in history (organizing meals for the poor), many parents place a box they call "St. Stephen's Box" next to the Christmas tree. The day after Christmas presents were opened, they encourage each of their family, in gratitude, to give away one of their choicest presents, so that the box may be shared with the poor or sent abroad to a mission country.

Classic Elizabethan-style Christmas Greeting card

On this night, during story hour, someone will read the story of "Good King Wenceslaus" (in the old Christmas carol) who "looked out on the Feast of Stephen," and then shared his meal with a poor peasant family. Afterwards, during the carol singing, they will sing that beloved carol (Chaney, 79).

The Third Day of Christmastide (December 28) is today called the Feast of the Holy Innocents. The early church called it *Childermas*, and has observed it ever since the fifth century. It commemorates the birth of the child martyrs in Bethlehem that the soldiers of Herod would slay after the king realized the Magi had left without informing on the whereabouts of the Holy Family. It is also on *Childermas* that the Boy Bishop and attendants elected on St. Nicholas Day end their period of church leadership.

New Year's Eve and Day (the fourth high day in our season) are in the very middle of Christmastide, thus New Year's offers everyone the opportunity to look backward through the old year and forward to the new. To take stock of what went well during the past year and what did not. To renew one's daily walk with God and make resolutions that are likely to be kept. In a very special sense, New Year's represents a second birthday for each of us, a rebirth, an opportunity to close the old book and open a new one. Appropriately, the ancients named this pivotal month January after the two-faced god, Janus, with one face looking back and the other one forward.

The Twelfth Day of Christmastide (January 6) is one of Christianity's highest days (comparable to Christmas Day and Easter). Every day in Christmastide leads to January 6 (Some celebrate it on the Sunday between January 3 and 8). Epiphany is taken from the Greek word *Epiphaeneia*, which means "manifestation," "appearance," "showing forth." Gospel writers used it when they were chronicling occasions when Christ's divinity was revealed to those around Him (principally the Adoration of the Magi, Christ's baptism, and Christ's miracle at Cana).

Christmastide celebration includes New Year's Eve and Day.

Western Christians celebrate the arrival of the Magi on Epiphany, thus it is called "Day of the Wise Men," *"Dia de los Reyes," "La Jour de Rois,"* or *"Fête des Rois."* Orthodox Christians, on the other hand, prefer to use the Greek word, *Theophania* for this day. Sometimes they call it "Feast of Lights" because of their belief that baptism confers spiritual illumination and because they celebrate Christ's baptism on this day. In fact, eastern churches have been celebrating with this emphasis ever since the fourth century. During the first 300 years of Christianity, believers celebrated *both* Christ's birth and Epiphany on January 6 (Culver, n.p.).

In Roman Catholic countries it is traditional for children to leave their shoes on a doorstep or balcony (with straw in it for the Magi's camels) on the eve of January 5. On Epiphany morning, the children awaken to presents on, in, or by their shoes. In many areas, for children, January 6 is the most significant present day of the entire year.

In Russia, rather than the Magi it is *Baboushka* (same figure as *Befana*) who brings the presents. In Germany and Austria it is likely to be that fearsome female figure known as *Berchta* (or *Perchta*). In Syria and Lebanon, Epiphany is known as *Lailat al Kandahr* (Night of Destiny) (Gulevich, 184–90). Also in Ger-

271

many and Austria, the initials C M B (according to tradition, the names of the Magi Kings are Caspar, Melchior, and Balthasar) may be written over doorways with chalk that has been blessed as a form of protection for that household. Orthodox Christians have a ceremony known as "Blessing of the Waters Day," during which a congregation may walk into a river or body of water that a priest blesses. In Roman Catholicism, a pastor may bless each room of a house with holy water, or incense, recite special prayers, or write C M B above the door in chalk that has been blessed.

Christmas historians generally describe the Wise Men thus: "Melchior, an old man, with gray hair and a long beard, brought gold in acknowledgment of the Savior's sovereignty. Caspar, young and beardless, offers frankincense in recognition of the Holy Child's divinity. Balthasar, who was dark—as if Moorish—with a long flowing beard, brought myrrh as a tribute to the Savior's humanity. Some say that they were respectively kings of Nubia and Arabia, Godolic and Saba (Sheba), and Tarse and Egypt" (Hadfield, 165).

An old English "jolly" Christmas card

Lots of fun on Christmas Day,
Happiness and laughter,
And a New Year   Soon to
bright and gay,   follow after.

A Jolly Christmas

Long ago, Twelfth Night celebrations in England took their cue from King Alfred the Great, who decreed that all merrymaking should cease on that night, since it commemorated the arrival in Bethlehem of the Magi. In many parts of England, people used to light bonfires as a way of celebrating the Star of Bethlehem. Inside, as evening drew near, the master of the house would place a pan of clear coals on the hearth, then burn juniper berries on it. The resulting sweet scent would remind everyone of the frankincense and myrrh offered to Jesus by the Wise Men.

While the juniper berries were still burning, the cake (called the "baby-cake," "bean-cake," or "twelfth-cake") was picked up by a member of the family or party, followed by another carrying what was called the "knight's cake." The other members or family followed, torches in hand, in procession, with three circuits through hall, buttery, kitchen, and the porch. Five pieces of cake were ostensibly cut for Baby Jesus, his mother Mary, and the three Wise Men, but were given to beggars on the street or the town's poor (done so to comply with Christ's promise: "Inasmuch as ye have done it unto one of the least of these My brethren, ye have done it unto me" Matt. 25:40 KJV).

But there was another Twelfth Night tradition so ancient that no one knows where or when it first began—the election of the Bean King and his Queen. Over time, the Anglo-Saxon wassail-bread evolved from its original yule-dough (white bread, with later additions of caraway seeds, cider, honey, ginger, and pepper) to today's twelfth-cake (long referred to as "The cake full of plums")—otherwise labeled "The Bean Cake." Kneaded into each one would be a bean and a pea.

Later on, at the Twelfth Night party, the cake is cut and each guest bites in, hoping to bite down on something small and hard. The male who finds the bean in his slice automatically becomes king of the celebration, and the female who discovers the pea in hers becomes the queen. If perchance a male finds the pea, he is permitted to choose his consort; a female who finds the bean in hers may choose her king.

In olden times, once the bean had been found, the king was positioned in a chair, then hoisted high in the air by the tallest men. During three circuits of the room the king would draw a cross (with chalk) on every beam and rafter. Then, with his queen beside him, the royal pair would choose their court. Some, ministers of state, some soldiers, some ladies of the queen's bedchamber, and one poor hapless soul was anointed as the knave.

Elsa Chaney suggests that parents plan a Twelfth Night program for their children and friends. The traditional dessert will be the Twelfth Night cake (which will contain three beans or three nuts). The three who find them in their cake are immediately hailed as the "Three Wise Men," and are attired in beautiful robes (perhaps made from drapery); round oatmeal cans covered with aluminum foil make suitable crowns. After this, the "kings" rule over the rest of the evening: choosing and supervising the games and refreshments. They may even demand additional favors from their subjects. Placecards with Epiphany texts may be positioned on tables (Chaney, 102).

P arents can plan a traditional Twelfth Night celebration for their children, complete with a Bean Cake.

No Twelfth Night evening was ever complete without singing the old English (though some maintain it had earlier roots in France) folk song, "The Twelve Days of Christmas." How sadly ironic it is that about the only way Christmastide has been kept alive till our time is through the stanzas of this carol. Today, though it apparently had its origins as a secular parody, it is even sung in churches. In Twelfth Night parties, it is the centerpiece of a game (played before supper and the eating of mince pies and iced cake).

Christians of many denominations have arrived at supposed second meanings to these lines. Here are some of them:

Dare to make a new beginning with 52 Days of Christmas.

On the first day of Christmas, my true love sent
to me
A partridge in a pear-tree [possibly Jesus Christ].
On the second day of Christmas, my true love sent to
me
Two turtle doves [possibly the Old and New Testaments].
On the third day of Christmas, my true love sent to me
Three French hens [possibly the Trinity, liberal arts, or faith,
hope and love].
On the fourth day of Christmas, my true love sent to me
Four colly birds [blackbirds]. [Today many of us misread it to
sound like "calling birds" (possibly the Four Evangelists or
the Four Gospels)].
On the fifth day of Christmas, my true love sent to me
Five golden rings [possibly the five senses, the Torah, or the first
five books of the Old Testament].
On the sixth day of Christmas, my true love sent to me
Six geese a-laying [possibly the six days of work or the six days
of creation].
On the seventh day of Christmas, my true love sent to me
Seven swans a-swimming [possibly sevenfold gifts of the Holy
Spirit; Scripture features many sevens].
On the eighth day of Christmas, my true love gave to me
Eight maids a-milking [possibly the eight saved in the ark, or
the eight Beatitudes].
On the ninth day of Christmas, my true love gave to me
Nine drummers drumming [possibly nine muses, nine kinds of
angels, or nine fruits of the Holy Spirit].
On the tenth day of Christmas, my true love gave to me
Ten pipers piping [possibly the Ten Commandments].
On the eleventh day of Christmas, my true love gave to me
Eleven ladies dancing [possibly the eleven faithful apostles].
On the twelfth day of Christmas, my true love gave to me

Twelve lords a-leaping [possibly the Twelve Apostles, twelve heavenly gates, twelve tribes of Israel, the Apostles' Creed] (Hadfield, 173; Bowler, 220–1).

It was the custom during Christmastide to give a gift each day to those you loved most, just as is true in the carol. That, too, is a tradition well worth reviving today.

The End and the Beginning

And so we come to the end of Epiphany (but not the end of the Season of Epiphany), to Christmastide, to the Advent, and to the season of St. Nicholas to the 52 Days of Christmas.

Compare the richness of such a season to the emptiness and disillusion that so often follow a Christmas season devoid of the spiritual dimension. What if? What if each of us dared to make a new beginning for our families with this one-seventh of the calendar year? Dared to pull the plug on the electronic distractions which cloud the season with chaos, frenzy, and seasonal greed? Dared to substitute for this a blessed serenity into which our families may retreat for refuge and peace.

Might each of us—*especially* each child—be a different person at the end of these 52 Days of Christmas?

Might it at least be worth a try?

German die-cut image of a musical Kris Kringle

275

POSTLUDE

We've come to the end of *such* a long journey.

We have seen that St. Nicholas may very well be the missing piece in the puzzle, the mosaic, of Christmas. We recognize that Christmas, as it is celebrated in much of the world today, is just not working very well. In other words, the end result (how our children emerge from it) is disappointing at best. By beginning our season with Nicholastide and concluding with Christmastide, we give what's between, Advent, a beauty and meaning it did not have alone.

For seventeen-hundred years, mankind has warmed to the flawed presence of St. Nicholas. Only now are we beginning to understand why.

Without being divine, he approaches it in his selflessness, in his willingness to give his all for the sheep God entrusted to his care. In 1 Corinthians 13, the apostle Paul states that though you give away everything you possess to others, without love it means absolutely nothing. St. Nicholas, in that respect, can be our ideal, for every act of his life was motivated by that purest form of love, something we all aspire to but find so difficult to achieve. All too often we belatedly realize that our love for others is tainted with agenda, ambition, greed, and pride. Subconsciously, we want something in return. We want to make sure our generosity is known, that we get that plaque on the wall for all to see. In fiction, both Henry Van Dyke in *The Mansion* and Lloyd C. Douglas in *Magnificent Obsession* have articulated such an ideal. St. Nicholas is our *nonfictional* prototype, the standard by which all giving may be measured, not just at Christmas but throughout the entire year.

Most of us enjoy giving things to others, especially if those others give gifts of equal value back to us. We feel shortchanged if the recipients aren't properly appreciative. We find it harder to give when there can be no reciprocity, harder yet to give when there is little likelihood of gratitude for such gifts—and hardest of all to give anonymously. It is because St. Nicholas did just that, that so many millions in Europe's Low Countries imitate him in that respect every St. Nicholas season.

Most of us also assume we deserve all the creature comforts, gadgets, and luxuries we can get. Advertisers capitalize on this by telling us over and over, "You *deserve*" whatever product they are pushing. Apparently, St. Nicholas never felt he deserved anything: *only God deserved.*

Though we live in an increasingly secular world, there remains a yearning for something more than the temporary custody of possessions—for a philosophy of life that transcends time.

As we have noted in this study, down through history, each age reinvented St. Nicholas. It appears likely that our century will reinvent him once again. For gone is the somewhat naive euphoria of the millennial turn— the expectation that things would somehow be better in this Brave New World. Instead, as our planet has contracted due to overpopulation and increased travel, deep ideological fissures—in some cases, chasms—continue to divide us. Yet the longing for a global community of kindred spirits and shared values remains—and for someone who can be the catalyst to make such a miracle happen.

In a certain sense, the world today is interviewing candidates for this seemingly almost impossible task. Two of these charismatic candidates are in a room. At first glance, Santa Claus, glad-hander that he is, appears to have the edge over the more serious St. Nicholas. But as the crowd watches them, listens to them, and hears their stories, ever so gradually a consensus is reached—one of the two has in him the wisdom of the ages, one does not. One has been tried in the fires of time and place, one has not. When the wolves of our age attack (as they always do), the flock will gather

***Right:** Unique stained glass in the England's famous "Boston Stump," the massive parish church with its huge steeple in Lincolnshire. The window in the Cotton Chapel shows St. Nicholas with the Virgin Mary and St. Francis.*

***Opposite:** Traditional cookie cover scrap from France*

for protection around the one with the shepherd's staff. Most significant is that one takes no credit, declaring that all praise, credit, and honor, should be given to God—the other accepts such adulation.

Let's look at other candidates who have stood the test of time. Some of them we've met in the pages of this book. Others we've read about elsewhere: Confucius, Socrates, Luther, Plato, Aristotle, St. Augustine, St. Francis of Assisi, Moses, St. Paul, St. Thomas Aquinas, Rabbi Hillel, Siddhartha Gautama, Kalidasa, Lao Tzu, Mohammad, and Zoroaster.

Study them all, asking the question: who among them could possibly be such a universal catalyst? In truth, there is only one.

The universal symbol of pastoral shepherding and selfless giving; the perceived protector of marriage, family, and children. The one ecumenical figure with the power to unite all peoples: Christians, Muslims, Jews, as well as East and West.

Christians know that Christ is the reason why we celebrate the Christmas season. That is a given. But, of all those who have selflessly served their Master down through the ages, might not St. Nicholas be the ultimate human prototype, approaching St. Francis's ideal?

"Lord,

>   Make me an instrument of Your peace.
>   Where there is hatred, let me sow love;
>   Where there is injury, pardon;
>   Where there is doubt, faith;
>   Where there is despair, hope;
>   Where there is darkness, light; and
>   Where there is sadness, joy.

O divine Master,

>   Grant that I may not so much
>   Seek to be consoled as to console;
>   To be understood as to understand;
>   To be loved as to love;
>   For it is in giving that we receive;
>   It is in pardoning that we are pardoned; and
>   It is in dying that we are born to eternal life."

—St. Francis of Assisi (1181–1226)

277

BIBLIOGRAPHY

Ancelet-Hustache. *Saint Nicholas*. London: Cassell, 1960.

Arnest, Mark. "The Many Faces of Santa Claus." *The Colorado Gazette*, Dec. 24, 2000.

Barton, Laurie. "St. Nicholas Day." 1993 (2000 RCA Advent, Christmas, Epiphany).

Blair, Walter, Theodore Hornberger, and Randall Stewart. *The Literature of the United States*. Chicago: Scott Foresman and Co., 1949.

Bowler, Gerry. *The World Encyclopedia of Christmas*. Toronto: McClelland and Stewart, 2000.

Burns, Thomas J. "The Second Greatest Christmas Story Ever Told." In *Christmas in My Heart 10*, edited by Joe Wheeler. Wheaton, Ill.: Tyndale House/Focus on the Family, 2001.

Chaney, Elsa. *The Twelve Days of Christmas*. Collegeville, Minnesota: The Liturgical Press, 1986.

Christmas in the Netherlands. Chicago: World Book/Childcraft, 1981.

Cioffari, Gerardo. *The Basilica of St. Nicholas: A Short Historical Artistic Guide*. Bari, Italy: private printing, 1997.

_____. *Saint Nicholas: His Life, the Translation of His Relics, and His Basilica in Bari*. Bari, Italy: Centro Studi Nicolaiani, 1994.

Coffin, Tristram Potter. *The Book of Christmas Folklore*. New York: The Seabury Press, 1973.

Creasy, Sir Edward S. *The Fifteen Decisive Battles of the World*. New York: Heritage Press, 1969.

Durant, Will, *The Story of Civilization* series. New York: Simon & Schuster.

Ebon, Martin. *Saint Nicholas: Life and Legend – The Fascinating Illustrated Story of How the Revered Bishop Nicholas Evolved into Jolly Old Santa Claus*. New York: Harper & Row, 1975.

Engleman, Dennis E. *The Saint Nicholas Secret: A Story of Childhood Faith Reborn in the Heart of a Father*. Ben Lomond, Calif.: Conciliar Press, 1999.

"Fifty Years of St. Nicholas." *St. Nicholas Magazine*, November 1923.

Grun, Bernard. *The Timetables of History: A Horizontal Linkage of People and Events*. New York: Touchstone/Simon & Schuster, 1963, 1975.

Gulevich, Tanya. *The Encyclopedia of Christmas*. Detroit: Omnigraphics, 2000.

Hadfield, Miles and John Hadfield. *The Twelve Days of Christmas*. Boston: Little, Brown and Company, 1962.

Highfield, Roger. *Can Reindeer Fly?* London: Metro Books, 1998.

Hole, Christina. *Early Saints of God*. Minneapolis: Fortress, 1998.

Janson, H. W. *History of Art*. Englewood Cliffs, NJ: Prentice-Hall, 1977.

Jones, Charles W. *St. Nicholas of Bari: Biographer of a Legend*. Chicago: University of Chicago Press, 1978.

Kirkpatrick, David D. "Whose Jolly Old Elf Is That, Anyway?" *New York Times*, Oct. 26, 2000.

McKnight, George Harley. *St. Nicholas: His Legend and His Role in the Christmas Celebration and Other Popular Customs*. Gansevoort, NY: Corner House Historical Publications, 1917, 1996.

Markou, Antonios. *Concerning the Relics of St. Nicholas, Archbishop of Myra*. Etna, California: Center for Traditionalist Orthodox Studies, 1994.

Miller, Olive Beaupré. *Tales Told in Holland*. Chicago: The Book House for Children, 1926, 1954.

Roberts, David. "He's the Word Sleuth." *Reader's Digest* (April 2002).

Robinson, Nugent, ed. *The History of the World*, Vol. 1. New York: F. F. Colliers, 1887.

Rosenthal, James. "Celebrating Christian Style." *Anglican World*, St. Nicholas Special Edition, Christmas 2001.

_____. "Who Was St. Nicholas?" *Anglican World*, Christmas 2000.

_____. "St. Nicholas, a Necessary Tradition."*Anglican World*, December 2000.

_____. "Come Home, Santa, All Is Forgiven." *Church Times*, December 24 and 31, 1999.

Spicer, Dorothy Gladys. *46 Days of Christmas*. New York: Coward, McCann & Geoghegan, 1960.

Stredder, Eleanor. "The Twelfth Cake and Its Story." *Little Folks*, 1875.

Strich, Marie-José. *La Legende de Saint Nicolas*. Rennes, France: Editions Oueste-France, 1998.

Suk, L' Tishia. "Celebrate Advent!" Colorado Springs: *Focus on the Family Magazine*, December 2000.

Thoemnes, Kristin. *Christmas in France*. New York: Grolier/Hilltop, 1999.

Wheeler, Joe, "From St. Nicholas to Santa Claus." In *Christmas in My Heart 6*. Hagerstown, Md.: Review and Herald, 1997.

_____. "Hans and the Trading Game." In *Christmas in My Heart 5*. Hagerstown, Md.: Review and Herald, 1996.

_____. "A Pennsylvania Deutsch Christmas." In *Christmas in My Heart 4*. Hagerstown, Md.: Review and Herald, 1995.

_____. "Scrooge at the Crossroads." Intro. to *The Christmas Carol*, by Charles Dickens. Wheaton, Ill.: Tyndale House/Focus on the Family, 1997.

_____. "The 36 Days of Christmas." In *Christmas in My Heart, Second Treasury*. New York: Doubleday, 1997.

Willis, Lloyd A. Professor of Archeology and Biblical History, Southwestern Adventist University. Interview by Joe Wheeler. June 22, 2002. Keane, Texas.